NEW ESSAYS
ON
SHAKESPEARE'S SONNETS

NEW ESSAYS

ON

SHAKESPEARE'S SONNETS

Edited by
HILTON LANDRY

AMS PRESS, INC.
New York

FIRST AMS PRESS EDITION: 1976

Library of Congress Cataloguing in Publication Data
Main entry under title:

New essays on Shakespeare's sonnets.

Includes bibliographical references.
1. Shakespeare, William, 1564–1616.   Sonnets.
2. Shakespeare, William, 1564–1616—Addresses,
essays, lectures.   I. Landry, Hilton.
PR2848.N44   821'.3
ISBN 0-404-09028-1
LIBRARY OF CONGRESS CATALOG CARD NUMBER 71-161767

We gratefully acknowledge permission to reprint
Rodney Poisson's essay, "Unequal Friendship,"
which first appeared in *English Studies in Canada.*

Contents

Preface

Contributors

Rodney Poisson
Unequal Friendship: Shakespeare's Sonnets 18–126   1

Martin Seymour-Smith
Shakespeare's Sonnets 1–42: A Psychological Reading   21

W. G. Ingram
The Shakespearean Quality   41

Winifred Nowottny
Some Features of Form and Style in Sonnets 97–126   65

Anton M. Pirkhofer
The Beauty of Truth:
The Dramatic Character of Shakespeare's Sonnets   109

Hilton Landry
In Defense of Shakespeare's Sonnets   129

Marshall Lindsay
French Translations of the Sonnets   157

Paul Ramsey
The Syllables of Shakespeare's Sonnets   193

Theodore Redpath
The Punctuation of Shakespeare's Sonnets   217

Notes   253

Preface

The essays presented here were written for this book by scholars who are either specialists in the Sonnets or in their chosen topic. I felt that it would provide an opportunity for those who have been making some of the chief contributions to offer further and perhaps better thoughts on the Sonnets, and for others to fill in obvious gaps by studying certain aspects of the poems which had been neglected or ignored. Naturally, there is among the writers considerable variety in approach and point of view, not least in the matter of which text of the Sonnets to use. But this is merely the inevitable salutary result of allowing independent and conscientious scholars to "have their say." And in the nature of the case some essays are more technical than others, yet I think it is quite accurate to say that lucidity generally prevails.

My thanks are due to the contributors, especially those who worked under severe difficulties, and to my wife. One member of our original group did not live to complete his essay. Professor Otto Schoen-René died shortly after he began the analysis of modern continental scholarship; his death deprived us of an honored colleague and a valuable contribution to the collection. Dr. Anton Pirkhofer, a versatile student of literature, died in April 1969, just when the goal he wished to attain seemed within reach. Those who knew him will wonder at the *lacrimae rerum* and regret the loss of his talent, kindness, and intellectual generosity.

H. L.

Contributors

W. G. INGRAM—Formerly Lector in English, Trinity College, Cambridge; Director of English Studies, Emmanuel College, Cambridge, and University Lecturer in Education

HILTON LANDRY—Professor of English, Kent State University

MARSHALL LINDSAY—Professor of French, University of California at Davis

WINIFRED NOWOTTNY—Lecturer in English, University College, London

ANTON M. PIRKHOFER—Dr. phil (Innsbruck), Dr. phil. habil. (Vienna); lectured on English language and literature in Stuttgart, Vienna, Berlin, and Salzburg universities

RODNEY POISSON—Professor of English and Head of Department of English, Huron College, London, Ontario

PAUL RAMSEY—Professor of English, University of Chattanooga

THEODORE REDPATH—Fellow, Tutor, and Director of English Studies, Trinity College, Cambridge; Lecturer in English, Cambridge University

MARTIN SEYMOUR-SMITH—Professional writer and editor, Bexhill-on-Sea, Sussex

UNEQUAL FRIENDSHIP:
SHAKESPEARE'S SONNETS 18-126

BY

RODNEY POISSON

SINCE Laurens Mills traced the genesis of the friendship theme in Tudor literature and Stuart drama, no one has enlarged upon the idea that the friendship material of classical philosophy can be fruitfully related to Shakespeare's Sonnets.[1] Yet when we consider that the main body of these sonnets (18-126) comprises a sequence devoted to a relationship not treated in any other sonnet sequence in Elizabethan literature (Barnfield's *Certaine Sonnets* being only a technical exception),[2] it is reasonable to consider important both the artistic problems involved in substituting friendship for the theme of conventional love and the implications of this new sonnet theme. By so doing we may shed light upon how the poet is shaping his material and so sharpen our critical appreciation of the Sonnets.

On first thought, friendship does not, like sexual love, involve the ritual of courtship, which is a significant element of the sonnet convention; in friendship, there is no *hortus conclusus,* no wall against touch as in courtly love. Yet it is precisely the tension and the disquiet of such a relationship (whether real or imaginatively conceived) that is the "motive and the cue" for the usual sonnet "passion." Barnfield attempts to keep the same tension merely by substituting an innocent boy for a coy mistress, but he gives up at the twentieth sonnet and admits that his muse has labored to a standstill. He fails to develop a relationship which is distinct from sexual love but which retains yet a comparably interesting factor of imbalance or tension necessary to hold a long series of sonnets in the focus of one frame.

That Shakespeare has achieved this focus is at least vaguely experienced by most readers, but the focus becomes clearer in the light of the established ideas about friendship.

Certain ideas about friendship, which we no longer spell out or with which we have lost touch, were commonplace to the *literati* of Shakespeare's day. This collection of ideas was a classical inheritance directly available to the poet through the publication of the more popular of the ancient authors, such as Cicero, and indirectly through English translations of French or Italian versions of the originals, and also through a growing number of translations by English classical scholars. Again, this material could have been found diffused through such writings of Renaissance philosophers and men of letters as the *Governour* of Sir Thomas Elyot; the *Essays* of Montaigne, translated by John Florio; Charron's *Of Wisdome*, translated by Samson Lennard; and Bryskett's *Discourse of Civil Life*, much of which is a paraphrase from the Italian. In fact, scores of books containing ethical precepts gathered from the ancients made available to sixteenth- and seventeenth-century readers the basic ideas that comprise the friendship material of the period. It may be assumed that Shakespeare knew what he was doing when he chose to exploit this material in the Sonnets, for some of his early plays also show his interest in the friendship theme.

In the first place, it is an axiom that friendship, properly speaking, is a rational and spiritual thing. Montaigne describes it as "all pleasure and smoothnes, that hath no pricking or stinging in it," as distinct from "lustful love."[3] By true friendship he means a friendship based on virtue, what Cicero identifies as "true and perfect Friendshippe" (*vera et perfecta*).[4] For, he says,

> Vertue . . . both getteth, and also kepeth Frendship. In it, is al agreement of thinges, al stability, al constancy.[5]

And Shakespeare is equally emphatic:

> Kind is my love to-day, to-morrow kind,
> Still constant in a wondrous excellence;
> Therefore my verse, to constancy confin'd,
> One thing expressing, leaves out difference.
> (Sonnet 105)[6]

Such a relationship is "the most goodly & most natural Frendship, which is of itselfe to be desired & sought."[7] Cicero saw it to be a function of reason to seek such friendship: for "Man . . . both tenderlye loveth himselfe, and getteth an other to whom hee may so francklye impart his mynde, as thoughe of two, hee woulde make (in a maner) but one."[8] This sentiment is reflected in Sonnet 39:

> O, how thy worth with manners may I sing
> When thou art all the better part of me?
> What can mine own praise to mine own self bring?
> And what is't but mine own when I praise thee?

True friendship, therefore, would be lacking the frustration of romantic love because it is based upon equality. "For nothing is more eager & ravenous of his lyke, then Nature."[9] Hence Montaigne's opinion that friendship is a higher thing than sexual love:

> To compare the affection toward women unto it [friendship], although it proceed from our owne free choice, a man cannot, nor may it be placed in this ranke: Her [sic] fire, I confesse it to be more active, more fervent, and more sharpe. But it is a rash and wavering fire, waving and divers: the fire of an ague subject to fits and stints, and that it hath but slender hold-fast of us.[10]

Thus Shakespeare's beloved is "not acquainted / With shifting change, as is false women's fashion" (20). For in these sonnets Shakespeare has adopted an established position: "the ordinary sufficienty of women" cannot answer the demands of friendship; "nor seeme their mindes strong enough to endure the pulling of a knot so hard, so fast, and durable. . . . But this sex could never yet by any example attaine unto it, and is by ancient schooles rejected thence."[11] There in few words is the distinction between what Thomas Elyot dryly refers to as "carnal affection" and true love or friendship. This distinction is also explicitly drawn in Sonnet 20:

> But since she [Nature] prick'd thee out for women's pleasure,
> Mine be thy love, and thy love's use their treasure.

The separation of sex and love is essential in this view because, as the philosophical writings deriving from Plato insisted, the physical pleasure is a barrier to ideal love.

Indeed, relationships "forged and nourished by voluptuousnesse or profit, publike or private need, are thereby . . . so much the lesse true amities, in that they intermeddle other causes, scope, and fruit with friendship, than it selfe alone."[12]

Again, as friendship requires communication, any disparity works against the ideal relationship. For this reason Montaigne thinks pederasty is not admissible, "because according to use it had so necessarie a disparitie of ages, and difference of offices betweene lovers, [it] did no more sufficiently answer the perfect union and agreement, which here we require."[13] Setting aside the unlawful sexual usage between the man and the youth (Montaigne would say), love of this kind is good only in so far as it ends in friendship, but in its initial stages it cannot be rightly called spiritual for it depends upon the physical beauty of the beloved. He is really commenting on the *Symposium* from some distance. Pausanias, in the *Symposium*, says of this relationship that it is bad where the lover is "enamoured of the body rather than the soul . . . since he loves a thing that is unstable. . . . But he who is in love with character because this character is good remains for life, since he is fused with what is constant."[14]

Ficino's commentary on the speech of Pausanias, however, clears up the ambiguity of the relationship over which Montaigne is somewhat troubled. Ficino explains that love is "the desire of enjoying beauty." And as "beauty is perceived by the eyes alone, the lover of the body is content with the sight alone."

Indeed the lust to touch the body is not a part of love, nor is it the desire of the lover, but rather a kind of wantonness and derangement of a servile man.

Further, we comprehend that light (and beauty) of the soul with the mind alone. Therefore, he who loves the beauty of the soul is content with mental perceptions alone. Lovers exchange beauty for beauty. *A man enjoys the physical beauty of a youth with his eyes; the youth enjoys the man's beauty with his mind.* The youth, who is beautiful in body only, by this practice becomes beautiful also in soul; the man, who is beautiful in soul only, feasts his eyes upon bodily beauty. Truly this is a wonderful exchange, equally honourable, beneficial and pleasant to both: equally honourable, indeed, to both, for it is equally honourable to learn and to teach. The pleasure is greater in the older man since he is pleased both in sight and intelligence, but the benefit is greater in the younger, for as much as the soul is more excellent than the body, so much is the acquisition of the beauty of the soul more valuable than of that of the body.[15]   (Italics supplied)

The speaker describes the relationship as ideally conceived. And it is an important idea. For Ficino interpreted Plato to the sixteenth century, and through John Colet, who met and corresponded with Ficino, his philosophy was disseminated in England. Read against this passage, the love in the Sonnets of the older man for the youth needs no equivocation; for pederasty here is *not* sodomy. The occasional editorial nervousness about this aspect of the Sonnets is unwarranted. Ficino, in fact, made the relationship respectable in literature. Still, the basic inequality of such a friendship is shrewdly noted by Montaigne, and the very argument held against the relationship, its essential disparity, proves a reason why it is good material for the Sonnets. The beauty of the youth is everywhere strongly present, constantly in the eyes of the lover, but the very nature of the friendship is potentially unstable, and it is around this uncertainty that Shakespeare conceives the tensions which determine the rhythm of the Sonnets.

Again, one would expect in this relationship that the lover, who is the older man, would normally be in the position of a patron to the youth, with some vantage as it were, being an established man. Such is the situation in the classical instances. The point to be observed in Shakespeare's adaptation of this relationship in the Sonnets is that his lover lacks the compensation of any acknowledged superiority. He is poor (we infer) and outranked by his adored youth, who appears to be a noble and a darling of Fortune. Thus the friendship suffers a marked disparity, which is a substantial obstacle in the way of an ideal relationship. In a highly stratified world intimacies among unequals are unlikely to be clear and unambiguous.

Considered as a fictional relationship, however, its advantage over the ideal has much to recommend it to the ambitious sonneteer. For the inequality of the friends makes for distance and the necessary tension. Shakespeare has gained here what he lost when he rejected the theme of conventional love.

Now from the beginning of the sequence the ideal love is objectified in the person of the beautiful and virtuous youth. The terms suggesting the calm loveliness of the boy bring to mind the golden friendship approved by Ficino. For the lover in the Sonnets, the love is absolute, and there are passages where Montaigne's great tribute to the perfect union of friends could serve as a marginal note (cf. Sonnet 39).

> If a man urge me to tell wherefore I loved him [that is, his friend], I feele it cannot be expressed, but by answering; Because it was he, because it was my selfe.[16]

Montaigne, of course, knew his Cicero: "For hee that eyeth and looketh upon his faythfull Frend," says Laelius, "doth (as it were) behold a certen pattern of his owne selfe."[17]

The strongest statements on the subject abound, especially on the spiritual identity of the friends. Colet writes on the margin of a letter from Ficino:

> So great is the power of friendship that men who love each other mutually may somehow, even when apart, mutually see each other. . . . for each holds the image of the other in his own mind and so has him with him and sees him face to face.[18]

In Sonnet 61, Shakespeare asks his friend,

> Is it thy will thy image should keep open
> My heavy eyelids to the weary night?
> Dost thou desire my slumbers should be broken
> While shadows like to thee do mock my sight?
> Is it thy spirit that thou send'st from thee
> So far from home . . .

Thus a popular conceit in the Sonnets is founded upon no trifling notion. Shakespeare uses it in more than one instance (see also 27). We should note, too, that the apparently extreme language in which the communion of this absolute friendship is described is not a peculiarity of Shakepeare. Read out of its proper context, for instance, the following passage might be mistaken as belonging to a precursor of D. H. Lawrence:

> It is I wot not what kinde of quintessence, of all this commixture, which having seized all my will, induced the same to plunge and lose it selfe in his, which likewise having seized all his will, brought it to lose and plunge it selfe in mine with a mutuall greedinesse, and with a semblable concurrance. I may truly say, lose, reserving nothing unto us, that might properly be called our owne, nor that was either his or mine.[19]

Whatever the sexual overtones discernible to a modern reader, they are, of course, irrelevant to the passage in its proper context, for the apparent violence of metaphor does not pertain to the physical properties of love as carnal desire but to the spiritual force of friendship. And the same applies to those passages in the Sonnets implying the absoluteness of the self-surrender. In the fair and beautiful youth we may see if we wish Pausanias' description of the "incomparably temperate" Eros.[20] Indeed, the fair youth is addressed as "lovely and . . . temperate" (18).

At the outset, however, a perplexity besets the speaker, who is both poet and lover, or perhaps lover and therefore poet (for surely Eros, the youngest and fairest the gods, is the maker of poets).[21] The opening line of Sonnet 18 has a characteristic spontaneity: "Shall I compare thee to a summer's day?" But once the lover enters on the exchange of terms, the poetic act of making, which is to immortalize in metaphor the beloved incarnation of Eros, then the very properties of youth and beauty are by a complex irony apprehended in terms of the transient; the similitude of the summer's day has raised a doubt even as it is proposed. The poet-lover's eloquence is foreboding: his purpose is to assert eternal love and perpetuate the beauty of his friend in timeless verse; instead, in the very act of framing the poem of praise to the "god of his idolatry" he betrays an awareness of a telltale imperfection in the basis of the poetic trope. To be sure, the perfect love of which he would sing is temperate, for it is spiritual rather than carnal and to be distinguished from the instability of sexual love. At the same time the apt figure of joy, the summer's day as imaged idyll, is troubled by harsh overtones of the actual:

> Rough winds do shake the darling buds of May,
> And Summer's lease hath all too short a date.

The serenity disappears with the legal term "lease," a *memento mori*, elbowing its way up to the threshold of the speaker's consciousness. The "summer's day" changes to a kind of moral emblem, spelling out the message of transience—*tempus edax rerum*. In the act of cupping the rose, he has caught the thorn. In the first two quatrains, then, the lover is trapped in a dilemma resulting from his own special awareness—that sharp consciousness of time that assails a man who is near thirty—especially an Elizabethan with perhaps one chance in a hundred of living beyond forty-five. In the last six lines of the sonnet he solemnly declares the faith of the poet and closes with a sort of doxology of eternal love:

> But thy eternal summer shall not fade
> Nor lose possession of that fair thou ow'st
> Nor shall Death brag thou wand'rest in his shade
> When in eternal lines to time thou grow'st.
>   So long as men can breathe or eyes can see,
>   So long lives this, and this gives life to thee.

Looking ahead through the poems in the sequence we may consider that the several greater pieces on mutability that follow are in effect a recurring emphasis upon this theme, which from the first intrudes into the praise of love. In Sonnet 19 as in 18, the concern with the impermanence of youth and beauty, "the fading sweets" and their surrender to Time, is already conceded because experienced by the lover previously. The elegiac note has the effect of damping the confidence of the poet's boast:

> Yet do thy worst, Old Time! Despite thy wrong,
> My love shall in my verse ever live young.

In Sonnet 30 the "remembrance of things past" warns the lover of his "dear time's waste," and he laments the loss of "precious friends hid in death's dateless night." As he looks backward with regret he may look forward with misgiving, and though the moment is sweet, the consciousness of Time is a shadow on the grass. The poignancy is a function of the disparity of age between the lovers. And where this feeling is sufficiently generalized, as in Sonnet 60, it becomes universal—especially when read out of context. But these sonnets gain force when considered against the precarious balance of the friendship. A fluctuation of feeling between the awareness of Time and the sweetness of the relationship is one of the features of the Sonnets which establishes the sense of pattern. Transience is a condition of a friendship of this kind.

In Sonnet 22 the predicament of the lover is confronted within the familiar identity conceit (cf. "My true love hath my heart and I have his").[22] But Shakespeare goes beneath the surface of the conceit: the external beauty of the youth has won the love of the poet (as explained in Pausanias' speech in the *Symposium* and in Ficino's *Commentary* upon the passage).[23] Even though he may know it is but a sign of the inward beauty, which is the eternal quality the poet seeks to immortalize, still he is captured in the moment of passing loveliness, "the seemly raiment of my heart," and wills to be blind to the reality of his own decay: "How can I be elder than thou art?" The statement, framed as question, is both wit and wisdom. A witty conclusion to the syllogism made out of the conceit, it is also a statement of the poet's age, at once admitted and denied. While he is glorifying the experience of mutual love, he seems to be glancing apprehensively at the falling-off to come:

> Presume not on thy heart when mine is slain
> Thou gav'st me thine not to give back again.

Knowing the kind of doubleness the mature dramatist is capable of, one is tempted to see a layer perhaps too deep: the ideal beauty with which the poet invests the beloved is indeed a raiment of the poet's own heart; that is, it is an illusion. Does the lover-poet of the Sonnets here apprehend how unstable the relationship is even as he celebrates it? The ideal and the actual coexist in the poem as a condition of self-conscious art.

It is not the death of the beloved that is feared, so much as the loss of the eternal moment caught in the features of the beloved, which, as experience has taught the poet, is changing even as he looks: he dreads the time when "all those beauties . . . / Are vanishing" (63).

The impression deepens with the increased mastery in later sonnets. In Sonnet 64 the reaffirmation in the couplet is missing, and the boast that poetry can defy time is forgotten in the acknowledgement of the inevitable:

> Ruin hath taught me thus to ruminate,
> That Time will come and take my love away.
>> This thought is as a death, which cannot choose
>> But weep to have that which it fears to lose.

In this mood the survival even of poetry is a hope against hope:

> O fearful meditation! Where, alack,
> Shall Time's best jewel from Time's chest lie hid?
> Or what strong hand can hold his swift foot back?
> Or who his spoil of beauty can forbid?
>> O, none! unless this miracle have might,
>> That in black ink my love may still shine bright.
>> (65)

But there is more to the imbalance than a disparity in age. There is a social gap which works against the relationship; for it robs the lover of the natural initiative that belongs to the elder. They youth is not only young but rich, and, we may infer, of great family. He seems to be courted by poets who bid for his patronage. This second feature of imbalance makes communication at times especially difficult and, idealized as is the poet's love for the youth, the relationship in which it has to be sustained is far from the ideal as conceived by the authors we have noted.

Mention of the special delicacy required in such an unequal friendship is made in Cicero, for instance, who is explicit about the need for an equality among unequal friends: "But this is a very high pointe in Frendshyp," Laelius cautions, "that the Superiour is equal with the Inferiour." He goes on to point out that despite his pre-eminence over friends of lower rank, Scipio managed never to affect any superiority.[24] Tact comes easier to the old than to the young, however, and when the poet-lover stands in the relationship of an older to a younger and is also of inferior social station, he has to devise his own protocol of praise and entreaty to avoid the perils of insolence on the one hand and flattery on the other. For the poet-lover now praises his love, now defers to his young lord, and now, saving his lordship, rebukes and corrects him as a friend is bound to do. The tensions consequent upon these situations are implicit in the composition of the verse, and the modern reader must beware lest in recognizing a convention he fail to observe the uses to which it is put. Shakespeare does not merely imitate; and there is less repetition in the Sonnets than is sometimes acknowledged. The relationship is not static; it changes. What is said here about certain sonnets in the earlier part of the sequence cannot be applied to later sonnets without noting that after the first estrangement, for instance, there is a perceptible change of tone. A loss of innocence, we might call it.

At the beginning, on the other hand, the boy is the very pattern of perfection. Shakespeare has the lover describe the object of devotion in terms of the ideal young courtier:

> A man in hue all hues in his controlling,
> Which steals men's eyes and women's souls amazeth. (20)

This is the youth whom he identifies as "the master-mistress of my passion"—a striking phrase to a present-day reader, who sees it as perhaps merely a wittily ambiguous allusion to the conventional mistress of the sonneteers; but it happens to be very close to Florio's version of Montaigne—"this soveraigne and mistris Amitie."[25] The phrase would, then, be nicely appropriate to the all-in-all friendship as distinct from romantic love—a courtly phrase newly minted for the occasion, for none had so far written friendship sonnets of this kind.

Unfortunately, the disadvantage of such a love is that the youth is the object of every kind of flattering tribute; and flattery has no place between friends. True friendship is not a matter of advantage. "In this noble commerce, offices and benefits (nurses of other amities) deserve not so much as to be accounted of. . . ."[26] But the "other [lesser] amities" can be very eloquent in their expressions of love and duty, and our lover finds himself in a situation comparable to Cordelia dumb before the fulsome flattery of her sisters. It is not so much that there is a rival poet who competes for advantage, for patronage, but that the lover finds himself cruelly aware how invidious his own position is. He must protest:

> So it is not with me as with that Muse
> Stirr'd by a painted beauty to his verse.
>   (21)

Actually, the term "rival poet" is misleading in that it suggests that the lover is competing. His difficulty, on the contrary, is that he would not be suspected of flattering: "O, let me, true in love, but truly write." He is the true lover, not the "other amities." "The union of such friends, being truly perfect, makes them lose the feeling of such duties . . . and expell from one another these words of division and difference: benefit, good deed, dutie. . . ." Hence the lover has to instruct the youth even while as lover and poet his role is to sing love's praise. So he says, "I will not praise that purpose not to sell." Montaigne is explicit: "Their mutual agreement, being no other than one soule in two bodies, according to the fit definition of Aristotle, they can neither lend or give ought to each other." In truth, "there is no greater Plague or mischiefe in Frendship, then adulation, glavering [smooth talking] and flatterye."[27] In a socially dependent position the poet of the Sonnets finds the friendship jeopardized by the youth's very proneness to poets and poetry, perhaps the very ground of their friendship. For this susceptibility leaves the boy open to a special kind of flattery— the most difficult to contend with. If the lover competes or seems to compete, then he is lost. His poetry is love, not a commodity.

Sonnet 26 is a courtly approach to the same problem vexing the relationship. Suspicion of flattery, again, is a risk the poet-friend will not take. Through the nice conceit of the "embassage," he is diplomatically correct in witnessing his duty in terms appropriate to his lordship's merit or degree: in so far as it is proper for the poet in his station to pay his respects to the lord, he does so without pretentious flourish; hence "all naked." If he resents the finery of the other poet he does not violate protocol. Instead, he relies upon his lordship's favorable opinion, despite want of art. The intention is a discreet mixture of devotion, decorum and irony with intent to give love that will not be mistaken for flattery by a youth who is suspected of failing to distinguish between the two. If the overtones are reminiscent of the formal dedication, they may be deliberately so, for the irony effected thereby becomes a way of pointing out the frustration which arises from the inequality that strangles the voice of true praise. The obliquity of the implications in the resolution of the sonnet supports the inference—the "time when" clause has for its themes Fortune ("Till whatsoever star that guides my moving / Points on me graciously") and the poverty of the lover, glanced at in the ambivalent "tattered loving," beneath which phrase is the traditional image of the lover as pilgrim, in poverty and humility. For worship he must, since, as Aristotle in his abstemious discourse has observed, "friendship depends . . . on loving . . . so that it is only those in whom this is found in due measure that are lasting friends." "It is in this way more than any other way," concludes the philosopher, "that even unequals can be friends; they can be equalized."[28] The sonnet may be taken, of course, as being an expression of an ambition to write better, putting "apparel on my tattered loving / To show me worthy of thy sweet respect." But within the framework of the Sonnets, as noted, writing *is* loving. Here again is a plea to be heard as a sincere lover who bids for love in return. "For no one, when he loves a friend, will bear to be neglected."[29] In sum, the language is skillfully adapted from the courtly-love convention and from the dedicatory epistle. At the same time it meets the stricture that in true friendship there must be no flattery.

The lover therefore would not ape the hangers-on in court circles and that other poet in particular whose tongue is so eloquent of praise. The fear of being confused among those who write to flatter, and the need to cultivate the powers of discretion in his difficult young 'friend turn up as the motives for sonnets both early in the sequence and later. In one instance he avows that his love outweighs other poets' skill and asks that his beloved weigh plain love over poetic artifice (32). Much later, in a different tone he taxes the boy directly with being prone to flattery:

> You to your beauteous blessings add a curse,
> Being fond of praise, which makes your praises worse.
>
> (84)

In another, a playful irony sweetens the rebuke:

> My tongue-tied Muse in manners holds her still
> While comments on your praise, richly compil'd
> Reserve their character with golden quill
> And precious phrase by all the Muses fil'd.
> I think good thoughts whilst other write good words,
> And, like unlettered clerk, still cry "Amen"
> In polish'd form of well-refined pen.
>
> (85)

The lover's anxiety grows naturally out of a friendship so unequal; "for friendship is said to be equality."[30]

Even in a mood where love seems sure and rapport achieved, as developed in Sonnet 25, there is some misgiving. The poet-lover meditates upon the superiority of love to the goods of Fortune, and the sonnet by itself is not remarkable, but in the context of the situation there may be read into the poem the imagined awareness of such a lover so placed. Though barred by Fortune from "public honour and proud titles," he is, himself, potentially the marigold in the sun's eye. Yet the distinction drawn in the poem serves as a tactful directive to the poet's young friend. A friend owes no such dependency as a favorite to a prince, even if the beloved is a great one. For love is not of the place but of the heart:

> Then happy I, that love and am beloved
> Where I may not remove nor be removed.
>
> (25)

The statement that love is secure where it is true and mutual distinguishes it from the ordinary amities: *verae amicitiae sempiturnae sunt.*[31] But in these sonnets it is not Shakespeare's way to state a theme pat. Even the famous Sonnet 116 is not to be read free of the particular context of the perplexed relationship which is so resourcefully explored throughout the sequence.[32]

Although the moralists all agree that friendship, like virtue, is one of the few reliable goods of this world, they warn us that the true friendship is as rare as the man of virtue. "But a real friendship," says Plutarch, "requires a sedate, stable and unalterable temper; so that it is a rare thing and next a miracle to find a constant and sure friend."[33] Fair and lovely though the youth is, "the observed of all observers," at seventeen (say) he is hardly likely to be "sedate . . . and [of] unalterable temper," and the lover stands in most danger of being hurt. It is no accident that the uncertainty of the weather in the first sonnet of the sequence proves an ironically apt comparison to return to in 33, on the occasion of what may be called the first strangeness. The grave propriety of the glorious morning, with its sun nobly condescending like a gracious prince, glances at the state of favor which the lover has enjoyed within the circle of the noble youth whom he adores, while repeating in a new context the idea of the instability of courtly favor. For it is subject to change without notice, as observed in 25. The reproof (which is denied in the couplet) is indirect and ambivalent in the body of the sonnet: it is in the nature of things that the lover should suffer such neglect, for princes treat their favorites so, only the enthymeme is not so stated; but the youth who apparently "steals away" from his friend is justified (ironically) through the sophism which derives its conclusion through an established correspondence:

> Suns of the world may stain when heaven's sun staineth.

Here is the thin edge of the reproof written to the youth, presumably a bright young man, who will get the point of his poet friend's nuance.

Between sonnets 33 and 34 we may assume a reply in some measure defensive, with a note of genuine contrition. The metaphor of the weather is now extended into allegory and the claim of honor is advanced by the hurt lover. He has suffered some kind of disgrace as a result of the behavior of his young friend—acknowledged, it is implied, by the offender. The reproachful aphorism is unavoidable, and the man of honor, the young gentleman, is stripped of his noble condescension and (we are given to understand from the poem) he surrenders. Then by a magnanimous gesture the ground of the friendship is restored in the loving courtesy of the poet:

> Ah, but those tears are pearl which thy love sheeds
> And they are rich and ransom all ill deeds.[34]

Cicero's Laelius understood this delicate situation:

> For freendes must often times bee both admonished and

chidden also. And this is to be freendly taken, when it is
done freendlye and of goodwill.[35]

Under the circumstances of the friendship as conceived there is
more to come, and the poet explores further complicated states of
feeling which derive from the pressures in this demanding union.
Sonnet 35, which follows, shifts the tone. A different mood and a
new point of view prevail. A weariness comes with the realization
that the youth as projected ideal and the youth as erring man are
not the same thing. The cankered rosebud is a reminder of man's
fallen state. The weariness extends into the tired, flat rhythm of the
line, "All men make faults . . .," and the irony is inclusive:

> even I in this,
> Authorizing thy trespass with compare,
> Myself corrupting, salving they amiss,
> Excusing their sins more than thy sins are;
> For to thy sensual fault I bring in sense—

If the offender's youthfulness is assumed to be the plea entered, the
"sense" or reason advocated in the defense to excuse the sensual
fault, then in a double sense the lover argues against himself, for he
as the older man must understand the transgressions of young
flesh. *Tout comprendre c'est tout pardonner.* The twist in this
expert sonnet is that the lover has to condemn himself as accessory,
for he condones the fault. It is the sharp dilemma of a relationship,
whether erotic or not, where the lover is bound by something analogous to what is called the tyranny of love.

> I an accessory needs must be
> To that sweet thief which sourly robs from me.

The inference that the youth, whose "sensual fault" commits a rob-
bery upon the friend, has in fact slept with his friend's mistress, is
born out by the treatment of the matter in Sonnet 40. In the latter
poem the complexity is explicit. The lover of the youth loves wholly.
The friendship is all in all. The mistress is not a rival. Though you
rob me of my mistress, he says, you are not in effect gaining any
love which I have withheld; for you had it all before. The sonnet
provides the explicit statement of the absoluteness of the poet's love

for the youth. It is love of another and greater kind than the love of touch reserved for the mistress. Yet there is the kind of bitterness the inferior has to stomach, and his dignity seeks the cover of an ironic wordplay:

> Then, if for *my love* thou *my love* receivest,
> I cannot blame thee for *my love* thou usest.
> (Italics supplied)

"That is, because of love for me, since you must love anything that belongs to me," then "you take my mistress" and make love to her. So Dr. Ribner interprets the two lines.[36] It is at once a witty and a savage rebuke masked under the conventional ruffle. The identity cliché is a classical commonplace, but in the context it is ironical. If one happens to have an example in mind where the conceit is used seriously, the effect of Shakespeare's irony is all the more acid. In a little-known narrative poem of no art by Edward Jenynges, for instance, two friends face just such a dilemma, but the lady is sought in honorable wedlock. The two friends are noble youths and all is socially equal between them. But the principle of likeness and mutual love in the perfect friendship operates so that the one falls desperately in love with the other's betrothed and confesses to him that he is dying of love for the girl. The girl's promised husband, however, loving his friend beyond all else, accepts the situation as stated—

> For lyke as God by hys great powr
>   hath formed us as one
> All lyke in everye forme and part
>   for men to look uppon:
> So hath he made our myndes agree
>   in every thynge alyke,
> For looke what one of us would have
>   the other ther to doth seeke.[37]

And he yields to the argument that he should give the girl over to his friend,

> Estemyng more our freyndshyp then
>   A womans love and lust.

The conduct of the friends corresponds to the bookish ideal. The poem, of course, is a versified paraphrase of the story of Titus and Gysippus as it appears in Chapter XII of Elyot's *Governour,* unacknowledged by Jenynges, who simply changes the names of the characters. The friends in both the prose version and the poem are (*mirable dictu*) alike in body as in mind, a circumstance deriving from the ancient original which allows the lady to be married to the other friend without her perceiving the difference! Thus the situation can be resolved, in so far as the men are concerned, in the peace of perfect amity. Euphues, in a similar situation, tries to deceive his friend and the friendship is sorely tried. But Shakespeare's variation is different again. In the Sonnets the lover is poor. His mistress is not a woman of honor and is therefore outside the courtly convention. But she shares the role of outsider with the lady in Jenynges' poem, for neither woman must be allowed to come between the friends. In the world of the older poem, the situation is an *exemplum* of perfect amity, which is a static relationship from the beginning of the poem. In the Sonnets, however, the situation, a plausible one arising out of the youth's beauty (he was made for women's pleasure—Sonnet 20), serves as a chance to explore the imbalance of the friendship between the two unequals. When the poet forgives the transgressor, it is to explain that true love is by its very nature a surrender; but the phrasing is designed to make the youth wince:

> I do forgive thy robb'ry gentle thief,
> Although thou steal thee all my poverty.

He is, indeed, gentle—a wellborn man; hence, "gentle thief" is an oxymoron which says in effect that his theft is contrary to generosity, that is, outside the laws of courtesy. Robbing the poor is, of course, the basest of conduct. The ambivalence of the lines is a measure of the barrier to be bridged. It is the retort courteous, which at once hates and loves, challenges and forgives.

> And yet love knows it is a greater grief
> To bear love's wrong than hate's known injury.

Perhaps Shakespeare meant this as an ironic comment upon the aphorism that Scipio confessed not to understand:

> A man oughte to love, as thoughe hee should one day
> again hate.[38]

Such interesting passages happen often enough in the Sonnets to give them a living nerve, and it seems to be obvious that the kind of tension is a coefficient of the variation in the relationship the poet chooses as the subject of the Sonnets. Deciding upon idealized friendship and beginning with a classic pattern of youth and older friend, he invests the relationship with the social disparity which puts strain upon it. It is the instinct of the dramatist at work Shakespeareanizing the substance of a sonnet sequence into something new and strange.

No external reason is needed to account for the youth who stands at the center of the 108 sonnets addressed to him by his friend. The special tyranny which he exercises over the older man proves a challenging theme, immeasurably superior to that of the conventional Lady.

SHAKESPEARE'S SONNETS 1–42:
A PSYCHOLOGICAL READING

BY

MARTIN SEYMOUR-SMITH

===============

SHAKESPEARE'S sonnet sequence is certainly uneven; no critic, I
think, has ever bothered to deny it. Equally certainly, it is the most
profound and sustained body of poetry in existence about various
aspects of love. So extraordinary is it that we can infer certain
priceless definitions from it: definitions of, among other things,
poetic irony, and even of the kind of relationship poetry itself bears
to the experience that prompts it. For, despite such limiting
evasions as "the intentional fallacy," poetry, like all literature —
whether we regard it as wholly an art or as a mixture of craftsman-
ship and individuation (I use the word without specific Jungian reference)—does bear a relationship to experience. This is so whether
"psychology" eventually "dissolves into symbol," or "god," or not.

In this essay I ignore questions of identity and date in order to
concentrate upon the meaning of the first part of the sequence as we
have it in the probably pirated edition of 1609. What I am concerned with is the relationship of Shakespeare's sonnets to life—but
not to the lives of specific people. The best evidence is to be found
in the language of the poems themselves.

It has been objected that the notes in my edition of the Sonnets
are "biographical" and "psychological," to the exclusion of the all-
important ideas that they contain; Mrs. Winifred Nowottny, an

admirable teacher and the editor of the forthcoming New Arden edition of the Sonnets, told her students at London University that my treatment led to "loss of the poetry." The question is, What is the poetry? I believe, on the contrary, that my treatment is necessary before the poetry can be found. To what extent are the Sonnets, poems of astonishingly and almost uniquely high quality, deliberate works of art—or, in Sidney Lee's perhaps unfortunate phrase, "literary exercises"? To what extent are they an essential part of an existential procedure? This essay, by examining the first forty-two sonnets in some detail, attempts to answer these and allied questions.

I

I accept the order in which Thorpe published the Sonnets for the simple reason that no other postulated order is as convincing. The most intelligent attempt to establish a new order was made by Brents Stirling in an essay in *Shakespeare 1564–1964* (ed. E. A. Bloom, 1964); this was based on a theory of the way in which the printer might have muddled the sheets, and it is supported by Dover Wilson in his New Cambridge edition. But the argument is not finally persuasive. There is only one "correct" order, and that is the order in which the poems were actually written. This is irrecoverable, unless we assume that the Sonnets somehow reached Thorpe in the right order, and were thus printed. Since it is highly unlikely that Shakespeare ever wished to publish the poems, he probably never arranged them into an "artistic" order. There is no evidence, even, that he would have thought this a proper thing to do. It is not difficult to defend the 1609 order from either a chronological or an artistic point of view, and as it is all we have that is not wholly conjectural, it should be accepted—if only on the principle of Occam's Razor.

How should we approach this apparently private, and eventually deliberately nonpublic, sequence as a phenomenon? We all have preconceptions about how literature ought and ought not to be read, but sometimes it is advisable to put these aside; sometimes, we may even feel, we almost willfully misread certain poems by not doing so. If this is true of any poetry, then it is true of the Sonnets. In their case it is particularly appropriate to shed preconceptions, both because of the poems' extraordinary quality, exemplary as poetry, and because it so happens that they are not likely to have been conceived by Shakespeare as any kind of public gesture. The latter fact may not be wholly self-evident; but that it is usually willfully ignored is not without its irony. There are few readings of the Sonnets that do not tacitly assume that Shakespeare's prime intention was to create art, few that would care to entertain the notion that he may have been writing, primarily, for himself, this being his natural way of learning how best to exist well. Philip Edwards writes that in the Sonnets "Shakespeare is dealing with great complexities of the mind and heart; on to which is added the driving need of the poet to use his art, with all *its* complexities, to make sense of his condition" (*Shakespeare and the Confines of Art,* 1968). This is a pertinent comment, although for "the driving need . . . to use his art" I would substitute "driving need to . . . solve his human problems by approaching them truthfully"; the art is incidental, and arises from the intensity, the seriousness, of the poet's approach. It is, primarily, less a matter of "making sense" of his condition than teaching himself to act correctly in his situation— of discovering, by means of the poetic process, what "to act correctly" actually means. The phrase "making sense" implies too abstract a procedure.

Literature has ultimately to be seen and responded to in the totality of its contexts. All this really means is that the Sonnets are about what they are about—a notion that W. K. Wimsatt, for example, would coldly deny. But then Wimsatt would not choose to subject these particular poems to his critical treatment, for—as I hope to show—their very nature, which is the very nature of poetry, militates against it. For reasons of space, and because they establish the psychological situation, I concentrate on the first forty-two sonnets.

Sonnets 1-17 differ from the rest of the sequence in that they are less complex; the author is less involved in his theme, which is, quite obviously, a rhetorical instigation to a young man to marry and procreate his kind. It is tempting to ignore this comparative lack of complexity (which becomes evident only when we have read the sequence as a whole) of the first seventeen poems: the recognition of it is based in an intuitive response, one which cannot be defined in the same way as can notions of "structures" or "icons."

But the mind obstinately returns to it, because, exactly definable or not, it is a reality. The very first sonnet of all is mechanical, self-consciously introducing a fashionable platonism ("Rose") in the second line. Nothing much happens in the next sixteen poems, except that the poet becomes intellectually (rather than, at this point, emotionally) interested in the theme of narcissism. The most striking lines (e.g., Sonnets 5.10, 12.7-8, 4.1-2) are self-conscious "beauties"; they do not have any very powerful function within their contexts. The clinching couplets dutifully but mechanically perform their ostensible function of persuading the recipient to marry —they have no more weight than this. Certainly in Sonnet 14 something is happening: the poet begins by trying to work out his attitude to luck and destiny; but he ends limply, dutifully returning to the official theme, which does not much interest him. One does not need to conjecture that Shakespeare had received a commission from someone to urge a young man to marry: the formal nature of the theme is obvious, for the exhortations to marry are clearly more rhetorical than invested with emotion. They are "boring" in the sense that they have little impact, even as arguments; we look elsewhere in them for what interests us.

Then, at Sonnet 18, there is a change in tone that is almost abrupt. It is not quite aburpt: in Sonnet 17 Shakespeare has spoken of "the beauty" of the Friend's eyes ("If I could write the beauty of your eyes"), and this was the first time that he unequivocally linked *himself* to the idea of beauty in the Friend—but it is to be noted that by the end of Sonnet 16 the Friend's procreative skill has become "sweet." Sonnet 18 is not complicated; on the contrary, it possesses an entirely new directness. If it is not a love poem it has nevertheless seemed to countless lovers to provide a highly convenient and evocative parallel to their own feelings—possibly it is significant that none of the first seventeen sonnets has been so regarded. It is the culmination of a transition, which it fully acknowledges for the first time, and which has been going on since at least 15.14 ("As [Time] takes from you I engraft you new [by my poetry]"): from the impersonally expressed urge to marry to the announcement that the Friend will be immortalized in the poet's own verse. Lines 1-2 of Sonnet 17 might even be interpreted as implying, among other things, tnat a note of sincerity (or, for those behaviorists who cannot stomach the term, interest) is now creeping in. The kind of critical training that would cause readers to ignore the introduction of this new tone can be seen as, among other ingenious and philosophical things, deliberately limiting: the new tone is there for all to see. The argument that the whole sequence is a planned "fiction," with many such consciously deliberate changes of tone, lacks merit simply because the changes of tone themselves are of the kind that we associate with "life" rather than "art." One can only really defend the "fiction" argument by asserting that there is no such thing as "personal" poetry; and that is a risky undertaking. There are, of course, planned fictions in poetry; and there is also an important sense in which every utterance is a fiction (words themselves, after all, are not identical with what they signify). But the fictional element here is not planned: the author of the sequence is experiencing the emotion of being carried away. He is expressing that emotion, trying (as Mr. Edwards points out) to make sense of it, to strip off layer after layer of familiar falsehood to reveal whatever skeleton of truth may exist, in the poetic manner that comes most naturally to him. That we may, if we wish, eventually infer abstractions from his efforts is irrelevant: first, we must acknowledge our own commonsensical as well as intuitive apprehension of his entirely personal note, and follow his series of personal statements. *Entia non sunt multiplicanda.* It is, after all, a coherent series.

If, in terms of tone, 18 suddenly relaxes tenderly from the somewhat strained rhetoricism of 1-17, Sonnet 19 is again self-consciously rhetorical; but its sustained magnificence evidently derives from a powerful pressure of emotion. The tender sweetness of 18 is resolved into grand simplicity. In the comparatively artificial Sonnet 2, time was certainly going to "digge deep trenches" in the Friend's brow; Shakespeare was distanced from his subject. Now the marriage theme is completely forgotten, and Shakespeare is finding excited reasons for defeating time: the Friend is now "my love."

In the unique Sonnet 20 Shakespeare tries to come to terms with what is an extremely complex situation. The poem can be understood only as a declaration, by a person who has previously imagined himself to be heterosexual (and whose experience has been totally heterosexual), that he is experiencing homosexual feelings. If we can fathom this key sonnet, then we can go a long way toward finally resolving the very vexed question of homosexuality. I therefore make no excuse for devoting a considerable amount of space to this topic and in particular to Sonnet 20.

Rollins, in his indispensable Variorum edition, calls the poem "filthy"; this is quite simply an expression of a pre-Freudian attitude, and it must be respected. Rollins may not have liked talk of pricks, or any other sexual puns, but he never kept quiet about what he saw. He was thus entitled to his preferences, even if members of a later generation can legitimately charge him with having severe critical limitations. What is matter-of-fact to us once needed great courage to state; like an even earlier critic, Dowden (over "country matters"), Rollins had that courage when it was needed.

Other editors and commentators are not always able to be as honest. Satisfactory discussion of the problem has been vitiated by the fact that homosexuality itself is a subject that causes most of us to become confused and overemotional. Few literary critics like to talk about it at all; others talk of it too aggressively, unsubtly, and unthoughtfully; some speak of it only in order to acquit great Shakespeare of a heinous crime against nature. When a naïve editor, such as A. L. Rowse, apodictically not a specialist in criticism or in literature, bluffly dismisses the possibility of Shakespeare's homosexuality, we need take little notice (life being short); but sometimes quite nonliterary—and critically questionable — motives may infect the approach of more sophisticated commentators, who sometimes go as far as to ignore the presence of what they do not like to see. There is plenty of general comment on Sonnet 20 by critics of modern literature, but not very much by Shakespearean critics. There is a particularly excellent and completely uninhibited essay by Patrick Cruttwell, reprinted in his *The Shakespearian Moment* (1954), which argues that the "homosexuality" is no more than "Renaissance friendship." Cogently though Cruttwell argues, I do not think that the meaning of the sonnets written to the Friend really supports this. For even if they are about Renaissance friendship (I think they are about something more specific) they are nevertheless "about" homosexuality, in the two senses that the former was, of course, to some extent about the latter, in any case, and that any intense friendship between two men is also about it. It seems pertinent to examine 20 in the very detailed manner that it has not been subjected to by either Shakespearean critics, or by the more modern critics who take it to be an unequivocal statement of homosexual love. What does it actually say?

We do not know very much about any but one or two very obvious and unambiguous kinds of homosexuality, and we know even less about the extremely complicated phenomenon of bisexuality. Perhaps we shall find that Shakespeare's sequence, and this key poem, make a unique contribution to our knowledge.

II

Sonnet 20 is, first and foremost, a love poem (as, of course, is 18). "Passion" means not only "sexual passion" (Tucker's gloss, "[strong] feeling," is simply an evasion) but also "love poem" (here, this poem). That it is a love poem, in the usual and very general sense, does not necessarily imply that the author has consummated or even wishes to consummate the love he is expressing. We need to see what the poem says in order to find out what kind of love poem it is. If we do not want to do this, we must simply agree with Richardson, and say "I could heartily wish that Shakespeare had never written it"—which is at least honest.

It is consciously a love poem, then, but it is a very curious one. The general message of the first eight lines is that the Friend has the physical attractiveness of a woman, but is spiritually superior. It is difficult to avoid the impression that Shakespeare is describing a situation in which the "Master Mistris" of his passion is physically attractive in the manner of a woman. This is the type of homosexual emotion in which a man is physically admired as a woman rather as a man: in other words, his masculinity is a frustrating, even a "defeating" factor. It is not admired as a reflection of the lover's own masculinity. The element of narcissim is not at this point apparent. The objection that the Friend is not in any way sexually admired may be simply met: he is described as the "Master Mistris" of Shakespeare's "passion," and passion does not mean just "friendship," or even "Renaissance friendship." And because the context is that of a love poem, the notion of physical admiration would be specifically denied—we can be sure of that— if it did not, or was not supposed to, exist.

At this point in the sequence there has been no suggestion of lust; only of love and physical admiration. But that is nevertheless

enough to make the sonnet overtly homosexual, even if the suggestion is that this man's qualities steal *all* men's eyes. But the praise
of the Friend is at the expense of women. His face is painted by
nature and not by art; his gentleness is feminine in quality but not
tainted with woman's fickleness; his brighter eye does not rove; his
gaze transmutes those upon whom it falls. Women are thus seen as
"gentle," ideal, perfect love-objects, but perverted by their "falseness" and vanity. In the octave the Friend is seen idealistically,
rather in the manner that the classical Greeks saw boys.

The paradox inherent in this attitude is the fact that although
boys are spiritually more lovely than women, as escape from the
man-woman conflict their lovers still use them lustfully. The relationship is not actually free of "sex"; it merely seems to make sex
less agonizing.

What, in this poem, is "nature"? The question is important. In
the first line it seems to function simply as a tribute to the Friend's
"natural" beauty, as opposed to woman's "false" and painted
beauty. And in this compliment to the Friend "nature" itself is
regarded, by implication, as "good"; a permanent standard by
which the quality of all beloveds may properly be judged. This
man, whom Shakespeare has already addressed as his love is—
paradoxically—all that woman ought to be.

But is he? In the sestet nature itself is seen as having erred: in
the process of creating a "perfect" woman, it fell in love with its
own creation, and so turned it into a man. If this is not merely a
conceit that fails because "nature" has not been adequately
defined, then clearly it has a deeper meaning. And so it does. This
particular poem is nothing less than an apprehension of the apparent flaw in creation (an apprehension neither metaphysical nor
"conceited," but experientially inspired): that the sexual, which
should join male and female, which in one sense does join them,
should drive them apart: the conjunctive "thing" is also the
instrument of a fatal disharmony.

The realization of the existence of this paradox is what, in the
last analysis, led to Greek "homosexuality," which was an unsuc-
cessful experiment, an abortive escape route. Since man is almost
certainly physically bisexual, the Greeks were able to exploit their
situation physically. Modern homosexuality is usually a result of

some sort of psychically arrested development: a sociologically con-ditioned drive toward heterosexuality becomes distorted. The female object becomes displaced by a male one. Modern homo-sexual situations can nearly always be explained in terms of the original heterosexual drive: investigation nearly always reveals that the homosexual himself wants to be "normal." There was none of this "Freudian" background to Greek homosexuality, despite Freud's own suggestion that it was caused by the habit of putting boys in the charge of slaves instead of that of their mothers: this was a deliberate attempt, by men, to avoid the spiritually disturb-ing consequences of procreation.

The above is relevant, because it is the subject—it became the subject—of Shakespeare's sonnet sequence. Certain poets—Catul-lus is one example, and Shakespeare another—have had the faculty of completely transcending their age: what they experienced they experienced, of course, in terms of their respective ages; but they felt impelled and had the capacity to solve their problems in eter-nal—or comparatively eternal—terms. But the only way to begin to understand Shakespeare's solution is to try to understand the psy-chological background that he at any rate, if not some of his critics, assumes.

Sonnet 20 is relatively abstract because it is a resolutely cerebral attempt to analyze a new situation. It says, in effect, "I am in apparently absolute love with you, because while you have women's beauty you lack their 'false' sexuality; instead of lusting after you—since I appreciate that love's ideal fulfillment should be with a woman" ("adding one thing to my purpose nothing") "—I shall invest my hopes of fulfillment in you: women by 'using' you, have a chance of abandoning their falseness." That is the main sense, despite the incidental irony of "Mine be thy *love.*" At this stage Shakespeare is idealistically making the best of his situation; but it is impossible to deny that the young man's womanishness, with its "Greek" offer of an erotic union that evades the usual sex war, has not invited his lust. So the poem does not state that Shakespeare is "not homosexual," but that he proposes not to desire physical homosexual relations in the interests of a high ideal. Dover Wilson's view that Shakespeare "expressly dissociates his affec-tionate admiration for the beauty of his Friend's physique from any question of desire" is, surely, simplistic: it mistakes a resolution not to be homosexual for a disclaimer. The psychology of one man's admiration of another man's physique that was in no sense homosexual would be an interesting one.

The next nineteen sonnets record the gradual erosion of the idealism of 20. Sonnet 23 states the position clearly:

> As an unperfect actor on the stage,
> Who with his fears is put besides his part,
> Or some fierce thing repleat with too much rage,
> 4 Whose strengths abondance weakens his owne heart;
> So I for feare of trust, forget to say,
> The perfect ceremony of loves right,
> And in mine owne loves strength seeme to decay,
> 8 Oer-charg'd with burthen of mine owne loves might:
> O let my books be then the eloquence,
> And domb presagers of my speaking brest,
> Who pleade for love, and look for recompence,
> 12 More then that tonge that more hath more exprest.
> O learne to read what silent love hath writ,
> To heare with eies belongs to loves fine wit.

The actor who completely fails because he does not know his lines perfectly is a metaphor for the man in love (Shakespeare) who fails because he is incapable of knowing what the "right" way to behave is; with savage irony "rage" equates in one word both "passion to behave rightly" and the "lust" that undermines this passion; if it had not been for the original, if strangely inspired, lust (which in 20 Shakespeare proposes to transform), there would have been no desire to celebrate "love's right [rite]". The pun on "right" is characteristic of this sequence, for it solemnly gathers together under one sign both "the good" and the human need that undermines this good. But the idealism, the decision to intellectualize the physical and emotional situation, is still maintained: in Freudian terminology, Shakespeare will sublimate his feelings into his "books" (poems: these poems), because for the Friend to "hear with eyes" (ayes: positively, fruitfully)—a marvelously appropriate description of reading poetry—is to get the "wit," the truth, of love—without lust. Of course, the sneering irony of "love's fine wit" again undermines the robustness of the idealistic intention; but that is no more than honest, since all fine intentions are thus undermined.

In 22.13-14 and 25.13 we are informed that the Friend has in
some sense returned Shakespeare's love; we are not at this point
entitled to assume more than that he has affirmed (whether sin-
cerely or insincerely, understandingly or stupidly, is beside the
point) Shakespeare's view of the matter. But 25 and 26, in their different ways, contain hints of disaster. The final couplet of 25
opposes the grimly foreboding suggestions made in the first twelve
lines with a defiant but somewhat bathetic-sounding platonic faith.
Sonnet 26 introduces a new note of irony, which has previously
been only at Shakespeare's own expense. In 23 the poetry was to be
Shakespeare's "eloquence," and the Friend was urged to read
"What silent [not active, unselfish] love hath writ." But 26, the sarcastic "written ambassage," is sent only "To witnesse duty, not to
shew my wit." It would be foolish to imagine that Shakespeare is
not here bitterly referring back to the mood of Sonnet 23. Now he
must "dare to boast" of his love, and must hope for a "good conceipt" from the Friend in order to have the nature of his "Duty"
made clear to him. The ironic element here is no longer a merely
undermining one: "Good conceipt" is, one feels, ostensibly completely sarcastic. Where previously irony, not entirely unpeevish,
has undermined seriousness, functioning as a ghostly intellectual-
ism (its type of function is in itself an irony), undermines irony. The
seriousness is contained in "I hope," and the hope is for the sort of
understanding of which poetry is composed.

The emotion 20 describes, with a coldness that is of course partially programmatic, is very newly felt; the poem is highly intellectual, almost "metaphysical." The sarcastic 26 is relatively devoid
of thought; here we see the idealism degenerating into a mood that
is not unlike petulance. But this is temporary. The next six sonnets
—although much more "personal" than 20, inasmuch as they refer
to no plan or ideal, and do not trouble to deny the writer's despair
at absence or neglect—are a fairly relaxed series of examinations of
the state of being in love. The project expressed at 20.14, however
richly it may still suggest the sort of loving generosity that Shakespeare wishes to achieve, has been shelved in the interests of a more
direct, less metaphysically complicated manner of expression:
Shakespeare simply wants to be read for his "love" (32.14).

But the confidence in his own work that Shakespeare expresses here, and his sarcasm about a more stylistically accomplished rival poet (the notion of him may be introduced as early as 21), must not be taken as a poetically nonfunctional egotism, an "understandable" bit of incidental self-conceit. All poets, if for them poetry is a process of self-illumination, must assume that their lines are eternal: they are trying to express the truth, and there is a sense in which only truth is eternal. Even 32.14, which is simple enough, contains an important statement about what poetry ought to be, whether it has style or not.

So far the Friend has not, according to the poems (and this is all that matters), made Shakespeare unhappy through anything worse than indifference—an indifference not exactly definable from the description of it, but clearly something between positive neglect coupled with overindulgence of a skillful flattery and involuntary absence coupled with polite (perfectly proper) attention to another admirer.

Since we now reach, at Sonnet 33, the beginning of the so-called "Estrangement" group, it will be appropriate to ask the question, Why should the Friend's behavior, in a sequence that I claim is personal, be "not exactly definable"? The answer is, simply, Because the sequence is personal. Circulated among other private friends or not (this may apply to some or all of 1-17, or to lost sonnets), this sequence is exactly what it continually says it is: addressed to the Friend, who would of course have known about the extent and type of his indifference. Critics may treat an "unfinished" (if only in the sense that Coleridge wrongly thought that "Kubla Khan" was unfinished), personally directed sequence as though it "ought" to yield biographical precisions that the writer would never have bothered to think of. Nevertheless, Shakespeare maintained confidence in the poetic process of writing these sonnets as he wrote them; had he himself decided to publish them — the consensus is that he did not—he might have made certain matters clearer. As it is, he apparently did not. But we must not use the occasional vagueness of the poems as they stand as an excuse for turning them into deliberately planned fictions; as deliberately planned fictions they simply do not make sense.

IV

When we come to Sonnets 33 and 34 something new has happened. Shakespeare is no longer just complaining: whatever the Friend has actually "done," it is something that would generally be regarded as "reprehensible," a dirty trick. J. Q. Adams noted nineteen "strong" words from 33 and 34—words such as "basest," "ugly," "stain," "rotten," "disgrace." Even Ingram and Redpath, whose commentary remains as uncommitted as possible, admit that "something dark and unworthy has come between the friends." The general sense of 33 and 34 is that the "sun" of the Friend's goodness has been obscured: all that we can really infer about the nature of his behavior is that it proved him *not* to be the perfect youth of Sonnet 20. Previously he was seen as gilding all that he looked upon; now he is compared to a sun that "flatters" the mountain tops, whose "guilding" of the "pale streames with heavenly alcumy" is therefore equivocal, delusive. Beeching decided that the Friend's "fault" was the one alluded to in Sonnets 41, 42 and 43 (going to bed with Shakespeare's mistress); this is tempting, but unlikely. For the sun of 33 and 34 has betrayed itself by *permitting* "basest" (the word brings together the senses of menial, worthless, selfish, degraded and degrading, dingiest—and just possibly even "plebeian") clouds to hide his visage from the world. His "fault" seems to have consisted in allowing a person—a person not only reprehensible in the eyes of the world but also actually reprehensible—to associate with him: this is a disgrace. I think it would be overingenious to conclude that this "region cloude" was Shakespeare's own mistress, although it cannot be entirely ruled out. The use of "him" at 33.13, and the way it is taken up, militates against, although of course does not disprove, the notion of the "region cloude" being either a piece of behavior, "something" (as opposed to an actual person) or a woman. Dover Wilson, following Beeching, confidently speaks of "an allusion to the liaison mentioned in 40, 41, 42"; he is thinking of 35.9, "For to thy sensuall fault I bring in sense"—but this is totally conjectural. All that we can certainly infer is that the Friend could no longer be allowed, poetically, to function as a symbol of "perfection."

The argument of the final couplet of 33 is extremely complicated, and depends on a full understanding of the subtlties of the preceding lines. As I have pointed out, the sun-Friend is not at this point charged with anything more than "permitting" "basest" clouds to obscure him, so that he "steals" to the west: we cannot see his furtive progress; he is, the pun on "steals" implies, ashamed of himself. The final couplet drops the metaphor, although it refers to it. The Friend is no longer the sun, but has become a person again, "my love." The "region cloude," "him"—the Friend's "fault" represented by, I think, another person—is not disdained by the Friend on the grounds, ironically, of the observation that Shakespeare himself has made in lines 1-12: if heaven's sun, the actual sun, can become corrupt, lose brightness through being obscured, become dim—then of course so can "Suns of the world" (there is a malicious pun on "Suns" here: "Christs," implying "so you think he's Christ, as well as a kind of sun, which I, who really love you, have called you") become corrupt. The verb "stain" is used both transitively and intransitively, and the transitive sense is of course "corrupt." Shakespeare's argument is: the sun-Friend is corrupt because he associates with a "base" person. Ironically, the Friend's bland argument is that, since (as Shakespeare himself has just shown) the real sun sometimes goes in, so why should not "Suns of the world" sometimes become corrupt.

We begin to get the sense, familiar to us from the later sonnets, of a potentially beautiful and "good" man, a heavenly sun, whose love is beneficent and morally uplifting, becoming subject to sickening corruption. The way in which lines 13-14 of Sonnet 33 abandon the metaphor, causing line 14 to represent, simultaneously, an argument of the Friend's and a bitter statement by the writer, brilliantly conveys the feeling of a Friend who can be worse than obtuse: who can betray himself by being willfully and cruelly blind to the nature of Shakespeare's praise of him—to his own goodness, in fact. The bland, flat comma at the end of 33.13 (Ingram and Redpath insert a colon, ruining—as they so often do—the original tone, and therefore sense, by their disastrous superimposition of twentieth-century logical punctuation on constructions that were conceived in unawareness that such a system would ever exist) perfectly expresses the Friend's capacity for slick, grieving glibness. (And, in view of the rather explicit "Suns of the world," I cannot really see the strength of the Beeching/Dover Wilson argument that the "region cloude" is either the Mistress or the Friend's behavior with her.)

My reading admits that there is no real clue, even in the nature of the imagery, as to what the Friend's fault has actually been; but this is unimportant in comparison with the main point: that the Friend is capable of corruption, is in fact to some extent corrupt, where Shakespeare had previously regarded him as perfect—perfect enough to be a recipient of his love, which the Friend would then, being capable of it, pass on to women to "treasure." (We shall see this theme taken up again very shortly.) Sonnet 34, which describes a mechanism of forgiveness in terms of the transitions of mood that lead to it, acknowledges the corruption, but mentions that the Friend is now ashamed. Nothing could more clearly illustrate the manner in which these sonnets, as a sequence, record a swiftly moving series of emotional events: in 33.13-14, the Friend was not ashamed; now, by 34, he is.

The "disgrace" of which Shakespeare is still conscious does not necessarily imply, I think, that he feels imself socially or even morally disgraced; his bearing of "the strong offenses losse [or perhaps 'cross']" refers mainly to his own feelings of having misled the Friend by considering him as perfect. This is really the theme of Sonnet 35, where Shakespeare admonishes himself for having justified the Friend's "trespass" "with compare [analogy]." To make the point more forcefully, he begins 35 itself with a series of analogies, and then immediately reprimands himself for doing so. He has seen the Friend as a summer's day, the lord of his love, the sun, and now as a rose, a silver fountain, the sun again, and so on: i.e., his love has falsified its object by describing it in passionate, "romantic" metaphors. The primary force of "thy sensuall fault" is not pejorative, although it does contain an acknowledgement of the Friend's sensuality (foolishly ignored in 20, as the pun involved in the last two words of the phrase implies: "I brought *incense* to what was actually your sensuality; I ignored the real you in an idealism that I now recognize was self-indulgent"). "Sensual" could mean "Endowed with the faculty of sensation (but not with reason)" (*OED*, 2) as well as "lewd," and the emphasis is thus put upon Shakespeare's original fault of having perversely viewed the Friend as a wholly "rational" being: there was even another use of sensual to mean simply "Sensuous; physical" (*OED*, 3a). We have seen how in Sonnet 20 Shakespeare attempted to deal with his situation too cerebrally; the Friend's masculinity was "to my purpose nothing." Now he recognizes that the Friend is sensual—both physical and "lewd": since the Friend's "adverse party" (his sensuality) is his advocate, and in a just case, we must read this as a new recognition of the realities—doubtless unconscious ones at the time 20 was written—of the situation. If the Friend is "sensual," if to be loved he must be loved for what he is (i.e., partly for his sensuality), then Shakespeare needs to be an "accessory" to his own sensuality:

> Such civill war is in my love and hate,
> That I an accessory needs must be
> To that sweete theefe which sourely robs from me.

Understanding this in the context of the sequence, Shakespeare's "love" in 35 is a combination of both his idealistic love in Sonnet 20 and his more guilty, "sensual" love; and his "hate" in 35 is both self-hatred (for his corrupting self-indulgent idealism) and hate of the sensual fault. Thus the "sweete theefe" performs a double function, clearly reflecting the agonizing muddle he is in: it is both his lust, ruining his love, and his love, ruining his lust.

The absolute forthrightness of Sonnet 36, in which he decides to make a break, is only fully explicable in the light of this. There is no need to be overliteral in interpreting this sonnet. The "seperable [separating] spight" may have had a basis in biography, as a social or other bar between the two men, or it may not. We shall never know. But its main function in the sonnet is, certainly, as a metaphor for "my lust for you." The phrase "one respect" could refer to the Mistress; but again, whether it does or not, it functions as an equivalent for the "thing" of Sonnet 20: it means "one relationship," "mutual regard" (Dover Wilson), but also "focus of attention" (Ingram and Redpath). The "thing" is no longer "to my purpose nothing." What has happened is that the Friend's "shame" and apologies have led to overt "sensuality": so Shakespeare now says, in the octave, "we must separate, although we are in love and 'one': in that way my sensualities [blots] can be borne by me without your having any kind of guilty complicity [Shakespeare was older, as he makes clear, felt responsible, and believed that he himself had now become a corrupting influence]. We both want the same thing, but our homosexual lust—although it could easily be consummated—robs itself of its own delight."

The difficult "sole effect," obviously a bitter allusion to the fact that the only definite, "visible" result of love is sensual, is well glossed by Dover Wilson as "emotions that no other experience can give," but—oddly— by Ingram and Redpath as "the identical working of our love."

Again, "Fortunes dearest spight" of Sonnet 37 need mean no more than Shakespeares's realization of the exact nature of his love for the Friend, and of the easy fall from his earlier virtuous idealism. Sonnet 37, an unusually simple poem, maintains the resolution of 36; the poet will once more enjoy his love vicariously, sublimate it by loving only the friend's just and deserved public glory. (This poem does incidentally give strong support to the biographical theory that the Friend was of high rank. Certainly it was not written to a sea-cook.) The next two sonnets continue to maintain the resolution of Sonnet 36, and to develop the theme of praise.

Then, in Sonnets 40, 41 and 42, we have a startling new group. Once again the situation is changed. The Friend has supplanted Shakespeare in the affections—and, probably, the bed—of a woman. Whether this woman was the Mistress of the 127-152 group is not clear; it is likely, in view of 133.2 ("my friend and me"); but we may treat her as identical, and lose nothing of the meaning. This is where Shakespeare returns to the theme of 20.14; we must read the poems directly in the light of the intention there expressed. Thus, in 42.1 he more or less acknowledges that the Friend, from whom after all he has just decided to separate, has some right to this heterosexual experience, even if he has shown some spite in taking it. But now, in the harsh light of actual experience, Shakespeare quite forgets his previous idealism, by which women were to "treasure" their "use" by the Friend: he is jealous of both the Friend and the Mistress for excluding him, and sourly so because she is "having" the Friend, a "losse in love" (here "love" means, sarcastically, lust) that touches him very "neerely." Lines 5-14 cruelly parody the old idealistic procedures, leading to the deliberately ridiculous conclusion that the bed-denied cuckold (Shakespeare) is sweetly flattered by being the sole love of the woman (who is sleeping with someone else).

Sonnets 127-152, whether written at the same time as this group or not (probably they were) could not have been interpolated here, where they would have interrupted the sequence to the Friend; the reader is, in any case, almost deliberately referred to them. They are rightly placed at the end, because, whatever feelings Shakespeare may admit to having about the Mistress, it is, as Sonnet 20 implies, the problem of the male-female relationship that he mostly wants to solve, even if the way to a solution involves homosexual experiences.

In my edition of the Sonnets I was inclined to think that Shakespeare and the Friend had, at some time, some kind of physical sexual relationship. I now think this less likely, since—as I may have helped to show in this essay—there is no evidence for more than a strong physical attraction. Indeed, the question of homosexuality must be acknowledged to be present only, perhaps, because it would be, in the light of modern psychological knowledge, simplistic to remove it. I have no doubt that Shakespeare did "fall in love with" the Friend; but, as the frankly lusting sonnets to the Mistress show, his heterosexual impulses remained intact. Whatever a "homosexual" was in those days, whatever sets of circumstances produced him, Shakespeare was not one; but he did experience homosexual emotions and desires.

Eliot once said of Donne that thinking was, for him, experience. So it was for Shakespeare in this sequence of poems. His situation led him to think, and his thinking led him continually to feel new emotions. For a time he sees "love," such as that between himself and his Friend of the same sex, as opposed to "lust" (between man and woman); then he tries to resolve the conflict between them, to cause them to function together. But as Sonnet 152 clearly states, the Mistress was not finally worthy. While he thought she was worthy, he made some notable attempts at resolving the problem; and if Sonnet 152 is a bathetic ending to so remarkable a sequence, then it is at least an honest one—as Shakespeare says, all his honest faith in this woman is lost.

The Friend, too, as we know, proved unworthy; but Shakespeare could with him reach serenity by resolutely abandoning sexual desire, and wishing—against even the possibility of hope—for the Friend's welfare and for his attainment of a state of goodness. At the very end (125) he can state convincingly that the relationship had not, finally, been a selfish one from his point of view.

An understanding of the so-called homosexual situation, as displayed in the sonnets I have discussed, is essential for an understanding of the whole sequence. I have tried here to trace some of the main lines of thought and feeling. Basically, it is a matter of following how "thinking," the thing that sicklies over experience with its pale cast, affected feeling—and vice versa; of acknowledging an extraordinary degree of seriousness and poetic idealism; of realizing that, because for Shakespeare these sonnets represented something very much akin to what prayer represents to a serious Christian, the writing of them eventually affected his attitude and his behavior to as great a degree as his situation prompted them in the first place.

THE SHAKESPEAREAN QUALITY

BY

W. G. INGRAM

I

"Fine Things" and "Inconsequential" Images

What is it that seems especially "Shakespearean" in Shakespeare's treatment of the sonnet, not in biographical (or fictional) theme, but in pattern of thought-development and structural movement? One aspect of this may be described in terms of that familiar Shakespearean characteristic, a highly individual use of imagery, and its effect on this pattern.

Detailed study of Shakespeare's imagery has mostly (and understandably) been directed to the plays: to analysis of its content,[1] to the associative quality of Shakespeare's habit of mind,[2] to its thematic significance,[3] and to the development of his mastery of it as a means of characterization, of dramatic symbolism, of sustaining dramatic unity of tone.[4] Invaluable studies have also been made of the relations between Shakespeare's employment of imagery and the contemporary art of rhetoric.[5] But allusions in all these studies to the Sonnets are few. Miss Spurgeon necessarily cited examples of their subject matter; Armstrong makes a few citations; Professor Clemen has two brief passing references; and the instances in Baldwin and in Sister Miriam Joseph are, compared with the plays, minimal. In studies of the Sonnets we naturally find attention directed to their imagery; but the interest has been largely thematic. Its effect on structure and on what I will call "movement" *inside* the sonnet form—on the nature of the thought progression that modifies content-pattern—has received but limited notice. Yet this is one of the features that markedly distinguish the "Shakespearean" feel of the Sonnets from the general run of contemporary sonneteering. Wilson Knight characteristically (and valuably) concentrates on the thematic symbolism of the imagery;[6] J. W. Lever, taking a hint from Armstrong, makes considerable use of "image clusters" in his discussion of probable groupings of the poems and in his interpretation of their themes.[7] T. W. Baldwin uses his discovery of "genetic images," of a discoverable sequence of image-subjects throughout Shakespeare's work which is almost organically progressive, to defend the Quarto order.[8] Yet by and large the analytical study of poetic imagery, such as the work of H. W. Wells, C. Day Lewis, and Rosemund Tuve,[9] and scrutiny of the structural pattern of the Sonnets have seldom been brought together with particular relevance to these poems' internal movement of thought, a notable exception being Mrs. Nowottny's article to which I refer below.[10]

Certainly, as G. K. Hunter says in prefacing his essay on the dramatic technique of the Sonnets, this is "because criticism has been overshadowed by biographical speculation. There have been few aesthetic critics and these . . . have disregarded or noticed only with condemnation the reactions of their biographically-minded fellows."[11] And he argues cogently that we shall appreciate the Sonnets justly only if we recognize that when Shakespeare is writing a sonnet "he is not being a quaint and elaborate lyrist . . . or a passionate biographical poet whose confessions are cut short by his conceits, so much as . . . a *dramatist.*" This is a valuable and timely reminder that in the Sonnets "a dramatist describes a series of emotional situations between persons (real or fictitious) in a series of separate short poems . . . raising in the reader the dramatic reactions . . . by his implication in the lives and fates of the persons depicted"; and he cites instances where such a poem "is not simply a better example of a conceited sonnet, it is a more affecting poem, and this is because he makes the conceit serve a felt human situation."[12]

Professor Hunter's thesis, or something closely akin to it, is developed at greater length in a valuable study, *The Dramatic Character of Shakespeare's Sonnets,* by Dr. A.M. Pirkhofer of Innsbruck. Theirs is a key argument, and it not only helps us to understand the Sonnets collectively and often individually, but it also aids us in our comprehension of certain individual passages in detail, sometimes pointing to an answer (not always self-evident) to the question, "What is the image Shakespeare is employing here?" or possibly in one or two cases to the determination of a textual reading. The theme I propose to discuss here is no contradiction to Hunter's and Pirkhofer's thesis, but is in some ways complementary to it. For one element of the characteristic Shakespearean quality can be found in what I have already called the movement of the sonnet, the thought progression that is an essential element of its structure as a poem, as distinct from the merely formal patterning of lines and rhyme scheme; and this thought progression is essentially linked with the way Shakespeare's mind works in the deployment and development of the imagery.

"The literary image,'" Andrei Sinyavsky is reported to have argued during his trial, "is best when it is widest and unconfined." An adaptation of this general theme may have some application to my topic. It is a commonplace that, of the many thousands of poems of the sonneteering vogue, most "confined" the image within the "wit" of a conceit,[13] reducing Leigh Hunt's "moment's monument" or the memorable recording of Hunter's "emotional situation" to a verbal-intellectual fancy in which any experiential intensity of the "moment" was replaced by a slight, conventional sentiment, an excuse for rhetorical intricacy or panache. Of the minor sonnet writers, the few poems that still carry conviction and vitality to modern ears—a few by, say, Daniel or Constable, or best known of them all, through anthologies, Drayton's *Idea's Mirrour* LXI, "Since there's no help, come let us kiss and part"—live just because they achieve that quality which Hunter identifies as the essence of the Shakespearean moment's monument of "generating in the reader a reaction more proper to drama," rather than for any skill in purely decorative conceits. (In Drayton's sonnet the "image", of love personified on its deathbed, is introduced in the sestet as supporting the dramatized situation. The poem does not begin with an elaborate conceit; there is no feeling that a conceit engendered the poem or was its total end and aim.) And this preference is largely the result of the modern reader's changed expectations concerning the function of imagery and its place in the "logic" of a poem.

Of the major poets who wrote sonnet sequences, Sidney more than Spenser evokes this reaction proper to drama. Yet in Sidney the manner of development, the movement of the sonnet, is distinct from Shakespeare's; and this largely derives from the difference in the degree of the poets' submission to their own imagery and from the different thought progressions that result. Sidney, consciously "a peece of a Logician," employed the wide gamut of Ramist rhetoric in his poetic practice. He employed it not just decoratively but, especially in the *Astrophil and Stella* sonnets, functionally in the structure of the poetic logic of his poems. Whether in sonnets that most seem to present a dramatized moment—such as *Astrophil and Stella* XXXVIII, "This night while sleep"; LIII, "In Martiall sports"; or CV, "Unhappie sight"—or in more elaborately conceited sonnets like XIII, "Phoebus was Judge"; XXIX, "Like some weake Lords"; or the kiss sonnets (LXXIX-LXXXIV) —the imagery where employed is potently integral to the unity of the poem. But the line of development, the flow of imagery, is also more direct, more translucent than Shakespeare's frequently becomes, and the result is something more evidently, more intellectually coherent than the complex undertones often evoked by Shakespeare. This quality of Shakespeare's imagery in several sonnets, indeed, disturbs some readers when they cease to read in a way that yields passively to the emotional impact, the sensuous first appeal, and begin to ask, "How does the image work?" With Sidney there is no doubt; with a number of Shakespeare's sonnets there is, at least at a first intellectual interrogation.

To illustrate just how this movement of thought through image works, a sonnet of Daniel's (*Delia* XXX) may be compared with one of Shakespeare's (12) which has some similarity of theme. Daniel is clearly remembering Desportes (*Cléonice* LXIII), but the theme is common enough in the sonnet tradition; what is even more noticeable is the recurrence of symbols, even phrases, that are commonplaces and which will crop up here and there in Shakespeare's sonnets, too. It is the difference of impact, and with it the whole progression of the sonnet, that ring deeper tones in Shakespeare's work.

> I once may see when years shall wreck my wrong,
>   When golden hairs shall change to silver wire;
> And those bright rays that kindle all this fire
>   Shall fail in force, their working not so strong.
>
> Then Beauty (now the burthen of my song)
>   Whose glorious blaze the world doth so admire,
> Must yield up all to tyrant Time's desire;
>   Then fade those flowers that deck'd her pride so long.
>
> When if she grieve to gaze her in her glass,
>   Which then presents her winter-wither'd hue,
> Go you, my verse, go tell her what she was;
>   For what she was, the best shall find in you.
> Your fiery heat lets not her glory pass,
>   But (Phoenix like) shall make her live anew.
>   (*Delia* XXX)

> When I do count the clock that tells the time,
> And see the brave day sunk in hideous night;
> When I behold the violet past prime,
> 4 And sable curls o'er-silver'd all with white;
> When lofty trees I see barren of leaves,
> Which erst from heat did canopy the herd,
> And summer's green all girded up in sheaves
> 8 Borne on the bier with white and bristly beard:
> Then of thy beauty do I question make
> That thou among the wastes of time must go,
> Since sweets and beauties do themselves forsake,
> 12 And die as fast as they see others grow;
>   And nothing 'gainst Time's scythe can make defence
>   Save breed to brave him when he takes thee hence.[14]
>   (Sonnet 12)

The phrases in Daniel that remind us (but often how thinly) of Shakespearean speech, the images that both poets select from the contemporary repertoire, catch the eye immediately: "Golden hairs" that "change to silver wire"; beauty's "glorious blaze" — subtly different from "the blazon of sweet beauty's best" in Sonnet 106; "tyrant Time"; the "glass, / Which then presents her winter-wither'd hue"; his verse's "fiery heat" which "shall make her live anew." But it is not the richer evocative language of Shakespeare's lines ("And see the brave day sunk in hideous night"; "summer's green all girded up in sheaves / Borne on the bier with white and bristly beard"; "That thou among the wastes of time must go") or the mere proliferation of images of concrete association that alone distinguishes the two styles. Nor is it such intrusive ornamentation as Daniel's almost tautological Phoenix in his last line. The progression of the Shakespeare poem has a complexity of verbal and conceptual associations that moves, unobtrusively and compulsively, from the concrete symbols of transience (the clock, the violet) to death, Time, and defiance of mere mortality. Temporality in the first line is simple, measurable, horological; the second line not only compasses the whole passing day but with its powerfully emotive contrast of adjectives ("brave day" and "hideous night") imposes an atmosphere of doom on the commonplace clock that just "tells the time." The next lines carry us further, from the transitory day to the passing seasons of nature and of man, "barren" in line 5 having a thematic undertone relevant to the matter of the first group of sonnets. And with line 8 Shakespeare's habitual verbal associativeness begins to take charge: "bier" seems to suggest to him "beard," and the ripened beards of barley are "white and bristly" with the hoar of age. We have moved from the immediate moment to the recurrent transience of all things, and this leads us into the contemplation of beauty passing "among the wastes of time," and, with the seasonal harvesting or ripened grain, to "Time's scythe." Such a progression, memorable though individual lines or images are for their emotionally charged phrases and their evocation of concrete nature, is far more than Keats's "fine things said unintentionally" while the poet's conscious art is absorbed in the intensity of working out conceits. It imposes a pattern on the thought by the very fact that the images are not confined within the wit of a conceit but extend and move almost with an impulse of their own.

An equally interesting progression is to be found in Sonnet 15. Again the multiple images grow one out of another, and with them this time the thought closes in from the general to the particular, from the world and its transience to the love of friend for friend. The first quatrain, enunciating in its opening lines the universality of transience and decline, in its third and fourth employs a meta-

phor that presents the general condition of man on an analogical
level:

> When I consider everything that grows
> Holds in perfection but a little moment,
> That this huge stage presenteth nought but shows
> Whereon the stars in secret influence comment;

The image of the next quatrain parallels this, but with a difference:

> When I perceive that men as plants increase,
> Cheered and check'd even by the selfsame sky,
> Vaunt in their youthful sap, at height decrease,
> And wear their brave state out of memory:

Where the former image was offered on an analogical level, this
one brings man into direct fellowship with the natural world that
had stood remote. The sky that commented, though with "secret
influence" from a distance, on the "shows" presented on man's
worldly state, now cheers and checks the players as directly, as
overtly, as the seasons promote and curb the growth of the plant
world. (Typically, the image of line 8 derives at least in part from
association with the actors in lines 3 and 4; for Elizabethan players
frequently wore the finery discarded by noble patrons when fashion
had demoded it.) We have moved *on*, not circled by the superficial
extension of a conceit; have progressed, not by a logical exploita-
tion of the former image in the manner of, say, Donne, but into a
different yet not inconsequent image; and with this progression we
have moved deeper and closer into the human condition and the
poet's contemplation of it—which is about to become his personal
involvement *with* it.

For now follows the sestet:

> Then the conceit of this inconstant stay
> Sets you most rich in youth before my sight,
> Where wasteful time debateth with decay
> To change your day of youth to sullied night;
>> And all in war with Time for love of you,
>> As he takes from you I engraft you new.

The general reflection on man's estate is now applied intimately to the poet, his friend, and the perpetual war of Time with youth and beauty. The vocabulary is still drawn from the world of nature and the universe—day and night and the engrafting of trees. But from the remote impersonal spectatorship of the stars we have moved, through the direct consideration of the human condition, to the active partisanship, in the war against Time, of the love of friend for friend; and it is through the shifting imagery that this movement is effected. This is the functional activity of imagery in pushing the thought-movement forward, not concentrically but in a more complex progression that characterizes a number of Shakespeare's sonnets. What Rosemund Tuve wrote of one of Shakespeare's metaphors in *Antony and Cleopatra* may be applied to a number of single images and sequences in the Sonnets: The metaphor "operates immediately to furnish many meanings—which are possible, not compulsory, suggested, not stated, uncountable, not limited. They are not even any longer under the poet's own control except as he reins them in with the tiny threads of the co-operating words. All tropes give the reader his head in this fashion. But it is precisely because they open all these dangers that metaphors are so powerful an aid (as is Shakespeare's) to suggesting the significance of appearance, to insight as compared with sight."[15] And she speaks of writers who "use metaphor . . . to fairly push one into an abstract progress." Now this is just what is happening in some of the apparently heterogeneous or (physically or logically) incongruous sequences in several of the Sonnets, and it is this which fits these sequences into a structural poetic unity.

Probably the most cited, among the Sonnets, as instancing Shakespeare's shifting imagery, as exemplifying what is apparently an almost completely inconsequential sequence of disparates, is Sonnet 60. It is also a striking example of the way the association of image with word and of word with image dictates the patterning of the thought progression while still retaining in fact an inherent unity.

> Like as the waves make towards the pebbled shore,
> So do our minutes hasten to their end;
> Each changing place with that which goes before
> 4 In sequent toil all forwards do contend.
> Nativity, once in the main of light,

Crawls to maturity, wherewith being crown'd,
Crookèd eclipses 'gainst his glory fight,
8 And Time that gave doth now his gift confound.
Time doth transfix the flourish set on youth,
And delves the parallels in beauty's brow,
Feeds on the rarities of nature's truth;
12 And nothing stands but for his scythe to mow.
   And yet to times in hope my verse shall stand,
   Praising thy worth, despite his cruel hand.

Beginning with a "straight" simile of the advancing tide creeping imperceptibly on the shore (the advancing tide, for time in Shakespeare is always the destroyer, the eroder), the poem with its succeeding quatrains presents a series of images that on the literal plane appear inconsistent, but which gain a thematic coherence as one studies how they are produced one from another. From the advancing tide of the sea (a concrete image) we leap first to the abstract nativity (whose submerged concrete association with the newborn babe is implicit, but not explicated, in the verb "crawls"), then to light that is "crowned" with maturity (another concrete / abstract conjunction), to eclipses that "fight" against light's glory, to gifts destroyed by the giver. Time personified is the giver and destroyer of these gifts, but immediately becomes a dart thrower, a digger of trenches, a destroying cankerworm, a reaper. And these are not presented as simple parallels, as a bundle of images almost paratactically disposed, as in the exceptional structure of Sonnet 66 (or as, say, the similes in Shelley's "Skylark," to reinforce the one concept by accumulation of alternatives). They grow one out of another in an ever-changing concatenation that may defy logic but leads the mind on emotionally to the climax of line 12.

A poem which can even more disturb the mind that demands strict logical coherence, that requires a progression as categorically consistent as the steps in a geometrical proof, is Sonnet 86. Put it beside a Donne sonnet and we see at once the intellectual coherence of the latter, the alogical incongruity but emotional congruence of the image sequence in the former.

Was it the proud full sail of his great verse,
Bound for the prize of all-too-precious you,
That did my ripe thoughts in my brain inhearse,
4 Making their tomb the womb wherein they grew?

Was it his spirit, by spirits taught to write
Above a mortal pitch, that struck me dead?
No, neither he, nor his compeers by night
8 Giving him aid, my verse astonishèd:
He, nor that affable familiar ghost
Which nightly gulls him with intelligence,
As victors of my silence cannot boast,—
12 I was not sick of any fear from thence:
     But when your countenance fill'd up his line,
     Then lack'd I matter; that enfeebl'd mine.
                  (Sonnet 86)

Salvation to all that will is nigh,
That All, which always is All everywhere,
Which cannot sinne, and yet all sinnes must beare,
4 Which cannot die, yet cannot chuse but die,
Loe, faithfull Virgin, yeelds himselfe to lye
In prison, in thy wombe; and though he there
Can take no sinne, nor thou give, yet he'will weare
8 Taken from thence, flesh, which deaths force may trie.
Ere by the spheares time was created, thou
Wast in his minde, who is thy Sonne, and Brother,
Whom thou conceiv'st, conceiv'd; yea thou art now
12 Thy Makers maker, and thy Fathers mother,
Thou'hast light in darke; and shutst in little roome,
Immensity cloysterd in thy deare wombe.
                  (Donne, *La Corona* II)

Donne's poem builds up a series of intellectual paradoxes: perfection bearing all sins, immortality that "Cannot chuse but die," infinity imprisoned, immensity cloistered in a womb, the Creator of all things Himself conceived in mortal flesh. The emotional depth of religious sincerity is indubitable, the sense of wonder (a powerfully emotional reaction) is awakened. Yet the basis of presentation of the whole, the very nature of paradox itself, is an intellectual apprehension: and throughout (the Christian mythology accepted) there is a complete conceptual consistency of the contraries. We are never pulled up short by the question, "How ever did he get from there to here?"

Shakespeare's poem, on the other hand, assaulting us with a powerful opening metaphor, proceeds with a literal or logical incongruity of images quite startling once we cease to let the resonance of the verse itself carry us onwards with the impulse of its own movement. The *stately* motion of the *galleon* of lines 1-2 performs in lines 3-4 the feat of *burying* the poet's *thoughts*—in the womb that engendered them, the poet's *brain*. The next lines forget the tall ship and see the rival's "spirit" inspired by *ghosts*, one of which acts as an intelligencer, a phantasmal intelligence agent. And the couplet turns for its diction to the "terms of art" of rhetoric. "What a gallimaufry is here!" the logician may well cry. And yet the poem stands squarely on its own feet throughout all its tangential movements by reason of its emotional coherence—a sort of *tonal* harmony. Shakespeare here is, to quote Hunter once more, "not a Metaphysical *manqué*": the sonnet has a structural progression that is individual, and, considered in this light, integral.

The Keatsian appraisal, then, will not hold in such cases. It too evidently, as the ensuing "Is this to be borne?" in Keats's letter proves, detaches the "fine things" from their context and delights in them in isolation from the tenor of the poem as an artistic unity. (Significantly, the example he cites is the second quatrain of Sonnet 12, which I have tried above to relate to the rest of the poem.) Keats's remark was made when he was finishing *Endymion* and his approach to poetry was still much under the influence of Hunt. But this way of reading the Sonnets continued long after Keats, and I suspect accounts for the frequently unrepresentative selections from them (as a corpus) in many popular anthologies.[16] The examples in collections later in the nineteenth century, and in our own, mostly reflect the post-Romantic taste that gave preference to this Keatsian culling of "fine things" for their emotive appeal over sonnets more conceited or those dramatizing the intenser moments of the personal relationships between poet, friend, and mistress. "Every schoolboy"—and any of us whose later estimate of Shakespeare is largely "what Teacher taught me"—knows this strong, concrete, evocative quality of much of his imagery. Donne, we remember, can convey strong emotion while arousing comparatively few visual or strongly sensory reactions. Daniel's Phoenix, we feel, is a literary bird. Shakespeare's Philomel (102.7) may have a literary name and her hymns be mournful because of a classical legend, but when she "in summer's front doth sing / And stops her pipe in growth of riper days" we begin already to forget her bookish origin. And when "wild music burthens every bough" the tone of our reaction is likely to derive as much from our experience of an English copse in full summer as from our intellectual recognition that what he is really referring to is the multitude of rival poets who are now singing his friend's praises. Indeed, one suspects that many readers overlook the latter (the ultimately relevant) meaning in submitting to the line's evocation of days when "summer" was "pleasant." In another instance, such a "tonal harmony" as I have described as distinct from a lucidly logical application of the image occurs also in Sonnet 73. Though the whole sequence here is far from incongruous, it depends primarily on the elegiac quality inherent in each image—late autumn, after-sunset twilight, a fire dying in its own ashes. And the difficulty commentators have found in disentangling the "Bare ruin'd choirs where late the sweet birds sang" from the "boughs which shake against the cold" is in strong contrast to our old friend the General Reader's immediate acceptance of the line for its evocation of his own mood in recalling a walk in the late autumn woods. We can each of us work out for ourselves afterwards (if on literal analysis we find need to) the exact meaning of line 12, and the exacting critic will be happier when he has done so. But a busload of Clapham-bound passengers is likely to contain few literal analysts of poetic imagery, and if it is unfortunate that such an uncritically passive acceptance of fine things in linear isolation often results in a wrong appraisal of the Sonnets and in disregard or oversight of the textural unity of some of them, they could (if they know) plead that Keats erred before them. It results from the later Romantic shift in expectation from and reaction to poetry, and from one quality of Shakespeare's writing that lends itself in this event to distraction from its own integral function in the construction of the whole. But read with a more critical eye this distractive element dissolves in the apprehension of unity.

II
VARIETY OF MOVEMENT

Perhaps the commonest, certainly the most persistent, of misconceptions about Shakespeare's use of the sonnet form is that he observes a uniformity of internal structure: that the rhyme scheme imposes a uniform movement and thought pattern, and one that is in effect disintegratory. The expectation persists, for many readers, that his organization of a sonnet will be found to follow an invariable pattern of three quatrains, somewhat discrete by reason that each uses a different pair of rhymes, but developing the same conceit or enunciating, restating, and applying a position, the whole arriving triumphantly on the rhyme of a powerful but sometimes redundant couplet. And this despite a number of critical demonstrations to the contrary. Even W.H. Auden could say in a broadcast talk (though he later modified the all-embracing impression he first created), "The Shakespearean form . . . with its seven different rhymes, *almost inevitably* becomes a lyric of three symmetrical quatrains, finished off with an epigrammatic couplet."[17] That "inevitably" and that "epigrammatic" mislead. The Sonnets show far greater mastery and variety of formal structure than such a near-generalization concedes.

First, such a judgment leans too heavily on the overt prosodic pattern; the internal organization within that pattern, the poetic logic of the thought movement and verbal design, is not sufficiently brought into view. Characteristically imposing wisdom upon scholarship, W.P. Ker said in his Clark Lectures of 1912, "When you speak of the Shakespearean or English form of the sonnet, you mean a sort of abstract diagram or pattern, in which no particular words are distinguishable—something that is identical in all the sonnets *of that form.* It is a form that you may recognise on the page when the page is too far off to be read. *This is of course a subordinate sense of the word 'form,' belonging to the subject of Prosody, and not to the larger subject of Poetics:* but . . . the more limited and technical sense is [often] confused with the larger. . . . So that it is not always easy to describe verse or stanza form without getting beyond Prosody into poetical criticism."[18] And in the London lectures on Form and Style he applied this further. "The sonnet is not a mere stanza. . . . It is a true argument. In the Italian sonnet there is obviously a form provided for a position in the first eight lines, and a contradiction or variation or conclusion in the last six . . . —protasis and apodosis. . . . The English sonnet of the Shakespearean type does not suggest the form of thought so obviously. In the three quatrains and a couplet the protasis and apodosis line of argument is not suggested. The difficulty of the English form is that the final couplet suggests a point, an epigrammatic conclusion, and the danger of it is that the sonnet will turn into an epigram in the vulgar sense, and an epigram that is too long, for you have to get through twelve lines of preliminary before the flash at the end."[19] This, at first, might seem to support both Auden and the still more extreme popular view; but Ker characteristically goes on to show the error of a generalized assumption that "the danger of it" takes full charge in Shakespeare's own practice. He cites two examples. Sonnet 33, "Full many a glorious morning have I seen," he writes, "has . . . something of epigrammatic point, ending in a sort of proverb. But the sonnet is arranged much in the same way as the Italian, the change in thought coming at the ninth line, 'Even so'." And Sonnet 29, "When in disgrace with Fortune and men's eyes," he notes, "is not epigrammatic or pointed except in so far as the couplet, being a couplet, gives emphasis." Little turning of pages is necessary to find other variants; yet half a century after Ker we still find the myth of the invariable pattern of conceit-plus-epigram persisting in the popular mind.

Mrs. Winifred Nowottny, in an important essay on formal elements in Shakespeare's sonnets, carries Ker's "poetical criticism beyond Prosody" into analysis of Sonnets 1-6 with respect to "Shakespeare's strong sense of form," his "many experiments with form," and the key principle of the organization of a sonnet.[20] She uses the first six sonnets to demonstrate that "imagery is subordinated to the creation of the form of the whole and that imagery is at its most effective when it supports or is supported by the action of formal elements of a different kind." Her essay concentrates on a number of sonnets that may rightly be considered as a group and points out an interrelation of the organization of the several poems.[21] I do not propose to cover ground that Mrs. Nowottny has already mapped out. My purpose here is to indicate a few of the ways in which, in individual sonnets, Shakespeare avoided the danger Ker pointed out—of the prosodic dominating the poetic form of the English sonnet pattern.

Sonnet 7 provides an example early in the Quarto of a single image developed through the quatrains, with application to its object in the couplet.

> Lo, in the orient when the gracious light
> Lifts up his burning head, each under eye

Doth homage to his new-appearing sight,
4 Serving with looks his sacred majesty;
And having climb'd the steep-up heavenly hill,
Resembling strong youth in his middle age,
Yet mortal looks adore his beauty still,
8 Attending on his golden pilgramage:
But when from highmost pitch, with weary car,
Like feeble age he reeleth from the day,
The eyes ('fore duteous) now converted are
12 From his low tract, and look another way:
So thou thyself out-going in thy noon,
Unlook'd on diest unless thou get a son.

Here the sun-king's daily journey in his chariot is related in three stages, morning, noon, and evening, to mortal homage and to time, age, advance, and decline. The couplet, scarcely epigrammatic, applies this sequence to the state of the willfully heirless friend. The various elements of diction maintain a consonant sequence. "Gracious light," "burning head," "beauty," and "golden" form one, the dawn-to-noon group. "New-appearing," "strong youth," "middle age," and "feeble age" mark the progression of time, as "Lifts up," "climb'd," "steep-up . . . hill," "pilgrimage," "highmost pitch," "weary car," "reeleth," and "low tract" measure it, as it were, spatially along the sun's course. Parallel to this sequence runs the homage group: "homage," "sacred majesty," "adore," "Attending," "eyes ('fore duteous) now converted" to "look another way." (Such a grouping is necessarily too crude, for "gracious" and "golden" belong as much to the last sequence as to the first, just as "reeleth" reverses the motion of "Lifts up" and "climb'd"; and the whole interrelation is equally intricate.) Finally, the couplet picks up the sequence and echoes it: "If you outlast your prime and pass middle age in heirlessness you will die unhonored and unregarded." How clumsily a prose paraphrase destroys the structural link when we lose the verbal echoes of earlier lines with "thou thyself *out-going in thy noon, / Unlook'd on diest.*"

Such a sonnet moves directly forward, through twelve verbally integrated lines, from its developed position to the "application" reached in the couplet. We may regard it as one of the simplest structures, but I have lingered over the word groups to emphasize how, even in so direct a structure, the verbal organization is delib-

erately controlled. For it is by the variant use of this verbal patterning, combined with the thought progression derived from or con-
trolling his use of imagery, that Shakespeare's art overrides the
limitations of the abstract diagram of his prosodic form.

By no means all the sonnets divide simply into octave and sestet,
quatrains and couplet, or position, counterposition, and conclusion. Some indeed do proceed, and proceed very effectively, by
three stages and a conclusion. Sonnet 7, we have seen, does so in a
direct forward movement that is verbally interlocked. Sonnet 49
begins each quatrain with "Against that time . . ." and Sonnet 64
with "When I have . . .," both sonnets accumulating the reiterative
impact to fall with greater emphasis on the final statement of the
couplet. Sonnet 30, "When to the sessions of sweet silent thought,"
expands the position of the first quatrain through two more, each
opening with "Then . . .," and delays the "turn" (here a reversal,
not as in Sonnets 49 and 64 a derived result) until line 13. But Sonnet 53, "What is your substance, whereof are you made," partic-
ularizes the image of the first four lines through the next two quatrains, while Sonnet 66 has no octave-sestet division at all. The first
line of 66, "Tir'd with all these, for restful death I cry," enunciates
the theme; the next twelve lines expand this with particular examples, and the turn is given only in the concluding lines—"Tir'd with
all these, from these would I be gone, / Save that, to die, I leave my
love alone." Sonnet 129, "The expense of spirit in a waste of
shame," is a variant of this structure, the syntax here more freely
crossing the linear division and scansion, and Sonnet 99, "The forward violet thus did I chide," varies this pattern freely. Shakespeare is perpetually experimenting with the crossing of the prosodic and the poetic structural pattern and the possibilities of his
medium.

The function and placing of the imagery in this patterning are
important factors in the variant movement. Sometimes used to present a position that opens the sonnet (52, "So am I as the rich
whose blessèd treasure"; 60, "Like as the waves make towards the
pebbled shore, / So do our minutes hasten to their end"; 148, "My
love is as a fever"), the single or multiple images are elsewhere used
to develop or to counter this position. In Sonnet 8, "Music to hear,
why hear'st thou music sadly?" for instance, it is not until the
second quatrain,

If the true concord of well-tunèd sounds
By unions married do offend thine ear,
They do but sweetly chide thee, who confounds
In singleness the parts that thou should'st bear:

that the idea "music" is developed as an image, where its function
is to reply to the position of lines 1-4 and enforce the reproof of
receiving "not gladly" what the friend loves; and it is extended in
the third quatrain in its application to the friend's obstinate singleness. Sonnet 15, I have pointed out above, parallels the image of
the first quatrain in the second, with an application of it in the sestet, but further links the whole by the relation of "shows" in line 3
to "wear their brave state" in line 8 and so to "most rich" in line
10. Sonnet 86, already discussed, shows a similar pattern but with
an *answer* to the first position provided, as in 33, by the sestet.
Sonnet 90, "Then hate me if thou wilt," and Sonnet 130, "My mistress' eyes are nothing like the sun," variantly, present several different but consistent or parallel images reinforcing that first used.
The use of imagery is constantly combined with the verbal patterning and subordinated or united, as Mrs. Nowottny observed, "to
the creation of the form of the whole" and "supports or is supported by the action of formal elements of a different kind."

The "disjunct quatrains" idea of a sonnet is quite inapplicable,
for example, to Sonnet 90.

Then hate me if thou wilt; if ever, now;
Now, while the world is bent my deeds to cross,
Join with the spite of Fortune, make me bow,
4 And do not drop in for an after-loss:
Ah do not, when my heart hath 'scap'd this sorrow,
Come in the rearward of a conquer'd woe;
Give not a windy night a rainy morrow,
8 To longer out a purpos'd overthrow.
If thou wilt leave me, do not leave me last,
When other petty griefs have done their spite,
But in the onset come: so shall I taste
12 At first the very worst of Fortune's might;
And other strains of woe, which now seem woe,
Compar'd with loss of thee will not seem so.

While lines 1-4 outline a position, lines 5-8 do not present a single

unit opposed to or balanced against the first. Lines 5 and 6 summarize in a strengthened form the hostility theme of 1-4 in a more
military metaphor which is in turn reinforced by the weather image
in line 7; and this image itself implies the idea "storm" already
present (in a somewhat different sense) in the military language of
5-6, and in line 8 reverts to the overtly military diction. In this sonnet the linking diction is of supreme importance in binding
together both the prosodic and the image patterns. "Spite,"
"make me bow," "after-loss," "rearward," "conquer'd," "overthrow," "might," successive terms of overwhelming conflict, make
it clear that the sense of "drop in" in line 4 is not just "come in
casually" (as T. G. Tucker suggests) but a definitely purposeful (cf.
line 8) military one, as when we speak of "throwing in the reserve"
(here the "reserve" acts on its own initiative and not under orders
from Fortune). And these terms relate directly to the storm sense of
line 7, which cannot therefore just be picked out as a "fine thing"
—and perhaps therefore superior to the rest of the sonnet—in isolation from the tenor of the whole.

It is worth contrasting sonnets like 60, which I have discussed in
Section I, with those organized like 64 or 65, "Since brass, nor
stone, nor earth, nor boundless sea," where the image sequences
are not tangential, and with completely conceited sonnets, such as
44, "If the dull substance of my flesh were thought," or 99. The
degree of variety in internal organization, in the relation between
prosodic and poetic construction and movement, then becomes
apparent. How untypical any one sonnet is I have already endeav-
ored to indicate, but a comparison of 64 with 65, both so apparently typical of the three quatrains and a "clinching" couplet, may
serve to close this part of my argument. Though both are well
known, I will for convenience quote them in full.

> When I have seen by Time's fell hand defac'd
> The rich proud cost of outworn buried age;
> When sometime lofty towers I see down raz'd,
> 4   And brass eternal slave to mortal rage;
> When I have seen the hungry ocean gain
> Advantage on the kingdom of the shore,
> And the firm soil win of the watery main,
> 8   Increasing store with loss and loss with store:
> When I have seen such interchange of state,

Or state itself confounded to decay,
Ruin hath taught me thus to ruminate—
12 That Time will come and take my love away.
This thought is as a death, which cannot choose
But weep to have that which it fears to lose.
(Sonnet 64)

Since brass, nor stone, nor earth, nor boundless sea,
But sad mortality o'ersways their power,
How with this rage shall beauty hold a plea,
4 Whose action is no stronger than a flower?
Oh how shall summer's honey breath hold out
Against the wrackful siege of battering days,
When rocks impregnable are not so stout
8 Nor gates of steel so strong but time decays?
Oh fearful meditation! where, alack,
Shall Time's best jewel from Time's chest lie hid?
Or what strong hand can hold his swift foot back?
12 Or who his spoil of beauty can forbid?
Oh none, unless this miracle have might—
That in black ink my love may still shine bright.
(Sonnet 65)

Sonnet 64 is integrated by the succession of parallel destruction images, of concrete associations, that comprise the first two quatrains, picked up and transferred to the abstract reflection of lines 9-10 and the intimate individual apprehension of decay in line 12, the couplet applying the thought to its ultimate personal dread of loss. Within this structure, reinforcing it, is intricate verbal skill. The powerful, evocative tones of line 2 are not produced by mere resonance of what might at first seem repetitive diction: "rich proud cost" is not idly redundant. There is a cumulative weight given by the several senses of individual words. "Rich" implies lavish intricacy of work as well as costliness of material; "proud" means "flaunting pride" or "in which pride is taken" and—to an Elizabethan—"showy" (as in "proud-pied April," 98.2); "cost" has the double sense of "expense" and "ornament" (cf. 146.4-5). There is the careful choice and placing of epithets—"eternal" qualifies "brass" and not "slave"; set thus against "mortal" it gives a half-realized antithesis, suggested by the chiastic order of noun-adjective/adjective-noun, which ironically derides human efforts to achieve monumental immortality of remembrance. There is the play on words ("such interchange of state, / Or state itself confounded to decay"), the antitheses and formal disposition of words ("weep to have that which it fears lose")—even the assonantal and alliterative link of "Ruin . . . ruminate." Every word, every cadence, is exactly disposed.

Sonnet 65, equally carefully organized and superficially similar in pattern as in theme, moves, in fact, differently. Its second quatrain does not so closely parallel its first: it inverts it syntactically, and picking its first symbol ("summer's honey breath") from the last ("flower") of lines 1-4, it works backward with its "rocks impregnable" and "gates of steel" to the first line of the opening quatrain. The rhetorician in the Elizabethan is at work, with the poet still in control, and the internal movement has been skillfully varied, "artificially" in the nonpejorative Elizabethan sense. The third quatrain, despite the appearance of "Oh fearful meditation!" does not merely repeat the pattern of that in Sonnet 64. It introduces the particular reference to beauty with new metaphors; and the couplet, whose paradox echoes the powerful antithetical form of line 11 while substituting the frailty of "black ink" for the "strong hand" of that line, provides a defiance and a hope to counter the despair of the couplet in 64. That the two sonnets are organized to follow each other it is hard to doubt: that they each and identically consist of three discrete quatrains and a clinching couplet does not adequately describe them.

One element of this variant organization, that of a verbal progression, is linked at times with a tonal quality that may best be described in musical terms as varying the harmonization of a word or theme, or as a change of key in its employment. With respect to words, this appears to work in two (by no means inseparable) ways, that of wordplay and that of association, the latter in turn closely linked to my argument in Section I about imagery. In commenting on 64.9-10 I noted the change rung on the word "state." The relation of such wordplay to musical key was well expressed many years ago by Professor W. H. Hadow in an admirable little essay, *A Comparison of Poetry and Music.*[22] Noting the recurrence of the words "heaven" and "state" in Sonnet 29, "When, in disgrace with Fortune and men's eyes," he observed, "In the space of a crotchet, in the turn of a semitone, the sonnet changes from minor to major, like a shaft of sunlight through an unbarred window. . . . 'Heaven' and 'state' occur both at the beginning and at the end of the sonnet; but in the two places they are differently harmonised." One might add

that "state" occurs not twice but three times, each time with a slight
turn of sense, and that the middle sense, "and then my state / Like
to the lark at break of day arising," marks the point of modulation, the transition from "[wretched] worldly condition" (line 2)
through "mood, or condition of mind" (line 10), to the regal glory
of the last line, "That then I scorn to change my state with kings."

Such a "musical" use of harmony and key change can be seen
in Sonnet 71, "No longer mourn for me when I am dead," a sonnet
the skillful modulations of which I have sometimes been surprised
to find overlooked by even sensitive readers. Whatever sound-
values one applies to the lines, and especially to the vowels —
whether Elizabethan or twentieth-century "received pronunciation"
—it makes no difference to the contrasts themselves that are
effected between the different quatrains, and with the couplet. The
dramatic alterations are there in either set of values, if our ear
remains constant to the speech, Elizabethan or neo-Elizabethan,
that we elect to "hear" the poem with. The first quatrain,

> No longer mourn for me when I am dead
> Than you shall hear the surly sullen bell
> Give warning to the world that I am fled
> From this vile world with vilest worms to dwell,

reverberates its dirge-like tones, the long-drawn open vowels (some,
like "mourn," "dead," and "surly," longer and more lugubrious in
conjunctive sequence in Shakespeare's pronunciation than in our
own) heavily tolled out in alliterative stresses, like the passing bell
itself. Then, suddenly ("in the space of a crotchet, in the turn of a
semitone"), the second quatrain leaps into a lighter music, tender
with love and renunciation, with lighter vowels, lighter stresses, a
swift tempo of exultant affection:

> Nay, if you read this line, remember not
> The hand that writ it; for I love you so
> That I in your sweet thoughts would be forgot
> If thinking on me then should make you woe.

The third quatrain recapitulates *both* tones, line 10 looking back to
lines 1-4, lines 11 and 12 to the gentler, un-self-regarding tone of
lines 5-8, while line 10 with its harsh alliterating c's and echoic

"compounded" contrasts with the soft alliterating *l*'s of line 12.

The couplet is superbly organized, both in the management of its rhythms and in its backward verbal relation to the patterning of the whole poem.

> Lest the wise world should look into your moan,
> And mock you with me after I am gone.

Line 13 is notable for the spondaic, alliterating "wise world"—the slowing of the meter by the spondee giving just the voice tone that the irony of the phrase requires—and for the wider-spaced *l*'s that catch up and, as it were, disperse the alliteration of line 12, the initial "*Lest*" forfending any tendency to detach the couplet from the preceding lines. Line 14 repeats this sonal linking: "mock" first picks up the *m* of "moan" in line 13 but also of "mourn" in line 1, and its short *o* and sharp succeeding guttural form another contrast to these. Moreover, "mock" must for mere sense carry a far heavier stress than "with" (to stress the preposition would imply a meaning "in conjunction with," which would make poor sense), and this alters the whole pace of the line. This patterning of vowels and consonants, tempo and stresses creates a final cadence that echoes, and transposes, the opening line of the poem—"mock" (of the hostile world) against "mourn"; "with" (instrumental) against "for"; "gone" against "dead." As with the contrasted quatrains, the thought has turned outward to the friend, and the movement of the verse lightens. What began in Acherontic plangency closes in gentle abnegation. The general organization of the poem is describable in terms of key contrasts and rhythmical changes, the particular in terms of verbal echoes and contrasts.

The qualities I have discussed in this essay—the musical tones, harmonies, and contrasts; the verbal echoes, interrelations, and wordplay; the deployment and thought progressions of the imagery —are qualities that Shakespeare develops and utilizes with cogent dramatic efficacy in the verse structure of his plays. This has been extensively studied and expounded elsewhere. They bear relation also to consideration of the Sonnets as a corpus, to the interrelation of such as demonstrably by their thematic material fall into recognizable groups, and in such context to the "dramatic" apprehension of the situations and experiences they record. Others have written convincingly about their relevance to these topics. What I have attempted is a consideration of how these qualities can be seen at work in the construction of individual sonnets, taken (perhaps too restrictively, certainly selectively) as separate lyrics. Those I have used as examples are, for the most part, poems of considerable power. Certainly by no means all 154 poems are of such intrinsic merit or so successfully integrated; but the reader of the Sonnets may still profitably examine with attention, even in the slighter numbers, the varying methods (and varying success) of their internal poetic organization and the quite extensively varied experiments Shakespeare made with relating this organization to his prosodic form.

SOME FEATURES OF FORM AND STYLE
IN SONNETS 97–126

BY

WINIFRED NOWOTTNY

<hr>

It has become a common practice to speak of Sonnets 1-126 of the 1609 text as being addressed to one (real) person, Shakespeare's friend, and in this essay I avail myself of the practice for its convenience. The core of this essay is to be a critical consideration of a handful of sonnets drawn from the last thirty "to the Friend."

Exactly this run, Sonnets 97-126, was settled on in an article by T. A. Spalding in 1878, and again by W. H. Griffin in 1895, as one of three main divisions into which Sonnets 1-126 seem naturally to fall. Griffin gave to this division the title "Reconciliation and Retrospect" and characterized it in these words: "Most of what follows is distinctly retrospective. . . . The past tense, not employed in the early portions of the sonnets, is here frequent. . . . The silence of the past is referred to; it continues (cii.), but is now accepted as no sign of diminution of love."[1] Earlier, C. A. Brown, "the first name of note"[2] among defenders of the 1609 ordering of the Sonnets, had declared Sonnets 102-126 to be a "Poem"—"To his friend, excusing himself for having been some time silent, and disclaiming the charge of inconstancy." Many commentators have seen some such "Poem," but more commonly with the starting point at Sonnet 100,

Sonnets 97-99 being regarded as a linked trio which, though it stands off by tone from preceding sonnets, is not admitted to the ensuing "group"—I suppose because that "group" begins with a reference to the long-forgetful Muse. The group tends to persist, though with some fluctuation. As recently as 1966, J. D. Wilson, after abstracting Sonnet 104 to link it with 97-99, reaffirmed the main limits 100-126, while insisting that, within them, the sonnets are "not in the right order."[3] Yet Tucker Brooke, who declared his edition (1936) to be "dedicated to the assumption . . . that Shakespeare's sonnets have been preserved in disordered sequence, and to the hope . . . that the real order can be still recovered," was content to leave the order of Sonnets 97-108 and 117-126 unchanged, and in the case of the intervening members to do no more than reshuffle, extruding none and introducing no stranger. Thus the limits within which I move about in this essay are sufficiently congruous with scholarly opinion to allow me to pursue a literary interest without the appearance of randomness of choice.

I do not, however, assume that Sonnets 97-126 constitute a group, in the sense of exhibiting the coherence of a "Poem," or as being in "the right order." Indeed, my essay is to have a kind of preamble debating the compatibility of certain sonnets, and, in its course, will comment on the pairing of some others. By "pairing" I refer to cases where two successively printed sonnets, both on one theme, have resemblances in treatment, too, the resemblances being of a kind to make it look as though one member of the pair is a continuation of the other or at least is intended to be its companion piece. The presence of such pairs in the 1609 text, both within the run 97-126 and elsewhere, has of course been frequently noted. My comment on matters of arrangement and compatibility is subordinate to the appraisal of certain selected sonnets: 98, 100, 102, 109, and 126. These I have taken for study because of their own animation and beauty.

These five sonnets are not characterized by grandeur, evident pressure of thought, or the "closeness of texture" nowadays admired. In them an absence is recorded, the Muse invoked, occasional silence gracefully excused, faithfulness affirmed (despite absence and faults), and, lastly, tender praise finely contrived, perhaps as a valediction. This summary, not unrepresentative of edi-

torial précis, leaves it a mystery that within their compass fall some
of the most beautiful lines that the Sonnets as a whole can show,
lines which distinctly haunt the memory when sonnets more famous
have lost their outlines in a collective image of "Shakespeare's sonnets." Nor are these apparently unambitious topics recommended
by striking originality of diction. Each sonnet, in some way, gives
an impression of lightness of touch, ease of style, and poise. There
is little ostentation of wit—whether of wordplay, argumentation, or
developed conceit (save in the latter part of 126). It might almost
appear that in this handful of sonnets "happy accident turns holy
art." Such a description may seem to suggest or even to concede a
want of force. True, there is no battering or agonizing here, as in
some famous sonnets on Mutability, but these sonnets are not, by
that difference, made lesser things. Their ease is not lax, though
they present a blander surface and retain composure even in the
occasional decisive gesture or appropriate flourish. An epithet
which fits them all is "elegant." This may explain why they have
not been placed at the peak of fame. Shakespeare's sonnets have
on the whole been valued for attributes not usually associated with
elegance—or with exquisiteness in the sense exemplified by Sonnet
99, a flower-piece of a conventional kind,[4] usually regarded as an
extension of Sonnet 98. The fact that the editorial tradition has not
rejected its claim to be read as a continuation attests the impression of airiness made by Sonnet 98 itself. Here Brooke may be
quoted, as voicing an unease likely to follow from airiness in a sonnet of Shakespeare's. Taking together Sonnets 97-99, he concluded
that "all these three . . . are written as if the poet's heart was not
much in them"; in so far as he discriminated between them, his
view was that "the moderate afflatus" of 97 and 98 "finally petered
out" in 99, leaving it "poetically the poorest in the entire collection." One reason for his asperity towards 99 appears in the
remark that "the thought is wholly superficial." Another reason
may be that it has nothing of "the tone of plainest earnest" that he
commends in Sonnet 108.[5] A tone "of plainest earnest" would, as I
suppose, commend itself even in our own demanding days and even
to our critical sophistication, which readily ascribes any successful
tone rather to the poet's power in his medium than to the "sincerity" of a declaration. Only one of the five sonnets I have chosen has
this tone, namely Sonnet 109. It has this and exquisiteness too, for

in it Shakespeare judges to a hair's-breadth the degree of gracefulness appropriate to the fine passion of the gentle heart provoked to a full avowal of its own integrity.

To all five of the sonnets I have chosen, some kind of "retrospect" supplies matter and furthers the establishing of tone. It seems reasonable, on considering the subtlety of Shakespeare's use of retrospect in sonnets of the run from 97 to 126, to suppose that his mode is a circumstance not simply attributable to "real-life situations" obtaining at the time of writing. Where art is so active as to result in elegance of form and in passages of memorable intensity, it may be inferred that the choice of mode is not fortuitous. Indeed, if we exclude the notion of the publisher's being responsible for throwing into one pile a number of sonnets somehow involving recapitulation of things past (together with oddments somehow connected with these), the very frequency of Shakespeare's recourse to this mode in this succession of sonnets may be held to go beyond what one might expect mood alone to prompt, or actuality to make necessary.

It is not my intention to minimize the significance, to Shakespeare or to his friend, of the matter wrought into these delightful forms. So far am I from recommending that readers should banish all concern with "what the poems say" about Shakespeare and his friend as human beings involved in real episodes and responses, that I think it necessary to consider whether all the sonnets I am to treat are compatible with one another in the sense that one can read them without having to switch from one mental picture to another as one goes along. The pleasure derived from one of Shakespeare's sonnets, and also the critical evaluation of it, is likely to be somehow bound up with the idea one has of its occasions within some kind of assumed continuum of the relationship between Shakespeare and his friend. The sonnets I treat are not altogether easy to square with one another, nor can one simply turn a blind eye to neighboring sonnets. Without prejudice on the question of whether the whole span of text from 97 to 126 is or is not a "Poem" (or even, broadly speaking, a homogeneous group), I shall now make some survey of impressions given by the sonnets I have chosen, and by others nearby which have some special claim to be associated with them.

The early days of friendship are seen as from a distance in Sonnet 102:

> Our love was new, and then but in the spring,
> When I was wont to greet it with my lays.

Sonnet 115 also implies a considerable passage of time, notably by its reference to former immaturity of judgment:

> Yet then my judgment knew no reason why
> My most full flame should afterwards burn clearer.

The opening lines of Sonnet 126 also suggest a comparison of "then" and "now," even though they weave a powerful illusion of the staying of Time's power:

> O thou my lovely boy . . .
> Who hast by waning grown, and therein showest
> Thy lovers withering as thy sweet self growest. . . .

This sonnet (really a poem of six couplets but generally agreed to be not defective, since its argument is complete and telling) is, further, akin to 102 and 115 in the impression it gives of a measured judgment, detached enough to be objective even though tenderest feeling pervades the utterance. (The skill with which a tone of summing-up is achieved and maintained here is attested by the fact that this sonnet is commonly regarded as an *envoi*.) In some respects, however, it stands apart from the other four of my selection, and indeed from the greater number of the sonnets from 97 on. Its focus is on the Friend almost to the exclusion of all else, whereas other successful sonnets in that run find their topic in a relationship, rather than in the youth alone, and give as much attention to the poet—often to his poems too—as they do to the Friend himself. Still, the poet is not altogether invisible in 126, for one may suppose him to be among the "withering" lovers (I use the word in its Elizabethan sense: "those who love you"). Another respect in which 126 stands somewhat apart is its tissue of figurativeness. The discursive substance of its latter half is largely made up of a myth of Nature's contention with Time, within which there

is set a conceit of the auditing of accounts and their "quietus" (settlement or discharge). More striking, as being more of a challenge
to that mental picture of the Friend likely enough to accompany a
reading of previous sonnets, is the fact that here the Friend's
beauty is presented—in the last three couplets at least—as being
still so remarkable as to make him constitute the proof of Nature's
skill and the settlement of all her "audit," whereas some preceding
sonnets may be read as suggesting a diminution of the Friend's
beauty. A "waning" is indeed referred to in 126 itself, but this need
not be beauty's wane; it need not mean more than the Friend's
having passed whatever point in time constituted noon or meridian,
the turning-point between the way up and the way down. Nor is
there warrant for inferring beauty's wane from the minatory
address in lines 9-10:

> Yet fear her, O thou minion of her pleasure:
> She may detain, but not still keep her treasure.

This could be indirectly a compliment, suggesting that the poet has
adopted a deliberate grimness to make an impression on the heed-
lessness of youth. Yet when put in the context of the series 1—126
as a whole, the waning of the Friend even if only in years (and even
those of no great account) cannot but be felt as a bit of a come-
down. This loveliness, preternaturally immune to lapse of time, is
after all something other than the total perfection which in other
sonnets Shakespeare dreaded to lose. In so far as this is true, the
poem may be regarded as being at once compliment and *conso-
latio.*

The question now to be considered is that of the compatibility of
Sonnet 126 with Sonnets 104 and 108, where there is reference not
merely to the passage of time (as in 102 and 115) but also to aging.
Both use the word "old." Sonnet 104 would fit well enough with
126 if one supposed that as the friend's "perfection" began to pass
away he felt a need of reassurance, perhaps out of proportion to the
amount of discernible change in his appearance—or one might
suppose that simply his sum of years put him in some such frame
of mind. Its implications as a whole seem not to be as autumnal as
the first line alone might suggest: "To me, fair friend, you never
can be old." In this line it is natural to suppose that a note of plain

reassurance can be heard, and that Shakespeare would not wish such a note to sound out unless there were changes which could not be denied. If emphasis is given to the opening words, "To me," the implication is that the poet excepts himself from a general opinion. If emphasis is given to "you *never can* be old," the line could be an answer to the friend's unnecessarily gloomy view of his actual age (in years). The sonnet as a whole seems to me to suggest a situation in which it was still possible to reply to the friend's fears of appreciable change by saying that it was hard to make out whether his beauty stood exactly at noon or not. The octave, despite the doubt implied in line 1, ends with a reference to the friend's youthfulness.

> To me, fair friend, you never can be old,
> For as you were when first your eye I eyed,
> Such seems your beauty still; three winters cold
> Have from the forests shook three summers' pride,
> Three beauteous springs to yellow autumn turned,
> In process of the seasons have I seen,
> Three April perfumes in three hot Junes burned,
> Since first I saw you fresh which yet art green.

The long suspension of the syntax, while the pageant of the turning seasons unfolds, proves to have maneuvered toward a contrast between process of Time and the almost unchanging friend. The sestet introduces a concession: Beauty is always in process of stealing away ("no pace perceived") from its "figure"—that is, the exact configuration it has at any given point within its duration. This general truth is then applied to the case in hand:

> So your sweet hue, which methinks still doth stand,
> Hath motion, and mine eye may be deceived.

These propositions too are general: the lines mean that, in the very nature of things, the Friend's beauty must be changing, and, in the nature of things, the eye is prone to error (the more so if one loves). From these propositions, not from anything the poet can see, it follows that there is some reason to make the assertion—addressed to an audience of the future—that in the friend, Beauty attained its high summer:

> For fear of which, hear this, thou age unbred:
> Ere you were born was Beauty's summer dead.

The ending, as in Sonnet 126, is a grand gesture. Both sonnets are epigrammatic in their turning of the tables at the close, after an admission of those general conditions of existence which work to extinguish perfection. The tables are turned in 104 by the poet's scorn for the hungry generations, and in 126 by his certainty that Nature will relinquish the Friend to Time precisely because his beauty justifies her management of all the potential of life. From 104 one may perhaps expect closer correspondence to the Friend's own feelings about the matter. Sonnet 126 is more distinctly of the epigrammatic mode, more generalized, more ringing in its repartee to the inevitable. There the situation of the "lovely boy" quickly takes on general significance, and the poet's riposte seems to derive directly from the components of the situation. Sonnet 104 has a more personal orientation, despite the amplitude of its background and despite the generality of the truths from which it reasons to the case of the Friend. Its couplet seems to aim at being an "answer" to what is keenly felt when the pride of youth first falters—the keen sense of being now at the point to be ousted from "the top of happy hours." To such a sense, the couplet applies appropriate balm, by taking the "summer" of youth and beauty away from everyone else. Those whose youth is yet to come will be born too late and be of no account; when the sonnet ends, it is as if the sweet vial of summer had been stoppered and sealed for ever. Different as these two sonnets are in their amplification, there is no bar to our relating both to the same phase of actuality.

These considerations are not advanced in order to press any very specific theory about the actual age of the Friend at the time of composition of these sonnets. I should not like anyone to think that my remarks so far, or my adoption of a comparative method in this essay, amount to a recommendation that one should

> Match the syllogisms duly and orderly,
> And put together systematically and minutely
> The chain or coupling, links of the argument,
> That is to say, the connaturals, concurrences,
> Correspondents, concatenations, collocations, analogies,

> Similitudes, relatives, parallels, conjugates and sequences
> Of everything. . . .
>   . . . and when he has
> Attentively sorted it, from the beginning to the end,
> And united and collected the dispersed and distributed
> Matter, which is mingled up and down in combination,
> It will be easy to make a translation of it.[6]

I should like only to have, and allow my reader to have, a reasonable degree of confidence that the sonnets studied in this essay are compatible in reference, and that the essay as a whole has not got off on the wrong foot by trying to distill a common quality from sonnets not really congruous with one another.

The attention I have given to the question of the friend's age reflects the importance I attach to the question of Shakespeare's tact. It appears to me that in no small number of the sonnets I discuss, Shakespeare's technique as an artist can hardly be appreciated without relating it to his tact as a friend. This need not imply that he fully intended that every sonnet he wrote should promptly be despatched and read as a kind of epistle. What I imply is only that Shakespeare was conscious of his friend both as audience ("the ear that doth thy lays esteem") and as a vulnerable human being, and I think it may be the case that the remarkable delicacy and delight which I admire in the poems put at the core of this essay represent the quality of Shakespeare's love at a time when it had become necessary to think of the vulnerability more attentively.

Sonnet 108 seems at first sight to resist the interpretation that the friend, as there addressed, is still young enough to make an issue of his "waning." Though, like 126, it addresses the friend as "boy," its diction, once it has passed on from the topic of exhausted poetic invention to the topic of lasting love, is such as to evoke in a reader's mind an image of a state far removed from youth.

> What's in the brain, that ink may character,
> Which hath not figured to thee my true spirit?
> What's new to speak, what now to register,
> 4   That may express my love, or thy dear merit?
> Nothing, sweet boy; but yet, like prayers divine,
> I must each day say o'er the very same,

Counting no old thing old, thou mine, I thine,
8   Even as when first I hallowed thy fair name.
So that eternal love, in love's fresh case,
Weighs not the dust and injury of age,
Nor gives to necessary wrinkles place,
12   But makes antiquity for aye his page;
Finding the first conceit of love there bred
Where time and outward form would show it dead.

Shakespeare does not make it as clear as he might have done that the sestet is primarily a general statement descriptive of Love in its disregard of change. Further, even if its generality is borne in mind, a reader is hardly to blame if he supposes that the changes Love can ignore are already there in the Friend for the ignoring. Some editors make it clear that they take this view. Brooke's summing-up of the sonnet's drift may be cited as an example: "the poet asserts his daily need of expressing his love and his patron's 'dear merit,' both of which have survived 'the dust and injury of age'."[7] The difficulty of making out the reference of the generality is neatly illustrated in two glosses from Dowden's editions of 1881. The earlier of these treats lines 13-14 thus: "Finding the first conception of love *i.e.* love as passionate as at first, felt by one whose years and outward form show the effects of age." In the revised edition (also of 1881), "felt by" becomes "excited by."[8] Thus the first gloss attributes "injury of age" to Shakespeare; the revised gloss attributes it to the Friend.

What makes the sonnet difficult is the want of a clearly-made-out connection between the octave and the sestet. Difficulties begin with the connective line, "So that eternal love. . . ." One might see the connection as consisting of "So that"—with the meaning "And so from my continuing to write we see that Love endures"; or one might take "that" with "eternal love" (giving the meaning "that True Love people talk about"), and "So" (now on its own) as meaning "In exactly the same way" and as introducing some parallel to the poet's continuing to love and write. The position of "So" at the point of transition from the topic of writing verses to the topic of "eternal love" seems to me to suggest very powerfully that some parallel is about to be made out, in which case the meaning "In exactly the same way" is appropriate. Even though there is no obvious parallel or "sameness" to be seen, I do not doubt that the

word 'So" introduces some action by, or quality of, True Love, which
is parallel to the poet's persistence in versifying.

"That eternal love" is next described as being always "in love's
fresh case" (i.e., "in that state of ever-fresh vigor always characteristic of love)." I take it that this transition—slithering from the
long-lasting ("eternal") to the ever-new ("fresh")—is meant to recommend analogy between well-worn verse and undimmed Love (an
analogy at which one might well balk) by making Love both "eternal" *and* "fresh," just as the verses are both worn *and* prompted by
a devotion that is as vigorous as "when first I hallowed thy fair
name." The link passage "say o'er the very same, / Counting no
old thing old . . . / Even as when first . . ." itself exhibits a slithering from verses to the relationship celebrated in them ("thou mine,
I thine"), and from that to the time "when *first* I hallowed thy fair
name." The care taken to make both the verses, and Love, long-
lasting yet fresh, would seem to indicate some striving to establish
common ground for a difficult analogy.

Possibly the impulse behind all this care was Shakespeare's wish
to make it somehow work out that his writings prove his love to be
undiminished even though they broke no fresh ground. (Sonnet 76,
"Why is my verse so barren of new pride," does not try to "prove"
anything.) One might conceive of such an impulse as being connected with a former situation in which love and poetic creativity
did go together, and perhaps the sonnet reflects some feeling on
Shakespeare's part that if he could write finer poems—poems
always finer than before—the friend would thereby be reassured
that something essential in the relationship remained just as it was
when "love was new." Certainly the Sonnets, generally, and in specific passages, too, indicate that the friend inspired Shakespeare, in
no remote sense. I see no reason why we may not suppose that the
friend was proud of that and wished it to continue. The involvedness of this sonnet may have arisen because of the sheer difficulty
of giving reassurance on this score. Yet if one tries to account for
the involvedness in this way, one has to see the purport of the whole
as having, so to speak, two prongs: reassurance that the friend is
still an inspiration, and reassurance that his having been touched
by "injury of age" does not matter. Though the two reassurances
might well be appropriate to one (complex) situation, I cannot quite

see Shakespeare setting out to purvey both in one sonnet, nor, if he did, can I quite see why all the particulars of the sonnet are as they are.

The couplet—to mention one particular—is something of a puzzle. If the Friend was to be reassured on the score of how well his beauty wore, precisely the thing Shakespeare should not have ventured to say would be this: that lapse of time and the friend's "outward form" were such as to suggest that love must be dead. Had the Friend been in the autumn of life, resigned to "necessary wrinkles" and the like, there would have been nothing galling in assurances that such things are unimportant—but this is a sonnet in which he is addressed as "sweet boy." Squaring up to the difficulty, T. G. Tucker came to the conclusion that what the sestet says is this: "love . . . makes nothing of the dust and injury worked by advancing years, . . . but regards an aging lover as a handsome boy for ever." If this were so, with all respect to Tucker's eye for a real difficulty, one would still want to say the more's the pity. Tucker's conclusion may be rejected; the difficulty, which he faced, remains. If this sonnet was written not as a tribute to an aging man but as a reassurance to a young one sensitive about signs of his "waning," then the couplet alone, coming down with a thump on the last word, "dead," is enough to make the angels weep. Shakespeare cannot have been unaware of the emphasis that a final rhyme confers. It is worth noting that in Sonnet 104, where the couplet rhymes *unbred/dead,* the emphasis on "dead" has the effect of deliberate panache: a door is smartly closed in the face of Emulation's thousand sons, who arrive too late to get a glimpse of beauty's summer, not because it is already over, or nearly over, but because—as Shakespeare is careful to say—they have not yet even been conceived. No doubt all men make faults, even Shakespeare, and perhaps in writing 108 his sense of dissatisfaction with the "deadness" of his sonnets might be strong enough to pop out in a place which, being emphatic, should have been accorded to the freshness of love which he seeks to assert. Yet this notion of a kind of "Freudian slip" in technique (whereby a real anxiety about dullness pushes compliments to one side) is a notion not accordant with the ready admission "Nothing, sweet boy," nor with the self-confidence other sonnets evince. The Muse of Sonnet 100 is busy elsewhere, not dead; she may be refractory but she has at her disposal "might,"

"fury," "power," "light," and "skill" to boot. There are other sonnets nearby which are imbued with easy assurance of poetic power
(as I hope to show).

There is a way out of these difficulties. The argument is coherent and in no way tactless if it is the poet, not the boy, who is
marked by the dust and injury of age. (It may be noted that
Wyndham, insisting "I am convinced that the Poet does *not* refer
to any change in the outward beauty of the Friend," related this
sonnet to others in which Shakespeare speaks of his own age and
the depredations of "antiquity" in his own case.)[9] The sonnet would
then turn on the point that the poet, loving as before, goes on writing the same old praises, and just so the boy lovingly welcomes
them, though the poet and the poetry look old. The poet's praises
are "like prayers divine." If either one of the two people concerned
in the sonnet is particularly representative of "that eternal love" it
seems more likely to be the worshiped than the worshiper. To
impute some loving action to the boy would make the state of
affairs reciprocal, and reciprocal action seems to fit with the phrase
"thou mine, I thine." The use of the epithet "boy" would be understandable if the poet is here very conscious of his own age, for in
Sonnet 126, where again the epithet is used, the boy by keeping his
beauty over the years shows up the withering of those who have
loved him. (In plain human terms I suppose this means that there
would come a point at which an older man would feel very sharply
the age gap between himself and a still smooth-faced youth.) In an
interpretation that makes Shakespeare himself the one whose
"injury of age" is to be disregarded by love, the sestet's observations about "that eternal love" are still in themselves general, but
this love is evinced by the boy who does not reject the worship or
the worshiper (more magnanimously, perhaps, than by the poet
who loves too much to tire of reciting his well-worn phrases). One
apparent obstacle to this interpretation turns out really to furnish
support: namely the words "Finding the first conceit of love."
"Finding" must be in some way related to the poet's invention (traditionally the "first part" of rhetoric, "the most noble werke / Of
. . . inwarde wittes"),[10] a term derived from *invenire,* to find. But
this does not mean that we must make it Shakespeare who does the
poetic "Finding" referred to in the couplet. There is another sonnet
of Shakespeare's (26) in which, apologizing for "wit so poor as

mine," he tells the Friend of his hope that what is amiss in the verses will be pieced out by "some good conceit of thine / In thy soul's thought." That idea, applied to 108, would provide the sonnet with its formal "reversal," for the boy will now find the "conceit of love" for which the poet vainly racked his brains in beginning his sonnet.

It should, however, be pointed out that a formal reversal of the kind suggested above would still obtain if there were no question of personal age in the poem at all—that is, if all mention of age were referred simply to old verses and a well-established relationship.[11] There is no insuperable objection to be derived from the presence, in the sonnet, of the word "wrinkles." The word was applicable to what we now call folds or creases. (Such "wrinkles" would be "necessary" if one had to fold paper(s) up.[12]) More convincingly, one might take "wrinkles" in the contemporary, figurative sense, i.e., "blemishes," referring it to faults in the poet's verses—either their jadedness, or, more likely (since "necessary wrinkles" immediately follows the specifying of "dust . . . of age") to other unavoidable imperfections. (If this seems far-fetched, one must ask oneself whether "dust," as an image for signs of personal aging, is not more so. As an image for antiquated style it is apt.) And if there is no question of personal age, perhaps True Love need not be "represented" by anyone (poet or boy), but in that case the sonnet is vague or misleading.

There is a further possibility (compatible with the idea of the poet as being the one who is aging). It would be normal Elizabethan English to use the expression "would show" in the sense "strive to show." If we make "time" and "outward form" into semi-personifications (or go all the way and give them capital letters), then instead of "time" and "outward form," meaning "lapse of years" and "looks," we shall have Time (the old enemy) and Appearance (in a Platonic sense, i.e., as distinct from Truth) in league with one another in striving to make out that Love must be dead—only to find that Love prevails in that very case where, by the look of things, it could not survive. (The construction *there . . . where* meant "exactly there where.") Love not only prevails just where it seems least likely, but moreover it is as new and vital there as if it had just come into being. The expression "the first conceit of love" is almost untranslatable. What one should think of is the quality of the very moment when one first falls in love. Of course, this does not extrude or exclude the meaning that the Friend's "conceit" mends the poet's invention. The two ideas can operate simultaneously. One could, of course, have Time and Appearance striving to show that the Friend is too passé to be loved, but this returns us to the difficulty of "boy" and to the question of tact.

If there is no such tissue of poetic logic to connect verse (in the octave) with love (in the sestet), then the sonnet is broken-backed. If there is such a tissue, then I think we must still say—even after making allowances for our slower response to meanings which an Elizabethan reader would take in his stride—that the sonnet is not clear in execution, however fine the conception of love it seeks to express, and however neatly it works out if one works at it. To say so is not simply to derogate from Shakespeare's art. Rather it should serve to make the point that the "ease" Shakespeare shows elsewhere cannot have been easy to achieve. It may serve also to make the point that a fine sensibility and a command of eloquence do not take one all the way to greatness. For greatness one must also command oneself to discard some thoughts because they fall short of the pure beauty of simplicity.

> Whiles others fish with craft for great opinion
> I with great truth catch mere simplicity.

So Shakespeare's own Troilus observed (IV.iv.105-6).

The several elements of a cluster of ideas on love, poetry, change, and seeming which prove too weighty to be managed all at once in Sonnet 108 recur frequently in outstanding sonnets of the run 97-126. The four sonnets to which I now turn—98, 100, 102, and 126—show various aspects of these ideas, contained within elegant forms, and subordinated to the poetic realizing, in qualitative terms, of the emotions or attitudes with which they are concerned.

Through these clear forms, each freshly inventive and distinct, Shakespeare conveys attitudes differing from those one thinks of as characterizing the Sonnets as a whole. One feels here a new freedom from strain, or at least an adjustment to it, and an easier stance toward the responsibility of having great poetic gifts. (I do not attach much importance, in this connection, to Sonnets 103 and 105, since in so far as they belong to a convention of compliment whereby the poet represents himself as nonplussed by the wondrousness of the beloved,[13] their self-deprecation is a ploy.) This easier stance is, I think, present in the sonnet I have just discussed (108). An ambience of freedom, maturity and self-confidence has been noted (in Sonnets 100-115) by Martin Seymour-Smith. Shakespeare, he says, addresses the Friend "as if he were now confident of his poetic prowess."[14]

In particulars of handling as well as in the drift of the sonnets I have undertaken to comment on, there is above all a quality of poise. It makes itself felt in quite different contexts. Sonnet 98 is buoyant with delight. Sonnet 100 is full of confidence in the Muse it invokes, upbraiding her with her defection in terms eloquent of her greatness. If this is (by indirection) an amends for neglecting to celebrate the friend, it is an amends proffered with remarkable aplomb—one might say, with zest. No less than three of the five sonnets are in one way or another connected with shortcomings or faults on Shakespeare's part, yet even in these—indeed, one might say, especially in these—one is aware of his poise. When he treats of his silences in Sonnet 102, he does so without painful apology or straining earnestness; instead, there prevails there a lightly-expressed certitude, finely unconcerned to unravel the twists of the self or the "paradoxes" of love. He is content to rest his case on the quality of his love, a quality conveyed through the use of an instance from common life—made new, it is true, by the sensibility of his treatment of it, and made timeless by recourse to the myth of Philomel. The strength of his assurance reveals itself here as if by accident—as for instance in the seemingly casual reference to the past: "Our love was new, and then *but* in the spring." Spring is now *merely* spring, when viewed from the vantage point of "riper days." Though this is thrown off as if it were said only to lead into something else, the grace of the gesture is deliberate: those many sonnets in which spring is virtually equal to perfection are lightly set aside, but to recall them in this way is to make "summer" outgo all their hyperbole. So assured is the manner that one almost forgets that this sonnet, under one aspect, is an apology. Now, when Shakespeare apologizes, he does so by whisking his friend away to the woods where the nightingale is still singing—in the depths of the poem. In Sonnet 109, his amends are fashioned as the impetuous and almost reproachful disclosure of the heart.

One might perhaps infer some shift of roles within the personal relationship from which the Sonnets spring. In some sonnets of, roughly, the first half of the 1609 collection, and in sporadic sonnets later (for instance, 92), there are suggestions of the desire of the moth for the star, or of obsessiveness and abjectness seeming to have little to do with conventions of compliment or with wry exaggeration. In the run from 97-126 and more especially in the sonnets studied in this essay, one receives the impression that the poet speaks as if on equal terms with his subject, or even as one who commands some height from which he looks down rather than up. The kind of difference I have in mind is perhaps best suggested by pointing to the difference between Sonnet 126 and another sonnet which has been held to be a kind of *envoi* or accompaniment to some number of sonnets within the main group to the friend, namely Sonnet 26:

> Lord of my love, to whom in vassalage
> Thy merit hath my duty strongly knit,
> To thee I send this written ambassage
> To witness duty, not to show my wit.

It seems a long way from "Lord of my love" to "my lovely boy."

The disclaimer, "not to show my wit," is worth pausing on. To some extent, the roles of the sonneteer are "allowed"—like the lèse majesté of the Fool—and the allowed role of the poet in any one sonnet may be distinct from his role in the personal exchanges of real life. One is on safer ground in relating changes of tone to a chosen poetic stance than in relating them to personal factors. Even so, since Shakespeare in the Sonnets lays so much stress on his "truth," and since the tone of these particular sonnets I treat is so delicately poised—"compounded of many simples, extracted from many objects, and indeed the sundry contemplation of my travels," as Jacques said in claiming his melancholy as "mine own"—one is not after all being reckless if one supposes that attitudes of equality, reassurance, even protectiveness, have a real correspondence with Shakespeare's personal dispositions toward his friend. I make myself explicit on this issue because I am about to emphasize a related but different aspect of Shakespeare's attitudes, namely the picture he now presents of himself as a poet. What he really thought of his own poetry is not to be directly equated with the picture his sonnets give, but one may suppose a correspondence (making allowances for literary traditions), and one may suppose, too, that what Shakespeare thought about his poetic powers would deeply affect his whole view of himself.

The elevation of tone maintained in these sonnets is connected with a sense of the dignity of the poet's calling. Shakespeare seems to present himself, in his role as poet, as one who carries his honors lightly and with grace; *sprezzatura* is the dominant tonal effect. The diction, temperate for the most part, is raised by touches of deliberate literariness: poems are "lays" or "song," love is "my flame." It also accommodates the familiar. Though the nightingale is "Philomel," she "stops her pipe" and (at least by indirection) holds her tongue. The expression "stops her pipe" half-recalls the colloquial phrase "to pack up [one's] pipes" (which one might translate into modern English as "pack it in"), but it can as well suggest simple plainness of expression, since the word "pipe" was in use simply as a way of referring to the singing of a bird. Yet at the same time, because of the context, Philomel's pipe carries some suggestion of mannered pastoral. This is a style at ease with the Immortals, seen plain: Saturn laughing and leaping, the Muse at fault, the "lovely boy." If in these sonnets Shakespeare is not in full singing robes, at least he carries himself as one well entitled to wear them; the persona of these "lays" is The Poet.

The metrics support this. They contrive to impart musicality to the rhythms of normal speech by combining them in patterns. The patterns are neither obtrusive nor set. They haunt the ear with an insistent intimation of something distinctive and individual, not quite revealing itself, playing through the iambic pentameter at will. One is reminded of Ferdinand's words:

> Where should this music be? I'the air, or the earth?
>   . . . sure it waits upon
> Some god o'the island. Sitting on a bank,

Weeping again the King my father's wrack,
This music crept by me upon the waters
                              . . . but 'tis gone.
No, it begins again.

                              (*The Tempest,* I.ii.387ff.)

I think that this "magic" may be more important to the success
of these sonnets than any other factor. For this reason it seems suitable to begin more detailed consideration of these particular sonnets with Shakespeare's invocation of his Muse in Sonnet 100. The
metrical effects, though not "magical," are decisive and impressive,
and within the range of at least some commentary. I shall point out
some features, in the hope that to do so will be better than simply
to assert my belief that prosodic art is the *sine qua non* of Shakespeare's art as a sonneteer.

Sonnet 100 is distinctive not so much by "content" as by the
energy with which it rallies and urges the Muse. This energy pur-
ports to be moral, in that the Muse is told to redeem the time,
repudiate base subjects, and resume her proper office, but the aim
of the poem is to make amends for going off duty, and its creative
drive seems to be sheer high spirits. Shakespeare upbraids his
Muse but contrives to glorify her, and the Friend, too, and, further,
to present his struggles with the Muse in a just-perceptibly comic
light, which, indeed, is becoming, in so far as Shakespeare made no
sharp distinction between The Muse and "my muse" (a term cover-
ing his abilities, his manner, and his output). He represents himself
as trying by the expenditure of considerable energy to get "might,"
"fury," and "power" into orbit—or, in the terms of his own time,
to conjure up and control an awesome but potentially biddable
familiar.

His muse has been off on a low spree. "Rise, resty Muse" is not
a summons to wake from sleep. "Resty" had two main meanings.
One was equivalent to *restif,* meaning "resisting control of any
kind," and was in common use as a term summing up the various
kinds of exasperating behavior exhibited by a recalcitrant horse.
The other meaning was "slothful," but it is clear from the context
here that his muse has not been torpid. ("Idly" in line 6 means
"frivolously" or "reprehensibly.") The charge against the Muse is
one of bad behavior. She has wasted the creative *furor* on worthless
things and in so doing has been diminishing ("Dark'ning") her

repute. (The *New English Dictionary* gives the meaning "To deprive ... of lustre or renown" [9b]). She has, moreover, resisted two summonses already ("Where art thou?" and "Return"); and "resty" might be adequately explained by this circumstance alone. The third command, "Rise," would be appropriate as a formula for conjuring a spirit. Other meanings of "Rise" are appropriate: "To recover from a spiritual fall, or a state of sin" (*NED*, 3): "To ascend to a higher level of action, feeling, thought, and expression" (*NED*, 15). The "gentle numbers" she is now to produce are no contradiction of her "might." "Gentle," in Shakespeare's time, implied status, culture, refined taste, and the well-born manner; "gentle numbers" means poetry with prestige, poetry that matters. (They would be at a far remove from the manner of the satirist —(cf. "satire," line 11—as the Elizabethans viewed the genre.)

The metrics abound in energetic inversions, which are elegant too, being repeated and so arranged as to set up a distinctive pattern. This is done without sacrifice of the "dramatic illusion" of the poet's invoking, since a formulaic cast is to be expected in his utterances in such a situation.

The "music" of the poem is calculated in terms of phrasing. The phrasing is perfectly natural; the music resides chiefly in the relation of phrase to phrase, whether in recurrences or in freer forms of balance and completion. Phrasing as such may be illustrated from the opening two lines:

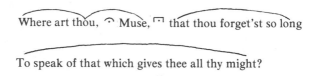

Where art thou, ⌢ Muse, ⌐ that thou forget'st so long

To speak of that which gives thee all thy might?

The second line, though it restores a sense of the iambic norm, is not really heard as having five beats; it is heard as speeding along toward the emphatic "all thy might," which has to balance the emphatic ending of the line before. There is no toughness of sense, or bright color in diction, to halt the attention and break the continuity. There is no point in the line, before "all thy might," at which the syntax is felt to be even partially complete. In so far as the line hesitates at all, it does so after "that" and after "thee," but such pausing is perceptible only as phrasing in music is perceptible. This continuity is necessary to offset the bold phrasing of line 1—phrasing that almost splits the line into two rhythmic parts. Subsequent lines repeat this cloven effect and establish a metrical motif:

Spend'st thou | thy fu|ry ⌐·⌐

Dark'ning | thy power | ⌐·⌐

Sing | to the eare | ⌐·⌐

Give my | love fame | ⌐·⌐

The urgency in this motif works toward giving the poem its emotional continuity. The sense of a distinctive recurring motif is related to what one might (for want of a better term) refer to as the conceptual music of the poem, by which I mean a patterned disposition of the chief concepts allotted to each line—indeed to each half-line. The lines tend to fall into two halves, each half offering one main concept. A relation of opposition or development obtains between the two halves of each line:

Spend'st thou thy fury ⌐·⌐ on some worthless song,

Dark'ning thy power, ⌐·⌐ to lend base subjects light?

Return, forgetful Muse, ⌐·⌐ and straight redeem

In gentle numbers ⌐·⌐ time so idly spent, . . .

There is no clop-clopping effect, because there is enough variety and enough connection to keep the interest swinging smartly between the conceptual poles of the whole. The current of sense runs through the poem in wave upon wave, "Each changing place with that which goes before," yet so that "all forwards do contend" (Sonnet 60). A related but virtually independent pattern is provided by the alternation (seen already in the first two lines, quoted above) of lines broken up by strong pausing and lines of continuous flow. The alternation is not regular (no pattern in this sonnet is mechanically regular) but it is effective. If one were to express this alternation in a formula (and the difference between the flowing and the pausing is marked enough to allow one to do this almost without hesitation), it would be seen that the pattern of their alternation runs independently of the rhyme scheme. By "independently" I mean that one never gets *a b a b* = pausing flowing pausing flowing. The successful avoidance of this would seem in itself to indicate that the two schemes, rhyme and rhythm, are meant not to coincide. In short, the aim is multiple structuring. Multiple structuring is a marked feature of the art of the group of poems I treat: here and elsewhere, the various structural elements seem to be arranged rather in the manner of the modern mobile, where a system of impulsions and balances produces movement which is at once elegant and apparently free. How far Shakespeare did this by conscious deliberation, how far "by ear," is not important; all that is important is to satisfy oneself that complex movement really is a principle of form, not merely an accident. I think that there is corroboration (of the view that multiple structuring is aimed at) in the repetitiousness and patterning of the diction. The fiction of apostrophizing naturally brings in repeats of "Muse." (It need not have done. One "O Muse" would have made the situation clear.) "Return, forgetful Muse" alongside "Rise, resty Muse" remains "natural" only because the poet represents himself in the act of invoking; still, this will not quite prove my point. Something more like proof may be seen in the repetition, linking, and placing of the words *Spend'st, song/spent, sing*. In line 3 they are given emphatic places, at beginning and end of the line:

> Spend'st thou thy fury on some worthless song,

whereas in lines 6 and 7 the order is reversed:

> . . . spent,/Sing . . .

The effect, as of a figure eight, is hardly likely to be accidental. Repetition of some elements of diction is marked enough to suggest that it has been deliberately cultivated; (cf. "gives thee all thy might"/"gives thy pen both skill and argument"; "forget'st"/"forgetful"; "so long"/"so idly"). Equal care is taken to maintain continuity and variety in patterns of alliteration, and to use these to enforce connected concepts.

The creation of interplay of patterns has been stressed in the remarks I have made, but one might also expatiate on the use of metrics for expressiveness, as in the tremendous pause after "fury," or in the sustained emphasis on the resonant imperative "Sing" in line 7: "Sing | to the ear |."

Minutiae of sound and metrics cannot be pursued in each of the sonnets I am to comment on. Subsequently I shall mention such things only when there is some particularly important bearing from them to other matters under consideration.

A possible objection to my estimate of the importance of metrics in Sonnet 100 is the fact that in Sonnet 101, usually regarded as a "companion" sonnet, to 100, the handling of metrics is not impressive. It will be as well first to consider the relationship between these two sonnets in a general way. Sonnet 101 begins, "O truant Muse, what shall be thy amends / For thy neglect. . . ." Thus the impression is given that it carries on where 100 left off: that the Muse will now in some way set about making up for her absence. Oddly, the idea of "amends" is not kept up; this sonnet has it out with the Muse all over again, as if 100 had never been. This is the more odd in that 101 is inferior in quality to 100; lack of logical advance is certainly not compensated for by any such development as might entitle us to regard 101 as a stage-two poetic rocket. The fiction governing the form in 101 (that of an argumentative dialogue with the Muse) is awkwardly introduced and continues to be awkward. The poet obligingly provides a feed-line, "wilt thou not haply say, . . ."; he develops the idea himself, he refutes it himself. It is not quite clear, while this is going on, whether the Muse is absent or present, and indeed if it were not for Sonnet 100, this last is not a question one would think of asking, for it is painfully clear that the poet in 101 is conducting a mere fiction of dispute. In Sonnet 100, on the contrary, what is perfectly clear is the situation: one which is "dramatic" in the sense that the poet can speak throughout in the persona of one adjuring the Muse (somewhat as Prospero adjures Ariel): "Where art thou?" "Return." "Rise." The energetic invoking in 100 is a truly sustaining fiction whose upshot is quasi-dramatic eloquence—eloquence far less forced and far more pleasurable than the word-thrashing display in 101 of a conceit of "color" versus "truth" (already quite sufficiently exploited in 21, 54, 67-68,[15] and 82-83). Admittedly one must allow for changes in taste, and to mention Shakespeare's frequent recourse to this conceit may perhaps serve only to suggest *per contra* that estimates of quality are no good basis for argument. However it may be observed that this particular handling of the color conceit falls into flatness (e.g., "But best is best, if never intermixed").

To come now to rhythm: Sonnet 101 is flowing enough in lines 1-7 and in the couplet, but in line 8 it starts bumping and banging about. The origin of the trouble seems to be that lines 5-7 constitute a completed rhythmical unit (in itself pleasing) and the quatrain is then pieced out with a single line which, rhythmically, belongs nowhere. On encountering that isolated line one has a feeling of having lost one's bearings, of not knowing where one is in relation to quatrain structure. The fact that the ensuing quatrain begins with another isolated line (followed by a rhythmical period made up of three lines) increases the confusion.

Before leaving the matter of Sonnets 100 and 101, it is to be observed that there is some conflict of content. Whereas 100 talks of the possibility of a wrinkle, Sonnet 101 is insistent on the Friend's beauty. (This might have come in very well, as a way of scouting the idea of wrinkles, if spoken by a Muse who, when called, returned, and spoke *in propria persona*—or, if that be impossible, had spoken in any way but the way she speaks in 101, namely as the ventriloquist's doll). Discrepancy—or at least non-agreement—of content extends to the couplets. Sonnet 101, consonantly with its own emphasis on beauty, tells the Muse to make the Friend "seem long hence *as he shows* now," whereas the couplet of 100, making no reference to what the Friend looks like, proposes simply to "Give my love fame." Further, Sonnet 100 makes emphatic reference to the duration of the Muse's defection ("thou forget'st so long"); Sonnet 101 neither says nor implies that "neglect" has been of long duration. If to a modern reader the word "neglect" seems of itself to imply duration, it is to be observed that Shakespeare elsewhere uses the word in the sense simply of an omission.

I do not believe that these two sonnets were originally planned to be read in succession. It is clear that they share too much to stand anywhere in the collection without drawing attention to their closeness of idea. It follows that if they cannot stand side by side, then they cannot both stand. In short, if one cannot accept them as a satisfactory diptych, one has to suppose that in some sense the two are alternatives.[16] I say "in some sense" because the history of the text of the Sonnets is unknown. (For all we know, Shakespeare may have written these as alternatives and yet at some time have come to think that he could get away with arranging them as a pair.) The relation I have tried to draw attention to—the relation of being too close to be separated, yet in some respects inimical—may sound like a too curious invention of a too minute reader. Anyone who has shuddered at two shades of pink which miss matching may be expected to view this line of argument as simple common sense.

In "pair" after "pair" of the run from 97-126 one could argue a comparable relation. (I will not say demonstrate.) So I am led by the prevalence of such relations—rather than by obviousness in any given case—to think that such "pairs" may represent "Shakespeare in the workshop" (though not as an apprentice). If this were true, it would be proper to regard each sonnet of a "pair" as a poem in its own right, and perhaps proper to regard the clearly better of a "pair" as a recension or rethinking of the lame or less good one. The decision to regard them so would bear on one's estimate of Shakespeare's art (in the sonnet) generally. Charges of monotony of conception and unevenness of execution would lose some ground. Some of these considerations—as also the difficulty of determination in the individual case—are exemplified in the case of Sonnets 97 and 98.

I shall not burden this essay with detailed comparisons extending over every case (i.e., Sonnets 113/114, 118/119, 124/125, and—though in this case the sonnets are separated—110/117, in addition to those already examined, 97/98, 100/101), but it may be of interest, and will demand no long discussion, to single out a particular feature to be observed in the case of 113/114 (the which feature, moreover, is matter of fact rather than of evaluation). Sonnets 113 and 114, both on the theme of the poet's being haunted by almost hallucinatory images, are closely connected in substance. Indeed, it may well seem to a modern reader that 114 is presented expressly as a continuation of 113, since it begins with the words "Or whether." But the construction "Or whether . . . Or whether" (lines 1, 3) can quite well be taken as a self-contained "Either . . . or." Sonnet 114 wittily complicates the theme set out in 113, but the necessary ground of the wit-work is (re-)stated in 114 itself (quatrain 1). Perhaps the oddest feature of the two sonnets taken together is the repetition of an allusion. Sonnet 114 in lines 5-6 makes and develops a clear allusion to a very well-known passage in Ovid. In his *Metamorphoses,* in the description of Chaos before the Creation, Ovid uses the phrase *rudis indigestaque moles* (Book I, line 7). To this, Sonnet 114 clearly alludes, in the words "monsters and things indigest," pointing up the allusion by the word "Creating" (line 7) and by the observation that the poet's eye makes, from monstrosities and misshapen things, cherubims (like "your sweet self"). In Sonnet 113 the Ovid passage is more diffusely recalled:

> For if it see the rud'st or gentlest sight,
> The most sweet favour or deformed'st creature,
> The mountain or the sea, the day or night,
> The crow or dove, it shapes them to your feature.

I find it very difficult to believe that if Shakespeare meant the two pieces to stand as companions he would have used this Ovid allusion twice, first diffusely in 113, and then distinctly, neatly, and to better effect in 114. It is much easier to explain these facts on the supposition that 114 represents a recasting of 113, worked up into a closer and wittier texture. (I do not think much of either of these sonnets, but 114 is at least not flat.) Sonnet 27 also takes up the theme ("my soul's imaginary sight") and achieves at least one vivid passage—the lines "Which like a jewel, hung in ghastly night, / Makes black night beauteous"—but on the whole one could do without these sonnets very well—though not without what looks like an offshoot, elsewhere: "It seems she hangs upon the cheek of night / As a rich jewel in an Ethiop's ear" (*Romeo and Juliet,* I.v.47-8).

Sonnets 97 and 98 share the idea that separation from the Friend makes a sweet season of the year seem hollow. In Sonnet 97 the sweet season is autumn. This circumstance is not disclosed until quatrain 2, while in quatrain 1 the poet describes a metaphorical winter of the heart ("How like a winter hath my absence been /

From thee, the pleasure of the fleeting year! / What freezings have I felt . . .''). Sonnet 98 pictures one season only, the (actual) spring, extending the description of it over ten lines—for we must count those which whilst ostensibly expressing alienation from its joys, in fact communicate them. It is a crucial difference in handling, that 97 surprises the reader when in line 5 it begins its ample description of "teeming autumn." The switch from a vivid picture of December to a vivid picture of autumn might possibly be due to some attempt to give the reader a sense of the disorientation felt by the poet. If so, the device works only too well—the more so for a modern reader who finds "summer's time," in line 5, a confusing term for "autumn," named in line 6. (Shakespeare himself used the term "summer" to cover all "the sweet o' the year," but might perhaps have spared the use of it here.) One has to pause to adjust one's imagination to the new demand upon it. Further, the sonnet as a whole bombards the reader with assorted seasonal terms: "winter," "December," "summer," "autumn," "prime," then back again to "summer," "winter." This series in itself is one that a great poet might come to rue. Might he not also see something to hesitate at in the series "abundant issue," "orphans," "unfathered fruit," "pleasures" (a term often suggesting the sexual), "wait on thee"? This narrowly misses making the Friend into the paramour of summer and the father of fruit in a way not so much mythic as grotesque; the compliment to the Friend almost topples over into pedigree-tracing. C. K. Pooler, viewing the matter differently, found the lines obscure. In a note on line 10 he writes, "Autumn may be understood as the earth in autumn and is evidently the mother, but who is the father? Possibly, the prime = spring." His verdict is that "the imagery seems blurred beyond recognition or recovery." I do not, of course, maintain that other features of the sonnet, which other commentators have warmly praised,[17] are quite outweighed by the element of muddle.

Sonnet 98 has a fine clarity of outline. It avoids a muddle of seasons by first imprinting on the mind the qualities of the real season, spring. In lines 5-10 it stresses, by repeated negatives, the poet's resistance to every solicitation of delight, his determination not to be happy, and in lines 11-12 it explains this resistance philosophically in attractive terms. The couplet refers lightly to the poet's nostalgia, not allowing it to trouble the fine airiness of the sonnet:

> Yet seemed it winter still, and, you away,
> As with your shadow I with these did play.

The construction "yet . . . still" means "as yet," and the point it introduces is that it cannot be spring until the Friend is at hand, for the Friend is the essence of spring. Though the couplet is not pictorial and makes no sonorous asseverations, it gives the poem its complimentary climax by quietly taking it for granted that all spring's delights are "your shadow," tossing this off almost parenthetically, as if it were said only to explain the poet's dégagé mood of "play." The style is limpid, placing its clear visual images sparsely, like "stones of worth . . . Or captain jewels in the carcanet" (52.7-8). Epithets are choice but not challenging. "Proudpied" as an epithet for April suggests the newness, color and gallant show of spring, but only as a kind of collective glory, not in particulars so concrete that April becomes too visible to be a "petty god" who can dance with Saturn. Shakespeare reserves keenly original description for the line that tells of the dance:

> That heavy Saturn laughed and leaped with him.

Saturn, as planetary influence and quasi-deity, was conceived of as the custodian of seeds lying in the earth; the line just quoted alludes, in an almost classical manner, to the quickening of new life. Yet the line is a catachresis (bold as the sudden sense of spring is bold), for Saturn was associated with all things heavy—"heavy" in the usual modern sense of the word, and in the common Elizabethan senses "gloomy," "sluggish," "dull." Saturn, against his very nature, laughs and leaps with the "spirit of youth in everything." The image gains in immediacy from the very remarkable metrics here. The strong emphasis which would normally fall in the last foot is transferred to "leaped." (Two negligible syllables, "with him," fill the last foot.) The rhythm of the whole line has to fall into place in relation to "laughed and leaped," and the mastery of this lies in the animation it sets up. "Laughed and leaped" is a unit: the alliteration emphasizes the gaiety of both words, which together describe the scene. This gives the line the structure:

> That heavy Saturn ⌐¬ laughed and leaped with him.

The fact that the last foot, where normally a strong emphasis falls, is filled by two unstressed syllables, adds to the prominence of the alliterative phrase. The mid-foot pause is important:

$$\text{Sat}\,|\,\text{urn}\;^{\sqcap}\;\text{laughed}\,|$$

To set this out on its own as I have done is enough to show that the syntax competes with the alliterative unity of "laughed and leaped," since syntactically one is impelled to run straight over the pause, and also straight on, beyond "leaped," to bring "with him" into a unit of sense running right through the line. Yet again, because there is a most striking antithesis between "heavy Saturn" and "laughed," there is a kind of explosion of significance at this point. This makes one want to pause ("That heavy Saturn laughed . ") but one is pulled on by "and leaped." The sense "explodes" again on "leaped," but again one is pulled on because, syntactically, "with him" goes with "laughed and leaped." The different pulls on the rhythm of the line give a tremendously vigorous gamboling effect. Might one also say that the metrically negligible "with him" (negligible in taking no emphasis) is the very phrase which completes and indeed focuses the brilliant picture of the sporting of Saturn with April? I find myself unable to particularize the remarkable effect of this except by saying that, because of it, the extraordinarily joyous and brilliant sense of the line reaches us as if it had flashed out like a vision (not like something put together phrase by phrase). Most of the effect of quatrain 1 depends on this line.

Similarly, quatrain 2 relies on a highlight: the phrase "make me any summer's story tell," fraught with a mysterious joy, hinting "I could an if I would." I don't doubt that the tale would have been a seductive one if told. Shakespeare knew well enough that in the spring (how young need one be for this?) the fancy lightly turns to thoughts of love. One can hardly make this out in detail without spoiling the deliberate catch-me-if-you-can with which the Poet-in-the-poem plays on the word "proud." An Elizabethan reader would hardly fail to take the connection when "proud" is associated with "lap." (Both words were capable, even without one another's help, of suggesting wantonness.) A reader sophisticated enough would presumably also enjoy the fact that what the poet gives with one hand he takes away with the other. He doesn't quite say that the flowers are wanton (for "their proud lap" is Earth's lap, and after all "proud" can mean simply "in fine array") and in any case he notices them only to say he isn't interested, either in telling the tale or in plucking flowers. And I hasten to add that when in line 14 he uses the word "play," which again is a word at home in wanton contexts, he provides an immediate context of philosophical terminology, all to do with the Real versus the Unreal, which accounts for "play" very solemnly. If Shakespeare were not, as I think, playing at *honi soit qui mal y pense,* the couplet might be a little lame, even though "play" earns its place and emphasis by its congruity with the terms "figure," "pattern," "shadow."

These little bubbles of double entendre are as proper, in the artistic sense, as Saturn's "leaping" with April, which conveys the "miracle" of Spring, and the liberation and approval of hilarity. The hilarity would not be as magnificent as it is, if the sonnet either lacked awareness of the senses or gave them a very important place. One of its pleasing strokes is its unobtrusive descent of the famous platonic "ladder" (by which one ascended from visible particulars of beauty to a notion of Beauty and so to love of Divine Beauty). Beginning in the mythical (quatrain 1), it proceeds through the generalized (quatrain 2, where the poet has a detached awareness of beauty everywhere), and in quatrain 3 it shows him noting the lily and pausing on the rose. This last is almost the undoing of his detachment. He does not, in a general way, see the color of the rose, but sees "the deep vermilion" *"in"* it (and, by some magic, his readers see the vermilion *deep in* the rose). His stance of unimpressionableness is, however, deftly saved, since in Elizabethan English one could praise a quality *in* a thing, where modern English praises a thing *for* a quality. So it is left beautifully ambiguous whether or not his glance went to the depths of the rose. This half-acknowledgement of intensity is vital to the argument of the poem, which is that however delightful the visible world may be, the friend is Delight itself. What the Friend surpasses must be made sweet indeed. After this moment of near-capitulation, the dégagé mood of the poet lightly springs up again, and everything that is merely pleasing is dismissed as not of the same order as the absolute value of the Friend.

It is a delicate question, whether or not the couplet brings this sonnet satisfactorily to a close. It shrugs off the visible beauties of spring as things which are only for "play." The word, as I have suggested, is appropriate in more than one way, and such slightness as it has is in keeping with the poet's slighting attitude to all that is "but sweet." Undoubtedly the word "play" has point enough to make the sonnet complete in itself; whether it is satisfyingly complete is another matter. I am inclined to think that the all-inclusiveness of the sonnet's sensibility, and its delicacy, would be spoiled by any pointed conclusion, and that its light finish is not in any damaging sense "inconclusive."

What then is one to make of Sonnet 99? Put together, 98 and 99 have enough by way of general resemblance of matter to lead one to look for real consecutiveness, and 99.1 seems to chime in with 98.14:

> As with your shadow I with these did play.

> The forward violet thus did I chide:

Sonnet 99 is sprightly and pretty. This is what makes it the villain of the piece. Because the beauty of 98 is cool, unobtrusive, and very much *sui generis,* when it keeps company with prettiness it is easy to pass it over and hard to take it seriously. It takes some temerity to challenge the traditional view that the two sonnets are linked. This linkage is commonly thought to be obvious. As grounds for the opinion one could allege that 98.14 speaks of play and 99 is playful; further, that in both sonnets the poet makes question of the relation between flowers and the beloved. It is not altogether easy to examine the traditional view, since commentators, assuming the obviousness of the linking, do not ordinarily set out the grounds of their opinion. I shall therefore confine myself to setting out some considerations that in my own opinion make it open to question whether 98 and 99 should be read as a continuous "poem" or not.

Sonnet 98 (as I see it) is a fine representation of a sensibility alive to the joys of spring but holding back from captivation by them. Sonnet 99 represents not the sensibility but the wit of the poet. He makes a prettily-colored picture from a blatant fiction (that the flowers have stolen the beauty they show), and the interest

of the poem is the prettiness and skill of its diverse compliments —
of which not the least is the dottiness of the poet, as inferred from
the elaborate "floweriness" of the compliment. One accepts his
"floweriness" as one accepts the ribbons, hearts, doves, flowers,
and sentimental messages that agreeably festoon a valentine. This
pretty, witty sentimentality seems to me to have nothing directly to
do with the dégagé attitude of the poet who, in 98, does not wonder
at the lily or the rose. These two poetic stances would be very difficult to reconcile if it were not for the suggestion in 98.14 that the
poet, being at a loss for something to do, puts in time by "play."
This connection (if such it be) is of such a kind as to point out in
advance that Sonnet 99 is less serious than Sonnet 98. One can
therefore allow that 99 is frivolous without at all allowing that it
makes 98 the same. In the dramas of Shakespeare one allows for
the convention of the play-within-the-play, and it is usual nowadays
to temper criticism of the style of such an "inset" by observing that
artificiality in the inset is a device whereby the main illusion, that
of the play at large, is not jeopardized by the avowed illusion of the
inset. Similarly, the introduction of 99 as "play" should make it
more than ordinarily necessary to be prepared for a change of tone
in passing from the one sonnet to the next. Since in these two sonnets, if they are connected, Shakespeare says that he "did play"
and then shows his playing, we should be careful not to project the
artificial mode of 99 backward to 98 and make that pallid.

I do not find it hard to think of Shakespeare as being sufficiently volatile to switch from one stance to another in the "breath-
ing-while" between 98.14 and 99.1. If volatility is taken for granted
it will do neither poem any harm to read the other alongside it. But
if one is in pursuit of a Shakespeare with one hand on his heart as
he pens each line, then of course the two sonnets cannot be read
together without damage to 98 (and 99 can hardly be read at all).

Yet even if one is prepared to allow Shakespeare to dash into
the wings between 98.14 and 99.1 to do a quick change into the
persona of the besotted lover, one has not quite got out of all the
difficulties. There remains the difficulty of having to read 98.14 in
one way in its own context, and in another way in the context of
Sonnet 99. In its own immediate context 98.14 means: "Though I
was in the midst of a glorious spring I could take no serious interest

in birdsong, flowers, etc., which to me were only simulacra of De-light. . . ." If the line is read as introducing 99, it means, "I passed my time by playing a game with flowers, accusing them. . . ." The agility necessary to take 98.14 first as a conclusion to 98 and then as introduction to 99 is rather more than I find myself able to exer-cise in reading, and I am happier to construe 98.14 in the meaning necessary to complete 98 itself, and to regard 99 as having no incontestable claim to the place it occupies.

A further difficulty lies in the relation of 98's idea of figure-pattern-shadow and 99's idea of theft. In this shadow relation the flowers are unreal projections of Delight. Whether they are "simu-lacra," "images," "appearances," or "imitations," they have not stolen anything, and the point, indeed, is in their unreality when compared with the Friend. In 99 the point is in their likeness: the "sweet" that proves them to be thieves is of the same order as the "sweet" of the Friend. I do not see how we can regard the "theft" as congruous with 98.11: "they were *but* sweet." There seems to me to be no way in which whiteness and redness, etc., can be so much like the beloved's beauty as to be deemed "stolen," and yet can at the same time illustrate the proposition that visible attributes are merely pleasant whilst true Delight is of another order of reality. On the other hand I can well believe that an only moderately atten-tive reader—Thorpe?—might pass over the philosophical meaning of "but sweet" and that, further, he might take "shadow" in 98.14 to refer to close resemblance between flowers and Friend, since in Elizabethan English "shadow" was applicable to a reflected image (as in a mirror) as well as to simulacra, figments, and so on. A reader so persuaded might think the two sonnets close enough in topic to be put together in print. If the theft conceit is as discrepant with the platonism as I suppose, then we should, if we connect 98 and 99 at all, connect them by way of a shift of mood from the ele-gant but fundamentally serious 98 to the witty froth of 99.

I have set out these considerations without making reference to textual oddities in 99, since I think is as well to rest no part of a lit-erary argument on uncertain inferences from textual data which may be variously interpreted.

I hope by making these remarks to have offered justification for treating Sonnet 98 as a self-contained sonnet. By justification I mean simply the proffering of reasons for saying that it is not binding upon us to connect 99 with 98; the question of "connection" is open. Shorn of 99, Sonnet 98 can the more easily be seen to resemble other sonnets of the five I treat, in its interest in Seeming and Truth, and in its technique. Particularly beautiful moments in the poem are set off by lines in which there is an apparent relaxation of style (seen, for instance, in leisureliness, generality of epithet, even in approximation to the prosaic). Musicality is preferred to conceit. The sophistication of the metrics, in particular, makes 98 comparable with 100 and with 102 (which I am about to consider); and with others to be treated later.

Metrical interest and musicality are the making of the first quatrain of Sonnet 102. Its movement is both distinctive and easy. The rhymes of this quatrain contribute to the appearance of ease. The effect of a smart clinch is avoided: in the *a/a* position by rhyming a two-syllable word with one of three syllables ("seeming/"esteeming"), and in the *b/b* position by the imperfect rhyme which, further, is made of words having different stress patterns ("appear"/"everywhere"). As in Sonnet 98, there is a distinctive metrical motif, established by running a word over the foot-division, before the caesura and again at the end of the line. This may be shown by abstracting the scansion of lines 1 and 3:

My love is strengthen'd, though more weak in seeming;

That love is merchandiz'd, whose rich esteeming

Such differences as are seen here are elegant variations rather than new pattern. The quick upward beat at the end of a phrase is important to the lilting effect of the whole—as one may judge by its frequency in the sestet:

Not that | the summer ⌐·⌐

But that | wild music ⌐·⌐

And sweets | grown common ⌐·⌐

The lovely last line of the sonnet, casual in expression, delicate in sentiment, yet "final," probably owes some of its "final" quality to the presence in it of a beautiful variation on this motif. The lilting phrase is extended, the "upbeat" now coming in the fourth foot instead of the third, but there is an echo of the original pattern since in the third foot one has to make a break between t/d in "not dull." The effect is that there is a double lilt, the caesura is delayed, and after the caesura all the emphasis is taken by the resonant "song":

Because I would not dull you with my song.

Verbal repetition of a kind fitted to advance musicality is also used, more persistently than in Sonnet 100, yet still without obtrusiveness. The repetition seen in "My love . . . I love . . . That love . . . Our love" is one instance; one can read the sonnet without consciously noticing it, even though it works to strengthen and animate pattern and to give continuity of timbre and argument. The quatrain reads simply, yet is agog with correspondences and contrasts, as for instance in

. . . strengthen'd, though more weak . . .

. . . not less, though less . . .

This close linking of patterned elements has variation enough to make the balance very delicate; the correspondences are as intricate as those of a dance. Pattern may be kept up even by so delicate an echo effect as that whereby "love is merchandiz'd" acts as a "repeat" of "love is strength'd." In addition to patterns of this kind, there is balance and variation in the arrangement of concepts, as when "new" is coupled with "but in the spring" and then

in turn the coupling gives place to the contrast, "in summer's front
. . . in . . . riper days." The analogy between Philomel and the poet
is expressed with the liveliest variations in the arrangement of
ideas. For instance, the description of the poet's time of song
occupies a whole line ("When I was wont to greet it with my lays")
but when Philomel's singing and desisting are described, the
description runs across the line-ending: "doth sing, / And stops
her pipe." No appearance of set equivalence, got by contrivance, is
allowed, and this is of importance; the effect is that Philomel
appears to be associated in the poet's own experience with the topic
in hand. Yet there is just enough balancing and repeating over the
second quatrain as a whole to make a kind of delicate music, freer
in this second quatrain, further from the rhetoric of verbal
schemes. There is a beautiful and almost indescribable effect of
recitative, fluent and rich, when the quality of love, as it was, floods
into the sonnet; now the sense runs line by line, leisurely,
continuous, slipping naturally into the mind, yet a recitative rather
than a conversation, in that the relation between line and sense is
evenly kept up. This freer but still formal arrangement is strangely
crossed with fleeting effects of onomatopoeia, so subtle as to need
another name: consider the subdued musicality of "in summer's
front doth sing," alongside the desultory "stops her pipe." The
line-by-line flow of sense continues in quatrain 3, first through a
line casual in connection and almost idle: "Not that the summer is
less pleasant now." This indeed could be conversation. It runs on
into the rare, intense song of the nightingale, throbbing through
distance of time:

> Than when her mournful hymns did hush the night.

It is art no less astonishing to have begun some of the alliteration,
lightly, in the preceding line. In patterns of sound, the summer and
the nightingale's song gradually become one, and are palpable. The
summer of love becomes more than metaphorical—it becomes
something lived and living still, the summer pleasant *now*. So the
distinction between analogy and reality is dissolved, and the
summer, no longer bound to any one context of meaning, floats
through the sonnet as a pure entity at once ideal and real.

Similarly, Philomel becomes that nightingale which sang when "love was new," and the song is indistinguishable from "Our love." And so the real point of the poem is made: love has not only continued, but has kept all the intensity of the beginning; yet, to that there is added now the poise of maturity (felt in the sensitive balance of form) and an uninsistent tenderness. The nobly offhand "Because I would not dull you" is to drop into place as the long-awaited "conclusion" of "Not that . . . But that . . . And . . . Therefore. . . ." The real conclusion, that of art, is on "song":

> Therefore, like her, I sometime hold my tongue
> Because I would not dull you with my song.

The singing rhymes carry the music of Philomel beyond the bounds of the poem. Song and silence meet, for this is "the stillness of the violin / While the note lasts." So compulsive is the illusion, that all things which have to do with summer and song now partake of the one diffused reality. The wonderful impressionism of "But that wild music burthens every bough" partakes of it, and contributes to it, despite the fact that it is a quip at the "common" "sweets" of other poets.

At whatever level of deliberation Shakespeare wrote, it can be no coincidence that made such likeness, both in technique and power, as is seen in "Not that the summer is less pleasant now" and "Nor praise the deep vermilion in the rose."

An interesting connection runs from Sonnet 102 to Sonnet 115. However different otherwise, they have it in common that in them the poet looks at his way of writing in the past, as well as his way of loving, and that the sonnet, in each case, is arranged so as to include a recall of the very quality of that former time. As, in 102, the intensity of new love is recaptured, so in 115 there is a harking-back to the theme of Mutability. The harking-back is confined to one quatrain, discriminated in style from the easier flow of the rest, and consisting of a forceful catalogue of the depredations of Time. While including this recall, 115 seems to belong with sonnets near to it in the 1609 collection, rather than with the famous "Time sonnets." Its affirmation that no intensity has been lost connects it with 102, and, less directly, with the passionate assurances given in

109. The quatrain that catalogues the works of Time may be compared, in form and in force, with the catalogue of misdoings in
Sonnets 110 and 117. Above all, the image of the clearer burning of
the poet's "flame" is a remarkable epitome of those attitudes,
toward love as it was and is, found in the great poems of the last
three decades to the friend. "Full flame" is that of the blazing fire;
the "clear flame," gemlike in radiance, is seen in the fire burning
at its steadiest, with greatest intensity and least noise. The image of
this clear flame is perfect as a description of Shakespeare's own
style in these closing poems.

It will not now require very detailed comment to show that Sonnet 109 succeeds in form as well as by strength of feeling. Here repetition is used not only to give musicality but also to present an
image of the poet making an impassioned declaration of the truth
about himself, and in its course returning almost to his starting
point ("O never say . . .," "Never believe, . . .") because he has not
come to the end of the impetus of his feeling, and because by putting his feeling into one form of words he finds out how much more
than that he could with justice say. The dominant feature of the
form here is that it represents the mounting of intensity and finally
its stabilizing in the declaration of the scale of value by which he
lives. The sestet does not simply restate what is said in the octave.
From heartfelt rebuttal of some charge of neglect during a particular absence, it moves on to a demand that the friend should at all
times have absolute belief in the unshakable orientation of the
heart which the poet declares. The diction in the octave is simple;
in the sestet it is insistently repetitive ("All frailties . . . all kinds
. . . all thy sum") and, at the climax of rebuttal, it couples the
strong moral term "stained" with the term "preposterously,"
which in Shakespeare's time meant both "illogically" and "against
the order of nature." The term is used because the poet finds it
strictly illogical that the friend should think it ever possible for him
"To leave for nothing all thy sum of good." It is as illogical to
think this possible as it would be in the poet to do it. This makes it
all the more moving and convincing when, in the couplet, there is a
return to the language of pure passion, pure quality, and pure evaluation, wrought to a simple intensity, expressive of the poet's passion for the rare quality of his friend, whom he calls both "para-

gon" (a current Elizabethan meaning of "rose") and heart of tender delight:

> For nothing this wide universe I call
> Save thou, my rose; in it thou are my all.

No act of asserting a value could be more sweeping, indeed absolute, than this. The poet, having on the tide of his emotion made impetuous gestures which sweep together all manner of things that threaten constancy—"*All* frailties that besiege *all* kinds of blood" —dismisses them by opposing them the "all" of the Friend. That "all" is at once the "sum of good" and yet a single thing: all that the poet has. The "frailties" the poet lists are obstacles in the way of constancy and of trust, and they are, though general, real: the nature of man, the weaknesses of diverse temperaments, the promptings of diverse ruling passions. The comprehensive and generalized citing of these obstacles is a demand for total commitment to the faith that should prevail between those who love one another.

It seems likely enough that this sonnet is connected with 110 and 117, where Shakespeare catalogues those things which he as an individual has in fact been guilty of. (Apart from the likeness of implied situation there is the further likeness that all the sonnets make something of an image of travel.) In those two other sonnets the emphasis is on the poet's scrutiny of his own cheapnesses. But in 109 nothing is specified, nor said to be of the poet's own committing. All we know is that he feels himself to be subject to reproach or accusation. It is only by inference that one may suppose *some* frailty. He admits to nothing, except the giving of an unfortunate impression: "absence seemed my flame to qualify." The adoption of a diction so dignified allows one to suppose what one pleases about the (uninteresting) details of his conduct in absence. For a comparison with the attitude here, one might go to that passage in the encounter of Antony with Octavius Caesar, where Antony without loss of dignity makes peace possible by admitting to "poisoned hours" which "bound me up / From mine own knowledge" and says he will "so far ask pardon as befits / Mine honour." Lepidus comments on Antony's speech: "'Tis noble spoken." It is by the adoption of a tone "noble" as Antony's is, that Shakespeare in Sonnet 109 convinces us that his ideal of trust is itself noble, whereas in Sonnets 110 and 117, where he both bares and beats his breast (admittedly, in vigorous and "nervous" language), the interest is in "Shakespeare's confessions," not in the ideal of trust. Indeed, in 110 the excuse given for his behavior is at best not clearly distinguished from that of *l'homme moyen sensuel*: "These blenches gave my heart another youth" (unless we take him to mean his heart only, and, at that, the better part of it). At worst, his promise of a better future is repulsively expressive: "Mine appetite I never more will grind / On newer proof, to try an older friend." But disgust with what is below the dignity of the self implies a fine ideal, and, toward the end of 110 and of 117, there is a sudden elevation—or rather an attempted elevation—of attitude and language, as pleading replaces confession, and the Friend's "virtue" (the dignity and efficacy of his love) is called in to make all well:

> . . . an older friend,
> A god in love, to whom I am confined.
> Then give me welcome, next my heaven the best,
> Even to thy pure and most most loving breast. (110)

> . . . shoot not at me in your wakened hate,
> Since my appeal says I did strive to prove
> The constancy and virtue of your love. (117)

The sentiments and the language here are such as to allow one to connect these sonnets with Sonnet 109. If it is indeed proper to make this connection and to make a comparative estimate of achievement, I think one might fairly say that 109 comes out of the comparison as the more accomplished and beautiful sonnet. Though its language is less taut, it is no less passionate, and it achieves a fineness of attitude not matched in the confessional mode of the admittedly vigorous 110 and 117. In form, too, it is finer. There is no such calamitous change of tone as is seen in the other two, where, after language of force and originality, and matter of much interest and power to move, the sestet in each case offers a bungling "compensation": Sonnet 110's repellent promise is much at odds with the language of its last three lines (quoted above); Sonnet 117 offers a plea couched in the conventional language of arrows which shoot from the beloved's eye, and then an excuse couched as a conceit.

The last fails, not because it is a mere conceit but because it looks like nothing more; the whole couplet looks pale and slight, as an offset to the force of such lines as "I have hoisted sail to all the winds / Which should transport me farthest from your sight." What the sestet of 117 needed to save it, and to offset the octave's force, is something more than a sestet can well accommodate: namely, the attaching of a sufficiently specific meaning to the words "constancy" and "virtue." Sonnet 109 stands as an example of how one may attach specific meaning and felt quality to such terms. Without these attributions, the terms of value cannot weigh equally with the particularized confessions: Sonnet 117, ending with what looks like mere lip-service to ideals, expressed in pallid terms, is hopelessly topheavy. Here again, in the comparison of (presumably) related sonnets, one may see from the lesser works what strength there really is, and what art, in the "ease" of the greater work. Sonnet 109 fully justifies that elevation of language adopted from the beginning ("never . . . false of heart"; "my flame"; "my soul"), and it successfully modulates into simplicity, as in "my home of love," and into passion, in "my rose . . . my all." These simple and passionate terms are justified by the form of the poem. Its essential form is that of the discovery of the deepest level of truth in the act of defending and affirming the truth as one has so far known it. The images, "my home of love," "my rose," are so placed in the course of the sonnet as to be, for the poet, "the fountain from the which my current runs." For the reader, these images are the deep pools where in stillness and translucence one sees truth. The form is the more powerful because these images are few.

Sonnet 126 presents perhaps the most difficult problem to anyone who would like to understand what kind of art or magic it is that wrests from almost incompatible components an illusion of ease and balance. It begins in tenderness and ends in a conceit which might have been expected to kill a poem by frigidity. If one asks oneself how it can have "come off" there seems to be no answer save an answer in terms of an attitude in the poet—an attitude understood as a way of comporting oneself so as not to deny either the real or the ideal, nor to minimize either of the two elements, the truth that is given and the truth that is chosen, which constitute the life of sensibility. This poem gives us the truth of the poet and the boy through hyperbole, and guarantees the clear-cut hyperbole by the delicate shading of rich human emotion conveyed by the opening words, "O thou my lovely boy, who in thy power. . . ." The vision of the boy holding the emblems of Time, as if they were his trophies, comes to the reader as vision rather than mere hyperbole because the very tenderness with which the opening words are suffused prepares us to believe that the poet speaks from insight conferred by loving contemplation. As the sonnet proceeds, his contemplation proves to have extended over a time long enough to show "thy lovers withering." Whether or not the poet is understood to be one of those "lovers," the tone is that of detachment, even in tenderness. The poet is present in the poem as the loving, admonishing, and finally elegiac voice. For my own part, I find him also present as one of a throng seen—or apprehended, for there is nothing visual—as receding or falling away from the timeless state of the boy. In the tenderness of the poet's address, more is said about the thing contemplated than about the seer. The opening words suggest such motives for tenderness as pride of possession, lovableness, beauty, youth. In all these motives together there is more than their mere sum. They seize the heartrendingness of boyhood as such, for they are conveyed to us as the responses of a moment in which the power and the vulnerability of this boy are in equilibrium, in a relation going beyond contention into the pure simultaneity of myth. The style of this first line is "plain" as an old song is plain. The sound of it is as lingering as its terms are brief and basic. Syntax has the marks of elevation: an extended periodic sentence sustains over the whole of the first quatrain a continuous dwelling upon the impassible quality of the boy ("O thou . . . who in thy power / Dost hold . . . Who hast by waning grown, and therein showest . . ."), and it is a beautiful feature of the poem that this description never really comes to an end. An anacoluthon breaks into it: "If Nature. . . ." The rest of the poem seems to follow from what is said about Nature's contention with Time, while the boy ideally remains as if "dreaming on the verge of strife," even though in a succeeding picture of him he goes "onward" and in yet another is Nature's "minion." Though the vision changes it is only as in a frieze. The art is directed toward an eloquence of arrested movement; the attitudes might almost be on Keats's urn. What sort of "coldness" this pastoral has may be judged by contrasting it with lines from Sonnet 65:

> O how shall summer's honey breath hold out
> Against the wrackful siege of battering days . . .
> O fearful meditation! where, alack,
> Shall Time's best jewel from Time's chest lie hid?
> Or what strong hand can hold his swift foot back,
> Or who his spoil of beauty can forbid?

In 126, though the poet counsels "fear," there is none of the terror, the short-taken breath, the almost hallucinatory vividness of the strong hand on the swift foot. Instead there is fact: decline will come. The boy, still Nature's darling, will be taken away from her as a toy is taken from a child. So the boy seems to diminish and dwindle. But only to grow. For it turns out that he is not a toy taken away nor a "minion" disputed over and given up like the "Indian boy" for whose sake Titania and Oberon quarrel. More, now, than "Time's best jewel," he becomes the settlement of all Nature stands to account for. Yet the tone here is not apocalyptic. It is set (by the content, by the couplet form, by the neatness with which "render thee" gives us the inevitable fact and the complimentary flourish in one breath) as being consummately elegant. No one need believe in the compliment. One need only believe in the attitude it expresses—the sort of attitude that makes a man determine to make no great fuss about aging or dying, beyond taking care to do the thing in style, to the discomfiture of his enemies and the consolation of his friends. There is nothing frigid in this "satire to Decay," even though the poet makes it not on his own account but on a friend's, for the Friend is "the better part of me." The poet has a right to his *sprezzatura*; we know from his "mournful hymns," elsewhere, that there was a time when he could say,

> This thought is as a death, which cannot choose
> But weep to have that which it fears to lose.   (64.13-14)

In Sonnet 126 he chooses not to weep. Should it prove, after all, that it is only by accident that 126 occupies the place of valediction, it is a beautiful accident.

THE BEAUTY OF TRUTH:
THE DRAMATIC CHARACTER
OF SHAKESPEARE'S SONNETS

BY

ANTON M. PIRKHOFER

AFTER all the extant works on Shakespeare's art, yet another study on the subject may need some words of justification.[1] The Keatsian. title of this investigation indicates the lines along which it proceeds: it epitomizes the fundamental struggle in Shakespeare between the mellifluous principle of Renaissance art which puts beauty first and the characterizing principle which is primarily intent on revealing the truth. Shakespeare's contemporaries praised his "sug'red sonnets" and his "well torned, and true-filed lines" whereas modern commentators stress the fact that more than any other Elizabethan author Shakespeare succeeds in laying bare the human heart, that he was out to expose the truth about human feeling and thinking and to represent man as he is rather than as he should be. In fact, no dramatist can afford to dedicate himself wholly to either of the two principles, to beauty of form or truth of character and incident, without endangering the balance of his work.

Even in the realm of the sonnet, the interaction—which at times may amount to a clash—of the two principles can be traced right into the outward flow of the individual line where the overall elegance of the phrasing is sometimes disturbed by clashing rhythms underscored by alliteration and the deliberate effect of ugliness or harshness required to express the "truth" of the individual sonnet.[2] With the true-born dramatist the aesthetic urge to create beautifully measured lines of poetry must be particularly susceptible to cross-influences stemming from his introspective curiosity and the ultimate desire to discover the inner "beauty" of created beings, to learn as it were what makes them "tick."

In the Sonnets, too, we are faced with a vision which congenitally saw the beauty of all things but which could not help penetrating beyond the outward semblance and appearances to the core —could not help seeing the substance behind the shadow both in the poet himself and the personages around him.[3] It will be seen in the course of this investigation that the claim of certain critics is justified, namely, that the poet-dramatist's truthfulness was irrepressible enough to make itself felt not only against his admiration of beautiful "facades" but against a vein of deference, a trend toward distorting the truth in order to please the addressee of the Sonnets (whether nobleman or commoner). This pull of conflicting impulses and principles should be sufficient to generate an interest in the Sonnets that must come near to that of an onlooker at a drama. Apart from this, there has of late been an increased tendency to regard the Sonnets under the same aspect as the plays, namely as the unfolding of the human mystery in the shape of stirring events set in a huge panorama of emotions and thoughts, presented predominantly as climactically structured action which excites suspense by employing—even in metaphorical contexts — human agents. This tendency should also be seen as part of the struggle of beauty versus truth; so should the literary outcome of that struggle, the line (or lines) of verse which both appeal and convince, which become "classical" for their very combination of dual qualities and are passed down the centuries as "haunting lines" bearing testimony to an unsurpassed "gift for imaged expression."[4]

In using the terms "lyrical" and "dramatic" (as distinct from an "epic") style, I draw on an earlier study dealing with the interaction of the lyrical, dramatic, and epic elements in the work of Thomas Hardy—a study indebted to the investigations of Oskar Walzel, Robert Petsch, and others.[5] Since then, a formidable body of research has accumulated in the field of literary aesthetics, mainly owing to the contributions of Bonamy Dobrée and F. W. Bateson in England, Austin Warren and René Wellek in the United States, Emil Staiger in Germany, and Herbert Seidler in Austria. Proceeding along different routes as some of them did, they yet combined to define and illustrate the fundamental approaches to literary art as well as outlining the history of single component parts of the literary artifact. Joining them were Wolfgang Clemen and his school at Munich University, who turned their critical attention to such epic or narrative elements in a play's structure as the *Botenbericht*.[6]

With regard to the subject under discussion here, it is of absorbing interest to observe the presence of the dramatic impulse even in the lyrical and narrative work of an outstanding poet-dramatist, all the more so since it has become customary to distinguish the more lyrical bias, say, of *Richard II* from the almost barely "functional" dramatic character of *Macbeth,* whereas with *Hamlet* one might speak of an "epic" expansion of the dramatic groundwork. It is one of the main tasks of this investigation to ascertain whether the dramatic instinct, chameleon-like as it is, has also found its way into more intimate spheres such as the poet's use of imagery which has so far—with the exception of Wolfgang Clemen's *The Development of Shakespeare's Imagery* (1951)—mainly been dealt with from a predominantly aesthetic or linguistic point of view, or in relation to the development of the meaning.[7] The ultimate purpose of research carried on in this direction should be to lead to a better understanding of the various means by which Shakespeare's ubiquitous impulse toward playmaking is translated into language, or—with particular reference to the Sonnets—employed to dramatize the sonnet form.[8]

I

THE DEFINITION OF "DRAMATIC"
AND ITS APPLICATION TO SONNET-WRITING

The modern trend toward regarding a number of Shakespeare's sonnets as hybrids between a verse epistle and a dramatic speech only partly echoes the pronunciamentos of earlier critics.[9] One of the most recent experts to deal with the Shakespearean poems, F. T. Prince, has a section on the Sonnets in which he stresses the fact that "they have in an unusual degree the tones of the speaking voice," a remark which leads him on to the cautious observation that "the Sonnets are essentially the poems of a dramatist."[10] His further statement, interesting as it is, is somewhat exaggerated, for it postulates no more and no less than that Shakespeare writes "each of them as he would write a speech in a play."[11] Another more pertinent observation of Prince's is the following: "He hears the poem spoken as he writes," the poem which is "conceived as a statement of fancy or impulse in a given situation." Prince's further remark—as he discusses Sonnets 109 and 97—on the "dramatist's gift and practice" giving Shakespeare's style its "immense *author-ity*: that resounding force of expression" (p.60) is perhaps a rephrasing, conscious or unconscious, of Mark van Doren's felici-tous pronouncement that "the volume of their sound suggests a deep, an almost subterranean hum of energy coming from the dark center of all the power there is" and that their subject is "the uni-verse pulsing under change." While skipping over my idea that the Sonnets may have dramatic value in themselves as miniature plays, Prince shrewdly comments on "authentic confusion" in them, "the confusion of strong emotions and conceptions which have not yet clarified themselves" (p. 60). He has thereby broached what I would rather call the poet's speaking in character, that is, with the voice of an assumed or fictitious personality instead of his own ("character-refracted" utterance). The "confusion" engendered is "dramatic" inasmuch as it rightly belongs to a person who is only partly identifiable with the author. Perhaps this is just another way of expressing what Arthur Mizener says about the structure of fig-urative language in Shakespeare's sonnets, that it "at least approaches in its own verbal terms, the richness, the density, the logical incompleteness of the mind."[12] There is, however, not only the dramatic "self-reflection" of one mind, but of many minds to be found in the Sonnets, an observation which throws new light on the old epithet "myriad-minded" as applied to Shakespeare.

As to J. W. Lever's and G. K. Hunter's criticism of the Sonnets, Lever's seems to be the more radical in assuming that there is "drama" proper in the Sonnets, whereas Hunter's is more restrained in claiming the Sonnets to be only "dramatic" in char-acter in so far as there are in them drama-like forces engaged in a struggle with each other.[13] Since these authors avoid a definition of what they mean by "dramatic," I propose to use my own definition.

I consider "drama" to be "structured action which is impersonated by actors (or one actor) who act and converse (or soliloquize on a stage." It now remains to be seen how this noncommital and elastic definition can be suited to the exigencies of sonnet-writing. That this is not too easy a task may be seen from the patent uncertainties which attach to discussions of the dramatic character of sonnets in general.[14] Thus there are contradictory findings as regards the dramatic character of Spenser's *Amoretti* which Hallet Smith judges to be "reflective, musical, flowing rather than impatient or dramatic,"[15] and of which J.W. Lever thinks that as a whole they are "undramatic." But Waldo F. McNeir maintains that they are "dramatic in method" even if they lack the "complex ambiguities" of Shakespeare's style.[16] This verdict and the similar one that Spenser's sonnets are "situational" and "circumstantial" in their explicit reference to the "events" are contradicted, however, by McNeir's other characterization of them as "chronological narrative" and "predominantly narrative." (The last characterization is as correct as the other is not.) I would suggest that the term "anecdotal" fits Spenser's procedure much better than does "situational," which I would reserve for Shakespeare's method. McNeir's terminological confusion cannot hide the fact that Spenser's sonnets are "narrative" in their basic method. It is for this very reason that they provide an illuminating foil to the description of Shakespeare's practice.

For in his Sonnets Shakespeare has little patience with, or gift for, the view of cyclical recurrence of natural and social phenomena (including love, hatred, and other emotions). Such epic formulas as "When I once met her in the garden . . . ," or "And many years passed until . . . ," or "X had received a shock but its impact was lessened with the healing effect of time" are of little use to him as a dramatic poet. The "once upon a time" attitude of the Oriental and aboriginal storyteller must be alien to the playwright, whose attention is fixed on the everlasting presence of the dramatic moment, the moment which is fertile in the sense that it holds a number of possible developments. The sonnet lines "everything that grows / Holds in perfection but a little moment" testify to the refined sensibility of the dramatist although they are blatantly untrue to the phenomena of organic revival and of the possibility of a man's or a woman's repeated "blossoming" both in an emotional and a spiritual sense, let alone a bodily one; for it is a matter of everyday observation that there is a perfection proper to young, middle, and even old age. In this connection it may be of interest to note the respect that was paid to wise old men in Germanic times as may be seen from such epic poems as *Beowulf*;[17] even the Wanderer's complaint is less about his old age than about the loss of his "gold-wine."

II

SHAKESPEARE'S CHARACTERISTIC PRACTICES

Thus, Shakespeare's prevailing use of the present tense in his Sonnets gives away the dramatist and his predilection for the "fertile moment," the gathering together in time of evolving and revolving things—which is at the same time an awareness of the dramatic moment, much as Shakespeare's Sonnets may strike one as being "chunks" from a more or less continuous and coherent confession. (This seems to be the view taken by most modern scholars, including Professor Prince and myself.) The present moment, then, fertile as it is with developments or reminiscences, is Shakespeare's natural starting point from which he looks back on the past or, with a prophetic stance, forward into the future. It is not a moment of timelessness as with the lyrical poet but a moment in time which is poignantly fraught with the consequences of past volitions and which contains the seeds of future actions or volitions—in short, a dramatist's present which, like the Weird Sisters in *Macbeth,* is concerned with the "deed without a name."

The fertile, the emotion-fraught moment, from which the action is ready to develop in various directions, may be exploited in different ways. One of them is the more-or-less straightforward presentation of a clash of wills and the endeavor of one will to overpower another (which underlies most sonnets of the so-called procreation series). Thus the "allo-persuasive" element which is the life and soul of drama is also the mainstay of Shakespeare's first sonnets. If it is argued against this—say, with Lee (ed. 1905)—that "nothing was commoner in Renaissance literature than for a literary client to urge on a patron the duty of transmitting to future ages his charms and attainments" and that this plea can be traced back to Erasmus and ultimately to Plato's *Symposium,* the reply is that in none of

these alleged parallels or models (certainly not in the clumsy contemporary versification of the increase idea as adduced by Mario
Praz in 1939) does one feel the clash of wills as one does with
Shakespeare, with whom one has the impression that the whole
thing is far from being a sham affair or merely put on for the sake
of complying with a literary convention. Nothing, then, could be
further from the truth than J.H. Chapman's verdict that "it [the
continuance of human species by this youth] is a joke" (1922). This
is best seen if Sonnet 1, say, is reduced to its "volitional" skeleton
while the "color" provided by the varied imagery is neglected. It is
necessary to do this in order to grasp the peculiar nature of Shakespeare's sonnets, whose dramatic character has so far been insufficiently realized whereas other traits have received even excessive
attention.

Here is the Quarto (1609) text of Sonnet 1:

> From fairest creatures we desire increase,
> That thereby beauties *Rose* might neuer die,
> But as the riper should by time decease,
> 4   His tender heire might beare his memory:
> But thou contracted to thine own bright eyes,
> Feed'st thy light's flame with selfe substantiall fewell,
> Making a famine where aboundance lies,
> 8   Thy selfe thy foe, to thy sweet selfe too cruell:
> Thou that art now the worlds fresh ornament,
> And only herauld to the gaudy spring,
> Within thine owne bud buriest thy content,
> 12   And tender chorle makst wast in niggarding:
> Pitty the world, or else this glutton be,
> To eate the worlds due, by the graue and thee.

Significantly, the very first verb of this sonnet ("we desire") is a
verb of volition representing the dramatic "will," after which the
"anti-will" is introduced in line 5 ("But thou . . ."). The basic
antagonism is even carried into the friend's self, which is seen as
split up in itself ("Thy selfe thy foe . . ."). All this constitutes a
highly tensional beginning which is hardly found in any other sonneteer. By way of comparison, Sidney is much less forthright in his
sonnets to Stella, which are almost all too "decorated" to allow of
direct utterance of emotion or thought. With him the prevailing

pattern is of narrative sonnets which are given an unexpected situational twist together with an awkward and often confusing changeover from the third person (indirect) to second-person address (direct).[18]

In delineating the basic conflict of the very first of Shakespeare's Sonnets it is immaterial whether "we" of the beginning stands for the poet and the family of the friend who would move him to get married or for the poet and the "world" (c.f. the accumulated references to the "world" in lines 9, 13, and 14) in which the matchmaking family might be indirectly included. (Neither Rollins nor Ingram and Redpath have thought this interesting term worth annotating.)[19] The simple antagonism of the beginning is rendered more subtle by the poet's repeatedly pointing to the biological paradox underlying the Friend's recalcitrant attitude, namely, the "famine-abundance" antithesis of line 7, the clash "bud buriest" of line 11, and the "makst wast in niggarding" of line 12. Thus the tensional buildup is rendered more complex by paralleling the clash of wills with a clash of paradoxic notions and even of alliterative sounds: in the contiguous *b*-alliteration of "bud buriest" the theme of the sonnet (refused procreation) is "compressed into the smallest possible antithetical alliterating formula."

Owing to the brilliant and hard elegance of its language, the structural organization of Sonnet 1 is a model of clarity. Compared with the blurred outlines of most of Sidney's sonnets, Shakespeare's first sonnet is already characteristically Shakespearean in the development of its theme, the statement of the will (lines 1-4) being followed by that of the anti-will (lines 5-12, with line 11 a variation of line 6). Both are rounded off by the peremptory note of the couplet in which the indicative of statement ("we desire . . . But thou . . . Feed'st . . . buriest . . . makst wast . . .") is replaced by the imperative ("Pitty . . . be") and the Friend is presented with an inexorable alternative between two courses of action (marked by "or"). It is the urgency of the allo-persuasive tone in Sonnet 1 which lends it the intensity of a speech in drama and which renders improbable Gildemeister's interpretation of it as "Arcadian" in mood and as aiming only at a symbolic "preservation of beauty."

Not always is the allo-persuasive tone as blunt or urgent as it is in Sonnet 1. Sonnet 2, for instance, opens with a prophecy couched in the future tense, the prophecy giving place to an insinuating use of the conditional which is kept up throughout the second and third quatrains to the end of the couplet. The initial bluntness of the cocksure prophecy in the first quatrain is mitigated by the conditional statements ending with the gently suggestive "This were to be new made," which contrasts strangely with the imperious "Pitty the world . . ." of the preceding couplet.[20]

> VVhen fortie Winters shall beseige thy brow
> And digge deep trenches in thy beauties field,
> Thy youthes proud liuery so gaz'd on now,
> 4   Wil be a totter'd weed of smal worth held:
> Then being askt, where all thy beautie lies,
> Where all the treasures of thy lusty daies:
> To say within thine owne deepe sunken eyes,
> 8   Were an all-eating shame, and thriftless praise.
> How much more praise deseru'd thy beauties vse,
> If thou couldst answere this faire child of mine
> Shall sum my count, and make my old excuse
> 12   Proouing his beautie by succession thine.
>   This were to be new made when thou art ould,
>   And see thy blood warme when thou feel'st it could,

Such nicely shaded variations of tone should not, however, blind one to the fact that most of Shakespeare's sonnets are generally either allo-persuasive or "auto-diagnostic" in character—in other words, they correspond to the duologue or soliloquy situation on the stage. I have coined the term "allo-persuasive" in order to have a convenient designation for those sonnets whose obvious function is to overcome the resistance of a second will by more or less pungent argument. But even in the allo-persuasive sonnets there is at times an admixture of the auto-diagnostic or—characteristically with Shakespeare—of the "allo-diagnostic" element. This note of diagnosis is already there in the very first of the Sonnets, where quatrains 2 and 3 diagnose the friend's state of mind, and the note increases as we leave the procreation sonnets behind. Still, the two types of sonnet do not cover the whole of Shakespeare's output. There are sonnets in between—not necessarily the most "Shakespearean"—which, like Sonnet 24, attempt the expression of a state of feeling or a situation of the mind by undramatic means, that is, by static conceits. These sonnets more nearly approach ordinary poems or lyrics, in which Spenser's *Amoretti* series abounds—poems, that is, in which the conflicting impulses of the waking world have come to rest, at least temporarily, in a vision more-or-less individual and original in character.

Thus Shakespeare's style as a dramatic sonneteer is firmly established from the beginning. There is in Sonnet 1, as I have already pointed out, the basic clash of wills; there is paradoxical antithesis, and an arresting life-or-death alternative in the couplet. The fact that the "herald of the spring" may have been a cliché in Shakespeare's time (a similar formula is found in *Amoretti* LXX) does not detract from the poet's achievement in dramatizing the issue in the way indicated. Moreover, he bestows upon the Friend the fleeting impersonations of an enemy to his own self, a herald to spring, a niggard, and a glutton. The line "Within thine owne bud buriest thy content" with its double meaning of "that which is contained" (potential child or progeny) and "contentment" is inimitably Shakespeare's own in that it ranges the basic forces of life and death against each other by making them cohabit in the smallest linguistic space ("bud buriest"). All this is evident although the clash of wills is mitigated by the use of metaphor whose rhythm moves from plant life (the rosebud) to inorganic existence (flame and fuel) and back to plant life (the bud of line 11).

The antagonism between the "we" of the first quatrain and the "thou" of the second raises yet another point which is worth pondering. For with the very first pronoun of his series of sonnets Shakespeare makes himself the spokesman of enlightened common sense. His voice thus takes on the ring of that of the chorus leader in Greek tragedy who warns the protagonist against impending evil although his pleading may be of little avail. This sense of a public function is absent from the more personal and individualistic pleadings of contemporary sonneteers, even if they occasionally employ the term "world" as does Shakespeare. Compared with the near-desperate struggle of the poet-mentor to avert a doom which is in store for his protagonist-friend, Spenser's and other sonneteers' worries dwindle to a storm in a teacup, leaving the reader amused rather than stirred. The affinity between such "pan-tragic" sonnets and Greek tragedy is even heightened when the duo of chorus leader and protagonist is imperceptibly replaced by the trio of chorus leader (the poet's "I" which is not often expressly mentioned but tacitly included in the argument), protagonist-friend (the "light" and thou" of Sonnet 7), and chorus proper ("each under-eye" and "eyes" of 7). Such formal affinity perhaps should not surprise us in view of the fact that in Sonnet 7 Shakespeare traces the mythic career of Helios or Phoebus, which seems to be the classical proto-type underlying the demythologized stories of *De Casibus Virorum Illustrium.*

Talking of classical affinities, there is yet another characteristic which also contributes to illuminate the incomparable range and depth of Shakespeare's sonneteering art, a range and depth that are inseparably bound up with the insight and stage experience of the great dramatist. For, to a great extent, Shakespeare's sonnets move between two extremes—both metaphysically and dramatically speaking. These extremes are represented by the "sonnet of fate" and the "sonnet of character," both of which have their parallel in the "tragedy of fate" (as exemplified by *Romeo and Juliet*) and in the "tragedy of character" (as exemplified by *Othello*), with *Macbeth* and *Lear* as mediating crossbreeds. The same tissue of events or sequences of happenings may now be looked upon as being decreed by outside fate, now as being forced from inside and deter-mined by a person's character; or, to put it in terms of the Sonnets, Time the Destroyer may alternate with the Friend as Trouble-maker. In harnessing both character and fate to the chariot of his inspiration, Shakespeare has brought to bear on his interpretation of the human predicament the two main forces which are decisive both for the individual and the community. This may be seen in a comparison of Sonnet 12 with Sonnet 13:

> When I doe count the clock that tels the time,
> And see the braue day sunck in hidious night,
> When I behold the violet, past prime,
> 4 And sable curls or siluer'd ore with white:
> When lofty trees I see barren of leaues,
> Which erst from heat did canopie the herd
> And Somers greene all girded vp in sheaues
> 8 Borne on the beare with white and bristly beard:
> Then of thy beauty do I question make

That thou among the wastes of time must goe,
Since sweets and beauties do them-selues forsake,
12   And die as fast as they see others grow,
And nothing gainst Times sieth can make defence
Saue breed to braue him, when he takes thee hence.

O That you were your selfe, but loue you are
No longer yours, then you your selfe here liue,
Against this cumming end you should prepare,
4   And your sweet semblance to some other giue.
So should that beauty which you hold in lease
Find no determination, then you were
Your selfe again after your selfes decease,
8   When your sweet issue your sweet forme should beare.
Who lets so faire a house fall to decay,
Which husbandry in honour might vphold,
Against the stormy gusts of winters day
12   And barren rage of deaths eternal cold?
O none but vnthrifts, deare my loue you know,
You had a Father, let your Son say so.

As nearly as possible, Sonnets 12 and 13 embody two extremes in philosophical and artistic attitudes toward the world; for in Sonnet 12 the responsibility is as ostensibly on the side of fate as it is put on the individual (the friend) in 13. Such tension as is found between the ceremoniously impersonal and almost ominously prophetic tone of Sonnet 12 and the unceremoniously personal pleading of Sonnet 13, between the pan-tragic attitude of 12 (which would be unnecessarily belittled by accepting Ernst Voege's far-fetched interpretation of its present-tense forms as "historic present") and the insistence on individual guilt in 13, bears out Robert Fricker's findings on polarity in Shakespeare's art—a polarity that exists simultaneously on various levels of understanding.[21] The contrast in basic attitudes between Sonnets 12 and 13 recalls the revulsion-of-mood sonnets and, more particularly, the "paired" sonnets.[22] This basic contrast is diversified and rendered more subtle, or even more tense, by the interplay of thematic and sonal organization.[23]

The preceding remarks might also serve as prolegomena to a typology of Shakespeare's sonnets, investigations of which have so far only been tentative. Perhaps scholars have up till now been hampered by the great variety of Shakespeare's approaches. Still, some valid results should at long last be within reach if the fundamental characteristics highlighted above are taken into consideration, together with the later discussion of the straightforwardly progressive versus the pivotal-turn sonnet—the sonnet, that is, in which the initial mood or situation is revoked by the mustering of an antagonistic force similar to the way in which the climax of a play may be followed by an anticlimax. (A good example of this is Sonnet 15.)

III
Dramatic Structure in the Sonnets

With the above remarks I hope to have established the peculiar, that is, the dramatic, character of Shakespeare's sonneteering style —its antithetical nature and the intense concentration on a second person (a "thou" or "you") which leads to the predominance of the allo-persuasive approach at least at the beginning of the series. Later on, the auto-diagnostic element comes to the fore, with an ever-increasing stress on the personality of the speaker which is at first almost nonexistent (as may be seen from the absence of the "I" from Sonnets 1-9). This is an attitude that befits the dramatist who only gradually—via the "world," by a painful process of discovery—attains the self-knowledge which has ever been the aim of great drama. *Gnothe sauton* (know thyself) may thus be said to be the prime impulse behind the Sonnets as well as behind the poems and the plays, more especially the great tragedies.[24] The proud confession of Sonnet 121 ("Noe, I am that I am, and they that levell / At my abuses, reckon up their owne") links up with Regan's contemptuous "yet he hath ever but slenderly known himself" and Lear's frenzied self-questioning ("Who is it that can tell me who I am?") and the most astonishing line in the Poems, "Before I know myself, seek not to know me" (*Venus and Adonis,* line 525).

In discussing Sonnets 1 and 3, 12 and 13 as paradigmatic I have taken for granted the legitimacy of my approach of treating each sonnet as an independent unit,[25] and in some cases of considering each sonnet as a miniature play. Such an approach would have been uncommon forty or fifty years ago when so many critics and scholars were keen on reading a continuous story into the Sonnets or were even in the habit of putting together, more or less arbitrarily, various sonnets so as to form consecutive groups or even whole stanzaic "poems."[26] In limiting my attention to the individual sonnet, one of the characteristics that strikes me as particularly Shakespearean is the tendency toward situational concretization and scenic climaxing. For, quite apart from whether we are dealing with a sonnet of the allo-persuasive or auto-diagnostic variety, of the straightforward progressive (as is the case in 12) or revelatory pivotal-turn species (with the couplet marking a "clinch to" or "wrench in" the development respectively), the power of visualization in many of them is such as to work up toward a scenic climax which should not be confused with the structural climax.

In studying Shakespeare's power of situational visualization it will be seen that it is coercive, that it has a way of immediately communicating itself to the reader or listener without the intervention of his reasoning faculty. This is demonstrated by Shakespeare's way of treating abstracts, which he forces down to the level of earthbound beings, less in the sense of Spenser's leisurely and static or epic presentation of pageants of pseudo-animated beings than by the swift establishment of a kinetic impulse which is imparted to the imagination in such a way that it goes on functioning in the manner of a visual *perpetuum mobile*. Examples of the length of chain reaction to which Shakespeare's power of empathy will carry him may be picked almost at random from the body of the Sonnets—26, 28, 31, 35, 57, 88, and 89 among others.

Thus Sonnet 26 has been taken to be a "frigid envoy" and, more fittingly, a "love-letter in the language of a vassal doing homage to his leige lord" by a number of commentators.[27] Still, it is conspicuously Shakespearean not only for the role assumed in it by the poet but for the fact that, on a second level that one might call the level of "stage visualization," through such arresting terms as "bare" in line 6 and "all naked" in line 8, a scene is built up in which the friend-star, after giving hospitable lodging to the "bare" beggar of a poet-vassal ("bestow," line 8), points on him graciously with fair aspect and provides the beggar in his torn garments with sumptuous or stylish clothing (line 11), whether the old "rags" are replaced or just covered up (as the phrase "puts . . . on" would seem to suggest). The scene which is thus, if only in a fragmentary way, conjured up recalls the Induction to *The Taming of the Shrew* where the Lord instructs the huntsmen to ask the tinker Christophorus Sly "what apparel he will wear." The finale of the scene has the poet, true to his part, not daring to boast of his love and hiding away his tattered "state" (line 12). Thus from the playful "vassallage" idea of the beginning—which may have been a half-legal cliché[28]—Shakespeare develops a scene involving two people and action which is not only symbolic but has stage reality or even the reality of life about it (lines 8, 10-14).

Dramatic visualization is also at work in Sonnet 28, where the scenifying impulse arises out of an almost casual personification of "day" and "night." The sonnet starts on a note of simple experiential realism (lines 1-2), employing the usual abstract terminology to denote an emotional state. But in the next line the metaphor has got out of hand, and the scenifying impulse, which may be said to have been dormant in line 3, begins to stir in line 4. It comes to life fully in lines 5-6, which suggest a torturing scene from one of the tragedies. The scenification is supported by the bestowal of a masculine pronoun upon "day" and also by its capitalization in line 9, and it is developed so as to include the poet who takes the part of the humble petitioner "on the rack" pleading with his torturers for release.[29] Almost imperceptibly, as the poet continues with his personifying jugglery, the tragic atmosphere changes to comic, and the oppressive tug-of-war between the two entities and the poet is mitigated as the familiar heterosexual tension between Day and Night supersedes the grim rivalry of two tyrants at court. The suggestion of a lively scene involving a trio of actors is, however, not kept up in the couplet, in which the moving figures of Day and Night are suddenly frozen, and the scene is "grammarized" and "devisualized" at the same time. The poetic effect is now made to depend on the repetition of the grammarized personifications and on the sound-symbolism they convey, while the figures of the previous scene fade into the background (although their shadows can still be discerned stirring uneasily behind lines 12-14).

There is a scenographic touch also about Sonnet 31, but there is more of it in 35, which is less subtle than 31 in thought, yet more dramatic in its basic confrontation of two personalities at strife and the painful sense it conveys of the poet's doing violence to his own. In their efforts to make sense of lines 8 and 9 in 35, commentators have generally failed to note the scene at court that is suggested by the wording of lines 8-13. The final result of such scenifying is that the friend is turned into a thief and the poet into his accessory — both being objectified by changing into something like figures on the stage of the poet's mind. Viewed from this angle, Sonnet 35 falls into three parts: the first consists of quatrain 1, which serves as a sort of introduction; the second consists of lines 5-8 and is in the auto- and allo-diagnostic vein using a moral and religious terminology; the third comprises lines 9-14, and it is only here that scenifying proper is started by the adoption of a legal terminology suggestive of a procedure in a law court.

In Sonnet 57 the embryonic scene grows out of the initial assumption of the stance of a slave (which continues into 58).[30] Here the scenification, which grows out of a disjointed meditation on time in Sonnet 12, constitutes the visual climax of a human drama involving two persons, the absent friend and the deserted poet. The actor Shakespeare appears to be almost deliberately merging his own individuality into that of a stage personage—"the speaker plays the unhappy role of the slave" where the comparison implies distinction of two individuals. Sonnet 58 revives or continues the identification, with a flash of transient personification at line 7 and a mounting tension between a spirit of toleration and a sense of injury which reaches its climax in lines 12-14.[31] Here, as is often the case with Shakespeare, the sonnet's development is clinched by an outbreak of linguistic fury in the phrases "self-doing crime" and "though waiting so be hell."

Certain climactic situations seem to have occupied Shakespeare's scenifying memory to such an extent that they recur in different sonnets. One of the most striking is the visualization of himself taking part in a court hearing and siding with the Friend against himself, as may be seen from a comparison of Sonnets 35,

49, and 88, more particularly lines 10-13 of the first, lines 9-12 of the second, and lines 3-4 of the third. The most graphic of these scenes is the second, where the poet is presented as raising his hand against himself. Here, for two reasons, I am afraid I cannot share the view expressed by Ingram and Redpath that "against" means "in front of." The first reason is that in the parallel passages from the other two sonnets, "against" clearly denotes "in an attack on" (taking up the "split-self" theme of earlier sonnets). The second is that the merely spatial reading of "against" instead of the combined spatial and symbolic reading would be detrimental to the climactic structure inasmuch as the antithesis between the poet's seeking shelter behind his "desert" (small as that may be—note "my defects" in line 2), yet siding with the friend in the imaginary lawsuit, would then be removed and make place for a dramatically illogical warding off of lawful reasons.

Next to the sonnets with a scenic and personifying climax or bent, it is important from my viewpoint to study hybrids—those sonnets in which the dramatist's impact upon the poet leads to a more-or-less unresolved dichotomy. How a lyric conceit can be lent dramatic force by personification and scenification is borne out by Sonnet 114, where the two psycho-physiological notions "mind" and "eye" are lifted to the plane of a stage action, thus taking their place beside such personified and scenified abstractions as "day" and "night" or "time"[32] and "death." In the process of scenification, the poet's mind is transformed into a monarch, with the additional flourish that the Friend is magically turned into the monarch's crown. What is of particular interest about Sonnet 114 is that it intensifies by scenification a situation that is set out in 113, where lines 9 and 12 as well as the couplet carry overtones of nascent personification. Thus the second of these paired sonnets, which are linked by the eye-mind antithesis and withal a palpable lyrical conceit, may owe its existence to the irresistible pull of the dramatist's instinct to improve upon the dramatically almost neutral version of 113, in which the final vision of a scenified relation between the mind and the eye as realized in 114 may have lain dormant. The doubling of the treatment of the eye-mind conceit is fully justified for the further reason that the second version (114), apart from introducing scenification on the visual level, widens the issue from an aesthetic and epistemological one (113) to one that openly stresses the moral aspect as the dimension proper to the dramatist and may thereby hint at more things (such as faults in the Friend) than meet the eye of the poet.

The overlapping of the poet's and the dramatist's outlook may also be studied in those sonnets where the poet's aesthetic urge toward beauty is not supported but counteracted by the dramatist's search for truth. This is the case in Sonnet 115, in which the play-wright's tone of immediate engagement clashes with the more detached tone of the reflecting poet—a "story" of personal involve-ment suddenly giving way to impersonal meditation and finally returning to the original vein. The problem of this sonnet, in my view, is the second quatrain, which appears to abandon the collo-quial origin and particular dramatic situation of the first (the situ-ation of the poet's feeling the tension of the fertile moment) for a compressed, if somewhat unimpassioned, meditation on Time. This might strike one as a poet's purple passage detachedly summariz-ing the content of more passionately engaged Time sonnets, if it were not for the impact of the preponderantly monosyllabic words suggesting the presence of a horde of monsters ("accidents") let loose by Time which creep, change, tan, blunt, and divert. More-over, seen in retrospect from the first line of quatrain 3, it would seem that "But reckening time" embodies a catch in the voice as if the poet had been unable to "grammarize" his fears properly, thereby involving him in a syntactic anacoluthon. Although the anacoluthon is made good by rephrasing the participial construc-tion (in "Alas why fearing of times tiranie"), the impression remains that the dramatist was not after all completely over-whelmed by the meditative poet. If the purple patch (lines 5-8) was inserted in cold blood, the "sutures" were skillfully glossed over by the dramatist in suggesting his own involvement by a syntactic slip and in concealing the workings of the poet's generalizing impulse behind the pangs of a mind struck with sorrow. Syntax that seems to have been thrown out of gear momentarily under the pressure of emotion—what a clever way on the part of the dramatist of reas-serting supremacy!

The hybrid character of a sonnet which demonstrates the tug-of-war between the poet and dramatist (and their final pacification or no) may be due to yet other causes than the particularizing-versus-generalizing pull as is the case in Sonnet 115. There is, for instance, in 36 no generalizing, purple-patch strain, but the sonnet appears to be firmly grounded in the interplay of volitional acts underlying human relations. Here the volitional impulse takes the shape of the "Let me confesse that . . ." opening where the "Let me" formula, frequent as it is in the Sonnets, gives the impression that the poet is assuming the stance of the playwright while indulging in an essentially private communication of the epistolary type of sonnet, inasmuch as the poet informs the friend of a decision as he would in a letter ("we two must be twaine"). The result is that, through the unconscious audience-orientation of the poet-dramatist, his voice is lent a heightened resonance as if the sonnet were a speech recited on the stage—more exactly, a "duologue" (or soliloquy delivered before a silent partner)—which constantly changes its direction like a meandering river that now pushes forward (in ascertaining the poet's will), now back on itself (in at once qualifying that will). Apart from this surging forward and backward of the volitional impulses which is of the very nature of dramatic speech, there is the interesting fact that the argument is not set forth in a purely ratiocinative way. Rather, the truth of the situation is given away underhand (as is often the case in stage speeches) and not without a certain air of contradiction, as if the poet were holding something back or making his revelation about his own "blots" which turn into "guilt." This leads to a tightening of the knot in the third quatrain, in so far as the confrontation of two persons which is already inherent in the first quatrain ("with me . . . Without thy helpe . . ."), but is there still overshadowed by the linguistic expression of a joint will ("we two," "our undevided loues"), is here outlined more sharply ("I may not . . . Nor thou . . .") at the same time as suggesting a scene (the behavior of two friends at an imagined meeting: "I may not . . . acknowledge thee . . . Nor thou with publike kindnesse honour me"). The couplet clinches the confrontation not only between the "I" and the "Thou" but between the poet and the dramatist; for the "But doe not so" in conjunction with "Unlesse thou take that honour from thy name" (line 12) and "Without thy helpe" (line 13) sets us wondering whether there is not perhaps here a subconscious appeal for both help and recognition that runs counter to the overt argument of the sonnet. The tension is solved, however, by means of a pun, in that the first "mine" in the couplet denotes possession whereas the second is the result of an illusion by which the poet feigns that the friend's "good report" is already his own so that there is no need for the friend to let him partake of, and thereby damage, his honor. Such sham solutions sometimes occur in hybrids where a real existential quandary is suddenly made light of by being dissolved in a pun (cf. the couplet of 43). This kind of poet-magician's trick may well be attributed to the beauty-adept who improvises nonchalantly to the detriment of the truth-seeking dramatist—even at the risk of engendering an air of disingenuousness in the artifact by preferring a sham-dramatic surprise turn to a more honest artistic solution in which the seriousness of the poet matches the genuineness of the man's experience.

IN DEFENSE OF SHAKESPEARE'S SONNETS

BY

HILTON LANDRY

WE call, for we see and feel, the swan and the dove both transcendentally beautiful. As absurd as it would be to institute a comparison between their separate claims to beauty from any abstract rule common to both, without reference to the life and being of the animals themselves,—or as if, having first seen the dove, we abstracted its outlines, gave them a false generalization, called them the principles or ideal of bird-beauty, and then proceeded to criticize the swan or the eagle;—not less absurd is it to pass judgment on the works of a poet on the mere ground that they have been called by the same class-name with the works of other poets in other times and circumstances, or on any ground, indeed, save that of their inappropriateness to their own end and being, their want of significance, as symbols or physiognomy.

Coleridge

The poetry of the feelings is not the one that the critic is compelled to prefer, especially if he can say that it taints us with subjectivism, sentimentality, and self-indulgence. This is the poetry . . . which we sometimes dispose of a little distastefully as "romantic."

John Crowe Ransom

In Shakespeare's sonnets we find both plain and ornate styles, sometimes in the same poem, but both, more often than not, in a state of decay; and we find also the only decay of rational structure which I can recollect among the major poets of the time.

Yvor Winters

Each of Shakespeare's works has long been public property, none more so than his Sonnets, the most admired and familiar collection of lyric poetry in English. Yet if everyone may, in some sense, read the Sonnets, few read them well; and fewer still, of the thousands who have published books and essays on these poems, have anything of critical intelligence to offer us concerning them. We may safely include among those who would accept this last assertion John Crowe Ransom and Yvor Winters, for they are concerned to lay particular stress on the uncritical and popular nature of the favorable reception generally accorded the Sonnets. Ransom and Winters are, in fact, the most articulate representatives of a small minority whose attitude toward the Sonnets is militantly unfavorable, although they are willing to concede that a few poems have a certain degree of merit. Their formidable criticism derives much of its strength from the firm but narrow base on which it is erected—a severely limited view of what poetry is and should be. For each of them, one kind of poetry is best and that kind is best exemplified by the work of a single poet. For Winters this supreme poet is Ben Jonson, for Ransom he is John Donne. No one would wish to deny these critics their assumptions and preferences, but we may legitimately inquire into the effect of their theory upon their practice and consider whether preference in some instances may not turn out to be a form of prejudice.

I

Ransom's "Shakespeare at Sonnets," the chief modern attack on these poems, was first published thirty years ago.[1] An apparently comprehensive treatment of the subject, it is divided into seven sections. The first presents useful preliminary distinctions and observations; the second deals with structural defects of the Sonnets; the third, with the deficiences of romantic poetry, the poetry of the feelings of which Shakespeare is the "most illustrious ancestor." A masterpiece of condescension, the fourth section takes up the presence of the metaphysical mode in the Sonnets, thus providing an opportunity for unfavorable comparison with Donne. It also considers the nature and function of feelings in metaphysical poetry in contrast to romantic associationist poetry. The fifth section moralizes on the Protestant distrust of the imagination and of that metaphysical particularity to which the Anglo- and Roman Catholic tradition always has been so hospitable. The sixth cites a dozen sonnets for their realization of the metaphysical image; and the last dismisses the opinion that Shakespeare was a "bold and successful contriver of metaphysical effects in his later plays." In my discussion of Ransom's "heresy and sins" I propose to follow the order suggested by my phrase and proceed from the general to the particular, beginning with his "moralization" on the imagination.

Problems raised by the fifth section of Ransom's essay are complex matters of intellectual history which cannot be adequately defined or, of course, resolved in a few sentences. Nevertheless, one may question certain statements of fact, especially in regard to the selection of facts and the distribution of emphasis. Despite Ransom's assertions to the contrary, the distrust of the imagination is neither a modern nor a Protestant phenomenon. If it is prevalent in the Renaissance, one must not ignore the fact that it is at least as old as Ransom's spiritual father, Aristotle, the philosopher whose conception of the mind dominated the West for more than two thousand years.[2] According to Aristotle's view, the imagination differs from both perception and thought, yet it always implies perception and is itself implied by judgment (*De Anima,* 427b); for reason depends on it to relay fresh sense impressions and to provide the images or schemata which must always accompany thinking (431a-b, 432a). Since imagination stands between the senses and reason, one might expect it to be either sensational or rational in character, and Aristotle does claim that all imagination is either sensitive or deliberative (433b).[3] Because no living creature is capable of appetite without imagination, it is also essential for the operation of both "will" and desire, or rational and irrational appetite, as the Renaissance would say.

Now even though Aristotle distinguishes between higher and lower functions of imagination (deliberative and sensitive) and thereby establishes an important precedent, he is also inclined to assimilate imagination to common sense (the root from which the five senses branch) and to regard it as decaying sensation (*Rhetoric,* 1370a) in the manner of Hobbes. It is just the natural relationship and sympathy between the senses and imagination which causes perennial alarm in both Catholics and Protestants, whether philosophers or theologians:

> there is such commerce between the fancy and the outward senses that they are never exercised in the reception of their objects but the imagination is drawn that way, and cannot present to the mind distinctly and with the calmness that is requisite those things on which our thoughts should be fixt.[4]

Another way of differentiating between lower and higher activities of the imagination finds the humble reproductive power associated with sense perception to be fairly reliable and the higher creative or productive power to be irresponsible. Medieval and Renaissance writers making this distinction (Albert and Vives, e.g.) use "imagination" to refer to the perceptual power which reproduces the reality known through sense perception, and "phantasy" to refer to the combinatory productive power whose activity is not limited to sensible reality.[5] The irresponsible activity of the highly subjective and creative phantasy, which operates freely in dreams, is exemplified by its combination of things never joined in nature to produce such mythical creatures as the centaur, mermaid, and griffin. Perhaps this is an extreme case of the notorious fallibility of the imagination (*De Anima,* 428a), a fallibility resulting from such factors as its ceaseless activity, combination of images, and dependence on the senses.

From my condensed account of what an educated man of the Renaissance might be expected to know of the imagination, the conclusion to be drawn is not simply that it was regarded as dangerous and fallible; it was also considered to be versatile and indispensable.[6] Both Protestants and Catholics are agreed on this point, so that there is far less difference between them than Ransom would lead us to believe. There are, in fact, some indications that, contrary to what he asserts, Protestants allowed the imagination a far more important role in religion than did the Catholics. If, for example, one compares the Puritan, Richard Sibbes, with the Anglo-Catholic, Jeremy Taylor, the prose counterpart of the metaphysical poets, there is no doubt about who takes the imagination more seriously. In *The Soul's Conflict with Itself* (1635), Sibbes claims "a sanctified fancy will make every creature a ladder to heaven," so that

> whilst the soul is joined with the body, it hath not only a necessary but a holy use of the imagination and of sensible things whereupon our imagination worketh. What is the use of the Sacraments but to help our souls by our senses and our faith by imagination?[7]

Taylor's very typical comments under "Helps to increase our Love to God" in *The Rule and Exercise of Holy Living* (1650) present us with a striking contrast:

> Lay fetters and restraints upon the imagination and fantastic part; because our fancy, being an imperfect and higher faculty, is usually pleased with the entertainment of shadows and gauds: and, because the things of the world fill it with such beauties and fantastic imagery, the fancy presents such objects, as are amiable to the affections and elective powers. Persons of fancy, such as are women and children, have always the most violent loves: but, therefore, if we be careful, with what representments we fill our fancy, we may the sooner rectify our love. To this purpose it is good, that we transplant the instruments of fancy into religion: and for this reason music was brought into churches, and ornaments, and perfumes, and comely garments, and solemnities, and decent ceremonies, that the busy and less discerning fancy, being bribed with its proper objects, may be instrumental to a more celestial and spiritual love.[8]

The historical perspective which I am recommending is completely ignored by Ransom. He sees the problem of the acceptance of the imagination and what it creates from the standpoint of a modern defender of the faith surrounded by the pagan forces of positivism:

> The deterrent to our reception of metaphysical effects is distrust; we do not believe in the validity of the imaginative organ. It is . . . a powerfully inherited distrust, going back to the tyranny of that modernism, . . . defined as scientific positivism, which killed the religious credulity of Europe, beginning in the Renaissance; it was going strongly by Shakespeare's time. . . . We cannot escape it. A nice exhibit of our scruples is to be found later in Coleridge's rejection of fancy as the irresponsible bastard variety of the image-forming faculty, though necessarily he discovered insuperable difficulties in drawing the exact line round it. And altogether proper must we think anybody's insistence that imagination must be representative, or realistic, in order that poetry may speak the truth.[9]

A discussion of the warfare between science and poetry underlying this passage is not relevant to my purpose, but I would like to question the accuracy and implications of a number of Ransom's statements. In the first place, the opening sentence embodies the enormous unwarranted assumption that "imagination" must be equated with, and reduced to, "metaphysical." Presumably, it is only the "metaphysical" (in religion and literature) which suffers from the alleged universal distrust of the imagination: the "romantic"—Shakespeare's sonnets—must thrive on it. Next, one must ask, to what group of modern men does "we" refer? Who are "we" who cannot escape from distrust of the imagination? I suggest that its false humility and democracy conceals a radical separation of John Crowe Ransom from the rest of the benighted contemporary world. This small "we" includes all Americans, the "general reader" of poetry, and the critic or special reader who disagrees with the writer; it excludes only Ransom and his coterie.

We who disagree with Ransom may be surprised to learn how early the modern scientific movement, of which we are the victims, got under way in England, especially since its father is Bacon, whose *Advancement of Learning* (1605) provoked nothing but indifference, and its first thorough exponent is Hobbes.[10] We are even more surprised to discover that Coleridge, the greatest English advocate and theorist of the imagination, shares our scruple about its validity and rejects fancy as a bastard variety. Coleridge's distinction between higher and lower functions of the imagination is not only traditional, it assumes that they are harmonious and complementary. In a very characteristic observation he says, "genius must have talent as its complement and implement, just as, in like manner, imagination must have fancy. In short, the higher intellectual powers can only act through a corresponding energy of the lower" (*Table Talk*, August 20, 1833). There is nothing here to which Ransom could take exception, even though his comment on Coleridge displays an unfortunate readiness to bite the hand that has fed him. If he can say that Johnson's poetry is a dependent of the metaphysical poetry he deprecated and repudiated, one may say much the same of Ransom's relation to Coleridge. Ransom's whole discussion of imagination reaps the benefit of Coleridge's exalted estimate of that power.

II

The second part of Ransom's essay, where he maintains the Sonnets "generally . . . are ill constructed," is a classic example of genre purism, of the kind of sonnet criticism that prevailed in the nineteenth century from the time of Capell Lofft (the elder) and Leigh Hunt to Robert Bridges and Theodore Watts-Dunton. (Genre criticism clearly has survived Croce's devastating attack on it, but it still remains more useful when addressed to genres of content rather than to those of form.) The trouble with this formal approach to the sonnet, especially as practiced in the nineteenth century, is that it tends to separate form and content. It also puts the critic in the awkward position of claiming that sonnets are to be judged by criteria which differ from those applied to other poems. In other words, one may find him claiming that X is a good sonnet while he resolutely ignores the fact that it is a bad poem. (The opposite case, conceding that a bad sonnet is a good poem, almost never occurs.) Now this is the anomalous position in which Ransom finds himself.

After asserting that the English sonnet requires the poet to write "three co-ordinate quatrains and then a couplet which will relate to the series collectively," he offers *Amoretti* LVI as an example of "what sort of thing could be done successfully in this logical pattern":

> Fayre ye be sure, but cruell and unkind,
> As is a Tygre that with greedinesse
> hunts after bloud, when he by chance doth find
> a feeble beast, doth felly him oppresse.
> Fayre be ye sure, but proud and pittilesse,
> as is a storme, that all things doth prostrate:
> finding a tree alone all comfortlesse,
> beats on it strongly it to ruinate.
> Fayre be ye sure, but hard and obstinate,
> as is a rocke midst the raging floods:
> gaynst which a ship, of succour desolate,
> doth suffer wreck both of her selfe and goods.
> That ship, that tree, and that same beast am I,
> whom ye doe wreck, doe ruin, and destroy.[11]

I have no wish to join the detractors of Spenser—his *Amoretti* is as much underrated as Sidney's *Astrophel and Stella* is overrated — but I suggest that this poem, if not one of his worst essays in the sonnet, is very far from his best. *Amoretti* LVI is a mere rhetorical exercise, superficial, frigid, and artificial, securing its logical pattern by sacrificing nearly everything else.[12] In short, I would say it is a poor or mediocre sonnet because it is a poor poem. But all this is of no consequence to Ransom, who is perfectly willing to separate "architectural design" from other considerations and to damn good poems for not having the proper structure. Two of Shakespeare's best sonnets, "Tyr'd with all these for restfull death I cry" (66) and "Th'expense of Spirit in a waste of shame" (129), are dismissed out of hand with the remark that they have "no logical organization at all except that they have little couplet conclusions." Although it differs from the neat pattern of distribution demanded by Ransom, Sonnets 66 and 129 do have a logic or structure of their own, and 66 also has the essential features of a traditional Provençal poem, the *eneug*.[13]

Ransom's discussion of *Amoretti* LVI and of Shakespeare's Sonnet 87 confirms my opinion that he is willing to stress the architectural design of a sonnet at the expense of other features of equal or greater importance. What recommends the Spenser sonnet to his approval is not only the three-and-one division of the "logical object," but also the simple substance, the "severely restricted" burden of the quatrains which permits the "summary comment" of the couplet to be adequate in its brevity. All this is to praise the sonnet for subordinating "content" to form. It leads, of course, to the obvious conclusion that "if the poet is too full of urgent thoughts, he had better use the two-part Italian form" of the sonnet, "which is very much more flexible" (p. 201). (This recommendation overlooks the practical obstacle of the greater difficulty of rhyming four words instead of two, especially in English, which has fewer rhymes than Italian.) He praises the "daring and clever" Sonnet 87 ("Farewell thou art too deare for my possessing") in similar terms when he says,

> It is legalistic, therefore closely limited in its range, yet the three quatrains all manage to say the same thing differently, and the couplet translates the legal figure back into the terms of a lover's passion (p. 202).

In this case Ransom has chosen a fairly good poem to illustrate the "perfect adaptation of the logic to the metre" which he finds in "only a large majority of the Sonnets." But even when he expands his brief description of 87, as he does in a later section of the essay, his rather conventional account of the poem remains unsatisfactory:

> . . . its substance is furnished by developing the human relation (that of the renouncing lover) through a figure . . ., a legal one, in which an unequal bond is cancelled for cause. Three times . . . the lover makes an exploration within the field of the figure. The occasions are fairly distinct . . . (pp. 207-208).

We do not need to be experts in the Elizabethan law of contracts to perceive the inadequacy of this view. We need only to read Sonnet 87 with care:

> Farewell thou art too deare for my possessing,
> And like enough thou knowest thy estimate,
> The Charter of thy worth gives thee releasing:

> 4 My bonds in thee are all determinate.
>   For how do I hold thee but by thy granting,
>   And for that ritches where is my deserving?
>   The cause of this faire guift in me is wanting,
> 8 And so my pattent back againe is swerving.
>   Thy self thou gav'st, thy owne worth then not knowing,
>   Or mee to whom thou gav'st it, else mistaking,
>   So thy great guift upon misprison growing,
> 12 Comes home againe, on better judgement making.
>   Thus have I had thee as a dreame doth flatter,
>   In sleepe a King, but waking no such matter.

The quatrains do not "all say the same thing differently" if only because to say something differently is to say a different thing. As a brief commentary will make clear, at least two different things are being said in the first twelve lines, yet one cannot intelligently assert that the "occasions" of the quatrains are "fairly distinct." The first quatrain, marked by the speaker's ironic resignation, concedes the friend's superiority and thus his right to release himself from any obligation incurred. In other words, the speaker's claims are no longer valid although that cannot be said of his emotional ties. Then the second quatrain, which appears to uphold and continue the legal and prudential view of the first by stressing the unworthiness of the speaker, quietly undercuts it by introducing the new idea of friendship as a free gift. Further development of the prudential view occurs in the third quatrain with its focus on the friend's initial error of judgment, but we are again reminded that friendship consists in giving one's self. For as George Santayana, among others, has pointed out, friendship should be a gift with no strings attached:

> A friend's only gift is himself, and friendship is not friendship, is not a form of free or liberal society, if it does not terminate in an ideal possession, in an object loved for its own sake. . . . To praise the utility of friendship . . . is to lose one's moral bearings.[14]

What Shakespeare gives us in Sonnet 87 is a simultaneous presentation of opposed views of friendship, one Aristotelian or utilitarian, the other Shakespearean or Christian.[15] Although it seems to be written entirely from the standpoint of the friend's selfish and practical conception, rendered in highly appropriate legal figures, the speaker's generous social and moral ideal of friendship is subtly conveyed by feeling, tone, and diction. (This strategy, incidentally, is typical of Shakespeare's procedure in a number of sonnets and represents a technique of which he is an unequaled master.) Then the speaker's unselfish ideal, more or less submerged in Sonnet 87, is embodied with purity and clarity in 88:

> When thou shalt be disposde to set me light,
> And place my merrit in the eie of skorne,
> Upon thy side, against my selfe ile fight,
> And prove thee virtuous, tho thou art forsworne.

It is evident that Ransom selected Sonnet 87 to illustrate his point for much the same reason that dismal texts on how to read poetry choose to analyze Sonnet 73 ("That time of yeare thou maist in me behold")—it seems to be normative, simple, and neat. But Shakespeare is never more deceptive than when he appears to be simple. However neat and simple 87 may appear in respect to its "architecture," in respect to a more fundamental kind of structure —that of feeling and argument—it is neither. And if it is architecturally normative in relation to a restricted number of the Sonnets, it is structurally normative for another but more important group. I do not propose, then, that one should abandon all discussions of form or structure. On the contrary, any adequate analysis of poetry cannot avoid considering form, even when it is not given specific attention. But I am suggesting that it is utterly unprofitable to be occupied with structure as architecture, with form in such an obvious, superficial, and generally insignificant sense.[16]

III

The middle portion of Ransom's essay—the third, fourth, and sixth sections—supports my contention that any serious discussion of poetry cannot avoid dealing with structure, for his principal concern here is with how poetry does and should provide a structure for feelings by the use of figurative language. This concern manifests itself in a whole series of opposed categories which gives us the coordinates or poles of analysis and defines the critic's predilection. Among the categories presented are subject and object, feeling and knowledge, association and system, romantic and metaphysical. Shakespeare's sonnets are mainly subjective, emotive, associative, and romantic, while the lyrics of Donne are objective, intellectual, systematic, and metaphysical. By definition, the romantic poetry of the feelings is self-indulgent: it seeks the "subjective satisfactions of the poet" and his many readers rather than the knowledge and expression of its "object." Nevertheless, it does have an object—one that is "rich and suggestive even while it is vague and cloudy" and which is suited to the "cognitive impulse . . . of low grade" found among the masses. Such poetry is based on the principle of association; the "pleasing if indefinite associations" of the "pretty words" loosely cohere, but they do not form a "logical or definitive object." Since "breadth of associations" is the breath of life to romantic poetry, it multiplies or compounds metaphors, presenting a "procession or flight of figures" instead of a single or systematic figure. Its saving grace is a meter whose function is to deceive us by lending its precision (and objectivity) to the poem as a whole. Shakespeare, alas, is a great natural master, and the "most illustrious ancestor," of this inferior kind of poetry (pp. 204-205).

To demonstrate the truth of these assertions, Ransom quite predictably elects for analysis the opening quatrain of Sonnet 33. But before I consider his comments on the poem, I must do what he refuses to do—place Sonnet 33 in its context, for if it leads a life of its own it also participates in the life of a group. Since the sonnets of this group (33-35) provide contexts of interpretation for each other, the group cannot be completely ignored if we are to understand any member. The speaker in Sonnets 33-35 has been offended by the masculine friend he addresses yet is willing to forgive him, and between the poles of a sense of injury and a disposition to forgive, the speaker's feelings move. Some assurance of forgiveness ends each poem, but the speaker finds it harder to give as he proceeds. In Sonnet 33 he forgives his friend freely and easily, in 34 with some difficulty, and in 35 with great reluctance. This progression indicates an increase in the intensity and complexity of the speaker's feelings as we pass from poem to poem. Sonnet 33, simplest in tone and feeling, minimizes the poet's distress, but Sonnet 35, "No more be greev'd at that which thou hast done," reveals the strength of the conflicting impulses within him.

To use the language of 35 (line 6), in Sonnet 33 the poet is simply authorizing his friend's trespass by comparisons:

> Full many a glorious morning have I seene,
> Flatter the mountaine tops with soveraine eie,
> Kissing with golden face the meddowes greene;
> 4 Guilding pale streames with heavenly alcumy:
> Anon permit the basest cloudes to ride,
> With ougly rack on his celestiall face,
> And from the for-lorne world his visage hide
> 8 Stealing unseene to west with this disgrace:
> Even so my Sunne one early morne did shine,
> With all triumphant splendor on my brow,
> But out alack, he was but one houre mine,
> 12 The region cloude hath mask'd him from me now.
>   Yet him for this, my love no whit disdaineth,
>   Suns of the world may staine, when heavens sun staineth.[17]

The quatrains of this sonnet constitute an extended simile containing metaphors within each of its members (lines 1-8 and 9-12), and the first sentence consists of the first and second quatrains. To quote only the opening quatrain as Ransom does is to split the first member of the simile in half and to isolate part of a complex sentence from the whole. One may allow lines 1-4 *some* degree of stylistic and syntactic independence, but that cannot justify doing violence to the sentence, the basic unit of meaning.

Ransom claims there is a failure of objectivity or realism in this first "fine-morning quatrain, with an all-ruling fair-weather sun . . . [as] the symbol of his false friend." The sun is "weakly imagined; rather, it may be said to be only felt, a loose cluster of images as obscure as they are pleasant." After briefly examining "in strict logic" the activities described in lines 2-4, he concludes that it is a "mixed and self-defeating figure." His remarks, in my opinion, are more or less beside the point and perhaps willfully obtuse. Here and elsewhere Ransom makes far too much of the objectivity or realism of figurative language, of the shaping of an image by "genuine observation." What is more important, as Coleridge pointed out long ago, is the extent to which the figures are modified by the main current of feeling:

images, however beautiful, though faithfully copied
from nature, and as accurately represented in words, do
not of themselves characterize the poet. They become
proofs of original genius only so far as they are modified
by a predominant passion; or by associated thoughts or
images awakened by that passion; or when they have
the effect of reducing multitude to unity, or succession
to an instant; or lastly, when a human and intellectual
life is transferred to them from the poet's own spirit . . .
(*Biographia Literaria,* Ch. 15).

In the speaker's effort to authorize the friend's trespass by comparisons, the role of the first quatrain, indeed of the whole sun figure (with its pun on "son"), is far from obscure or vague. The sun
in the first eight lines of Sonnet 33 is anthropomorphic, as it often
is in Shakespeare, and it is designed to present a contrast between
the full and free manifestation of powerful beauty and the obscur-
ing of that beauty by something which pollutes it. The metaphorical description of the opening quatrain may exceed the demands
of strict logic, yet it serves admirably the purposes of *realization* —
the vivid and "concrete" presentation of the sun's sovereign
power.[18] It is a *sovereign* eye not merely because it is regal (and
hence flatters what it looks on, responds to) but also because it is
noble or excellent and powerful, and that radiant power is conveyed by the third and fourth lines. If one wished to go behind this
sun to the son it symbolizes, one might say that it suggests that the
friend is a "man of sovereign parts" like Longaville in *Love's
Labour's Lost,* a person of radiant beauty whose presence flatters
and delights, a king to whom the speaker is subject, and so on.

The next quatrain of Sonnet 33 seems to encourage such a double reading of details, for "permit," "basest," "ougly," and "disgrace" may be taken as signs of disapproval, as strong pejoratives
which are elicited by the friend's fault. This is also the case with
"staine" in the couplet; when applied to "Suns of the world" it signifies "become soiled or blemished" as well as "grow pale,"
"become obscured." Yet the speaker's regret for the friend's loss
and his own is clearly subordinated to his desire to forgive, and the
simile of the quatrains forms the basis for the duplex excuse of the
couplet. His friend's behavior is as "natural" as the dimming of the

sun; when even the sun has imperfections, we must expect them in sons of this world.

A more spectacular example of misunderstanding a poem because of failure to consider either the immediate or wider context occurs when Ransom deals with one quatrain of Sonnet 53, "What is your substance, whereof are you made." He quotes lines 5-8 of 53 as an example of the literary or conventional image "not really shaped by a genuine observation"; states that such "asseverations . . . are the right of a literary lover, but . . . do more credit to his poetry than . . . wit"; and deplores the delusive phrasing, subjectivity, and lack of particularity in these lines (p. 205). A careful reading of Sonnet 53, especially in conjunction with the closely related 54 ("Oh how much more doth beauty beautious seeme"), reveals that he has missed the main point of the poem, and hence his acid generalizations are utterly worthless:[19]

> What is your substance, whereof are you made,
> That millions of strange shaddowes on you tend?
> Since every one, hath every one, one shade,
> 4 And you but one, can every shaddow lend:
> Describe *Adonis* and the counterfet,
> Is poorely immitated after you,
> On *Hellens* cheeke all art of beautie set,
> 8 And you in *Grecian* tires are painted new:
> Speake of the spring, and foyzon of the yeare,
> The one doth shaddow of your beautie show,
> The other as your bountie doth appeare,
> 12 And you in every blessed shape we know.
>   In all externall grace you have some part,
>   But you like none, none you for constant heart.

This sonnet is not the poem of unqualified praise that Ransom, Krieger, and Dover Wilson take it to be. Like the sonnets which precede it (43-52), Sonnet 53 is written in absence, the fact which governs its thought and feeling. Separation from the friend leads the poet here and in other sonnets to find images of his beauty everywhere, and in this case it also leads to grave doubts about the friend's fidelity.[20] After the serious opening question (lines 1-2), most of the sonnet dwells on images of the friend's beauty, as the summary twelfth line suggests. But the closing lines ironically question his internal or moral beauty (as constancy) after stressing his participation in external beauty: "In all externall grace you have some part, / But you like none, none you for constant heart." Instead of the conventional pious praise which most readers find in the last line, there is a genuine fear that the friend may be all shadow or physical beauty without any moral substance or fidelity. It is precisely for this reason that the next sonnet, 54, is a short sermon on the superiority of beauty which has *truth* (fidelity or constancy) as its center.[21]

IV

I have been indirectly propounding the view that Shakespeare's sonnets are not romantic in Ransom's derogatory sense; now I wish to dispute his claim that some are metaphysical as he understands this loose term. Of course, his basic strategy in the essay is readily recognized: the label "romantic" is reserved for sonnets which he dislikes, while those which he admires are called "metaphysical." In short, "metaphysical" stands for whatever is good or superior in poetry, "romantic" for everything bad or inferior. But if Shakespeare "honestly realizes the metaphysical image," his metaphysical poems still have the same qualities as his romantic ones, as one can perceive if he makes allowance for the variety of the Sonnets. Even Ransom concedes the indistinguishability of these styles in some poems, although he would prefer to say they are "mixed in effect" or "uneven in execution" (p. 207).

Metaphysical poetry "commits the feelings in the case . . . to their determination within the elected figure," the figure being presented systematically. It "elects its line of action and goes straight through to the completion of the cycle and extinction of the feelings." As these assertions clearly imply, Ransom assumes that "metaphysical poets are self-conscious and deliberate, . . . very like technical psychologists." Since these statements suffice to establish his essential position, a few observations on the limits and weaknesses of that position are now in order. First, it is certainly the case that this simple general account of the basic character of metaphysical poetry fits neither all of the poets traditionally grouped with Donne nor all of the poems written by him. "A Valediction Forbidding Mourning," for example, presents different, not obviously related figures rather than a single figure, and only the compass image is developed systematically.[22] Further, at least one segment of the poem is joined to another by a kind of association, for "move" of the second stanza probably suggested "moving" and "trepidation" in the third. Of course I am not implying that "A Valediction Forbidding Mourning" or any other poem is a paradigm of Donne's work; on the contrary, I would insist that his lyrics, like Shakespeare's sonnets, exhibit considerable variety within limits. I must also insist that relatively few poems handle figures, especially single figures, "systematically." Sonnet 54 is a poem that does so and meets Ransom's other requirements as well, but it is so obviously homiletic and undramatic that he would never dream of calling it metaphysical.

Now if Ransom's first statement about committing the feelings to the elected figure is so broad as to include both more and less than he intends, the second, with such phrases as "line of action," "completion of the cycle," and "extinction of the feelings," is vague enough to virtually defy sensible interpretation. Behind the sentence lies his definition of the feelings or passions as "calls to action" which want to "turn into actions and vanish." This definition must be what the mysterious cycle refers to, but in what respect can any poem result in the "extinction of the feelings"? A poem can channel, order, discipline, discover, present, or transmute feelings through its "line of action,"[23] yet it can never lay them to rest or extinguish them. The extinction notion seems to be put forward in opposition to what Ransom takes to be the case in romantic or associationist poetry, where one is offered an unhealthy "half-way action providing many charming resting-places for the feelings to agitate themselves" (p. 211). I suggest that this half-way action, in which feelings are partly relieved and partly exploited, is what in fact we find in all good poetry, however it may handle figures and whatever one may choose to call it.[24] As for "action" as he uses it, one must have some doubts about its meaning, for his thinking is militantly Aristotelian and his vocabulary may be also. At any rate, we are supposed to distinguish between action in ordinary life and its presence in poetry: metaphysical poets "start with feelings" and "objectify these imaginatively into external action."[25]

In this and other essays Ransom appears to assume that poets, especially metaphysical ones, construct poems in the manner of

Ben Jonson or Beaumont and Fletcher, writers who have the sense and perhaps the strategy worked out in advance of composition. Such an assumption attributes more self-consciousness, deliberation, and foresight to poets than the poetic facts seem to warrant, and it leads to excessive emphasis on the cognitive and objective— even to the point where one refers to the subject of the poem as "the object." It leaves little or no room for discovery during composition, for significant imaginative activities lying beyond the focus of attention. In short, it suggests that distrust of the imagination which Ransom laments in the fifth section of his essay. Above all, it does not do justice to a poet like Shakespeare who works with the utmost freedom or *sprezzatura,* discovering exactly what he wishes to say in the process of saying it. There is, therefore, a salutary warning as well as a relevant truth in Coleridge's acute comments on Shakespeare's action:

> In Shakespeare one sentence begets the next naturally;
> the meaning is all inwoven. He goes on kindling like a
> meteor through the dark atmosphere. . . . Shakespeare's
> intellectual action is wholly unlike that of Ben Jonson or
> Beaumont and Fletcher. The latter see the totality of a
> sentence or passage, and then project it entire. Shake
> speare goes on creating and evolving B. out of A., and
> C. out of B., and so on, just as a serpent moves, which
> makes a fulcrum of its own body, and seems forever
> twisting and untwisting its own strength (*Table Talk,*
> March 5, 1834).

For a good example of what Coleridge is talking about, consider Sonnet 125, a superlative poem woven out of a variety of related figures:

> Wer't aught to me I bore the canopy,
> With my extern the outward honoring,
> Or layd great bases for eternity,
> 4   Which proves more short then wast or ruining?
> Have I not seene dwellers on forme and favor
> Lose all, and more by paying too much rent
> For compound sweet; Forgoing simple savor,

8   Pittifull thrivors in their gazing spent.
     Noe, let me be obsequious in thy heart,
     And take thou my oblacion, poore but free,
     Which is not mixt with seconds, knows no art,
12   But mutuall render onely me for thee.
     Hence, thou subbornd *Informer,* a trew soule
     When most impeacht, stands least in thy controule.

Ransom cites this poem in his rapid survey of sonnets in which Shakespeare has the most conspicuous success in realizing the metaphysical image, remarking that it is "admirable though not unitary enough to be metaphysical" (p. 216). Once again he is making the mistake of equating variety in imagery with a lack of coherent structure. There are perhaps ten different figures in the poem, but it is closely argued and has a manifest integrity. Sonnet 125 continues 124 in the sense that once more the speaker's true love is contrasted with that affection which depends on "state"—here, all outward displays of loyalty and devotion. In the rhetorical questions of the first two quatrains he rejects the devotion that displays itself in forms and ceremonies, mere shows of service; in the last, he offers the alternative of his simple, wholehearted love. And the suborned informer of the couplet is the ineffectual jealousy against which he is protesting.[26]

The case of Sonnet 125, one of Shakespeare's finest sonnets, is a forceful reminder of Ransom's inveterate prejudice. Even when he cites the dozen poems in the "most conspicuous success" category, he is still Dr. Ransom examining a collection of sick patients and finding a few surprisingly healthy. Of the dozen sonnets he approves, only two excellent ones (57 and 94) escape censure; the remainder, he finds, betray such obvious weaknesses as multiple or confused figures, triteness, amateurish ignorance, obscure arguments, and so on. But in Ransom's strictures on some of these poems Shakespeare has been misrepresented, and as usual it is because he has been misunderstood. One instance of this is the comment on Sonnet 121, "'Tis better to be vile than vile esteemed"; another, surprisingly enough, is his statement concerning Sonnet 94, "They that have powre to hurt, but will do none."[27] Once more, then, we return to the fundamental question we must ask about the critic—how carefully and accurately does he read the particular work? For it is on the strength of his specific interpretations, not his flights of speculation, that a critic must stand or fall.

V

Yvor Winters' last extended discussion of the Sonnets appears in a published lecture delivered some years ago, "Poetic Styles, Old and New."[28] It is a very typical performance, beginning with Winters' peculiar, not to say idiosyncratic, version of the history of the lyric in the Renaissance and his taking the occasion to disparage Donne—"Jonson could have said more in two lines than Donne says in twelve"—and to assert the decadence of Shakespeare in the sentence I quoted as an epigraph. He claims that the short poem from the late middle ages through the early seventeenth century "was usually rational in structure, and in fact was very often logical"; within this "rational frame" were two main schools, "poets of the plain style" and poets of the "courtly, ornate, sugared, or Petrarchan" style (p. 44).[29] Donne's style is ornate, Jonson's is plain, and Shakespeare's mixed. Donne is dismissed in the short introduction; Shakespeare attacked at length in the second part; and Jonson is extolled in the third.

Winters' increasing dissatisfaction with the Sonnets, despite their traces of "unusually beguiling" genius, stems from three basic weaknesses in the poems: (1) the poet's attitude of "servile weakness" to the person addressed, (2) Shakespeare's failure to take the sonnet form "with any real seriousness," and (3) Shakespeare's subordination of the "necessity for sharp denotation" to his "sensitivity to the connotative power of language" (pp. 47-48). Concerning the first point, he alleges that a "large number" of the sonnets betray servile weakness in the face of the addressee, an attitude "so marked as to render a sympathetic approach to the subject all but impossible, in spite of any fragmentary brilliance." The obvious objections to these assertions are forestalled by his next remarks: we cannot say this is merely a courtly convention, for if it is, it is still a weakness in the courtly style. Furthermore, it is "not an invariable quality" of courtly poets, for it is rarely found in poets of the plain style. But Shakespeare not only exhibits this attitude, he "seems to mean it seriously." Since Winters does not list or give specific examples of the sonnets pervaded by servility—he deals only with a handful of favorites—one cannot tell what he means by this quality or by a "large" number. J. B. Leishman, in the third part of *Themes and Variations in Shakespeare's Sonnets* (1961), considers twenty-five poems under the heading "'Hyperbole' and 'Religiousness' in Shakespeare's Expressions of His Love," but no one would regard all or even many of them as servile or weak. On the contrary, Leishman asserts that among these sonnets and those in his two other categories "are many, if not most, of the finest in the collection" (p. 23). For example, Sonnet 57 ("Being your slave what should I doe but tend") and the paired 58, ironic presentations of the poet's resentment of emotional domination, are excellent poems which reveal no signs of servile weakness despite their subject.[30]

Refusal to take the sonnet form seriously, the second objection Winters raises, consists in extreme simplicity of conception and development, a weakness frequently "aggravated" by Shakespeare's tendency to "solve" the (moral) problems he poses by "an evasion or irrelevant cliché" (p. 48). Shakespeare's sonnets are generally developed through "simple repetition or antithesis," which fails to achieve the "closely organized treatment of the subject" found in the "best of Jonson and Donne." Here Winters is beginning to sound like Ransom, but it is clear that they have quite different notions of what constitutes good sonnet "form." Ransom praises in sonnets qualities Winters plainly condemns: simple substance, a severely restricted burden, a closely limited range (p. 137 above). As we shall see in his comments on 116, Winters believes sonnets ought to be packed with meaning as well as closely organized. The difference between them is also suggested by their treatment of Sonnet 66; Ransom dismisses it as having "no logical organization at all" except for a little couplet conclusion, while Winters asserts it "would be a fine example of the plain style, except for the couplet" (p. 49).

Sonnet 66, "Tyr'd with all these for restfull death I cry," is regarded by Winters as one of those Elizabethan poems "dealing with disillusionment with the world," like Gascoigne's "Woodmanship," Raleigh's "The Lie" and Jonson's "False world, goodnight." But where these poets "offer the best solutions they can," Shakespeare (typically) "turns aside from the issues . . . raised" to a "kind of despairing sentimentality," a revelation of "poetic and personal" weakness. The trouble lies chiefly in the couplet, an example of the "sentimental degeneration" of courtly rhetoric; but doubtless the "element of genius" in 66 also raised Winters' expectation so that he was unable to "take this sort of triviality with good grace"

(p. 48). Although I freely admit the couplet may seem like a weak anticlimax after Shakespeare's harsh enumeration of the world's evils, I fail to perceive its sentimentality:

> Tyr'd with all these, from these would I be gone,
> Save that to dye, I leave my love alone.

Both the strength of the poet's devotion and the moral weakness of the friend he loves are implied by these lines, and the friend's weakness is probably the chief concern. Apparently it never occurred to Winters to ask why the speaker should be reluctant to leave his friend alone in the infected world. The answer, suggested by the next four sonnets, especially 67 and 69, is that the friend is in danger of succumbing to corruption, for a discrepancy between his external beauty and his moral character has already appeared (69).[31] There is no "personal" weakness here simply because the poet is not primarily concerned about his own stance before the world. Characteristically, he considers the subject of the sonnet from the standpoint of his love and his friend, and thus Sonnet 66 should not be lumped indiscriminately with Gascoigne's "Woodmanship" and Jonson's "False world, goodnight."

Sonnets 66, 116, 129, and 146 are named by Winters in 1939 as some of the "greatest sonnets"; twenty years later they are all condemned, the first two by means of some analysis, the last two by brief derogatory assertions. Sonnet 116 receives the most attention, mainly because it provides a notable example of the third and greatest of Shakespeare's weaknesses, the one that sets him apart from his great contemporaries and casts a "veil of uncertainty" over a number of poems. This serious fault, conceived as an abuse of the normal functions of language, is the "use of words for some vague connotative value, with little regard for exact denotation" (p. 50).

Underlying Winters' distaste for the way Shakespeare exploits the resources of language is the conviction that sense or reference is always prior to feeling and attitude. As a result of this conviction, two sets of correlative terms appear in his vocabulary: "denotation," "rational" or "conceptual content," "idea," "motive," and "connotation," "content of association," "feeling," "emotion."

From such terms he often constructs assertions which may be rather confusing to those who do not share his assumptions, assertions like "the idea is a conceptual statement of the motive of the feeling" (in Jonson); but they become perfectly intelligible once we know that in all poetry the relationship of "rational meaning to feeling" is supposed to be "that of motive to emotion."[32]

The difficulty in 116 "resides in the word *worth*" (line 8):

> Let me not to the marriage of true mindes
> Admit impediments, love is not love
> Which alters when it alteration findes,
> 4 Or bends with the remover to remove.
> O no, it is an ever fixed marke
> That lookes on tempests and is never shaken;
> It is the star to every wandring barke,
> 8 Whose worths unknowne, although his higth be taken.
> Lov's not Times foole, though rosie lips and cheeks
> Within his bending sickles compasse come,
> Love alters not with his breefe houres and weekes,
> 12 But beares it out even to the edge of doome;
> If this be error and upon me proved,
> I never writ, nor no man ever loved.

"Worth" is a bone he worries for more than half a page before he moves on to brief disparaging comparisons with Greville, Donne, Jonson, and Sidney, claiming that here in lines 7-8 "one loses the thought" as Shakespeare contents himself with a "vague feeling of the mysterious and supernatural." He then proceeds to draw these general conclusions:

> The sonnet is characteristic in other respects. The successive quatrains do not really develop the theme; each restates it. This makes, perhaps, for easy absorption on the part of the more or less quiescent reader, but it makes also for a somewhat simple and uninteresting poetry. The sonnet form is short, and the great poet should endeavor to use it more efficiently, to say as much as can be said of his subject within its limits; such efficiency is never characteristic of Shakespeare. . . . The high reputation of the sonnet is due about equally, I suspect, to its virtues and its faults (pp. 51-52).

Winters is right when he observes that 116 is not packed, but wrong when he finds it simple and uninteresting. One must also agree with his earlier contention that the poem's feeling or emotion "cannot have force when its nature and origin are obscure" (p. 51), yet one must ask whether they are obscure in this instance. Although the poet's strategy in 116 requires him to speak from a position of apparent confidence and strength, the context which Winters characteristically ignores makes his true situation quite clear. In short, Winters' general and specific comments on the poem reveal that he has nothing to offer but the usual interpretation, or rather misinterpretation, and hence he is in the awkward position of condemning what he does not understand.

Although it is impossible to give a full and reasoned interpretation of 116 here—I have done so elsewhere[33]—I can sketch briefly the main lines of an accurate reading and indicate what Winters has ignored or overlooked. Sonnet 116, despite its ostensible "universal significance," does not stand alone as Winters and many others assume. It stands in the natural context of a group beginning with Sonnet 109, "O never say that I was false of heart," and ending with Sonnet 121, "Tis better to be vile then vile esteemed"; within this group are clusters of related sonnets, 109-112, 113-114, 115-116, and 117-120. The general subject of these sonnets is the poet's temporary offense against friendship, an offense including moral sin and prolonged absence from his friend. He freely admits his "wilfulnesse and errors" (117), as the many references to his sins reveal, yet he also insists that these "worse essaies" proved the friend his "best of love" (110), that his love has been purged, renewed, and strengthened by his divagation.

> O benefit of ill, now I find true
> That better is, by evil still made better.
> And ruin'd love when it is built anew
> Growes faster then at first, more strong, far greater.
> So I returne rebukt to my content,
> And gaine by ills thrise more then I have spent. (119.9-14)

However certain the poet may be about his own love, he cannot be certain about the friend's, for the quality of that love has been severely tried by grievous sins of omission and commission (117).

Both the seriousness of his own sins and doubts concerning the strength and nature of the friend's love are uppermost in the poet's mind in the eloquent and misleading Sonnet 116. One of the most misleading and surprising features of the first sentence, "Let me not to the marriage of true mindes / Admit impediments," is the subject ("Let *me* not"), for all the impediments lie in the speaker's past. He refers to them repeatedly in Sonnets 109-121, claims that they have increased his love in 115, and in 117 presents them as a bill of particulars with an excuse appended. Thus, if anyone is to allow impediments to the marriage of faithful, constant minds, it must be the friend addressed, not the unfaithful poet. The remover in question is the speaker, the one who recently changed allegiance, and the one who is guilty of alteration. It is his friend's love for him which must not alter in the face of alteration or be inclined to seek a new object.

How one takes the opening quatrain of 116 is important because it determines how the rest of the sonnet will be read. Since the third and fourth lines are clearly related to lines 5-8 of Sonnet 115, where the poet's sins are implicit, the connection with that sonnet should be decisive even if the wider context is ignored. Yet Winters has little or nothing to offer on this crucial quatrain; he merely says, "the first four lines have precision, dignity, and simplicity, which are moving" (p. 52). As for the second quatrain, his pedestrian remarks on "worth" and the figure of lines 7-8 (pp. 50-51) are undercut by his failure to grasp the point of the opening lines, and they simply provide an example of his devotion to myopic common sense.

His common sense appears to have deserted him, or to be subordinated to his critical obsessions, in the case of Sonnet 77, a poem which he uniquely "suspects" to be "the most impressive of all" (p. 58). He admits that the subject of this undistinguished sonnet is not important, but says that it permits "certain perceptions" to enter. Of course "perceptions" means moral perceptions, and he finds them in what he calls the "moralizing" of the last six lines:

> Looke what thy memorie cannot containe,
> Commit to these waste bla[n]cks, and thou shalt finde
> Those children nurst, deliverd from thy braine,

   To take a new acquaintance of thy minde.
   These offices, so oft as thou wilt looke,
   Shall profit thee, and much inrich thy booke.

His crude summary of the first eight lines ignores the poem's obvious rhetorical pattern:

> The first quatrain states the ostensible theme of the poem: time passes and we age, yet by writing down our thoughts, we take a new acquaintance of our mind, acquire a new learning. The second quatrain enlarges upon the passage of time; the last six lines revert to the moralizing (p. 59).

Clearly, the first quatrain of 77 presents mirror, sundial, and book with "vacant leaves"; the second picks up the mirror which shows aging and the dial which shows "Time's theevish progresse to eternitie." The third quatrain then gives us the book which offsets the loss of memory, and the couplet seems to sum up the profit to be derived from the functions of all three. Winters, however, talks of the "enemy" (Time) invading the mind in line 9, a "brilliant and terrifying suggestion" of the "destruction of the mind itself" due in part to preceding lines and no sooner made than dropped (p. 59). This distorted reading of the third quatrain stems from his desire to see a progression or climax in a series where none is intended. On the contrary, there is a contrast or gap in the first quatrain between the mirror and dial, which show how beauties wear and precious minutes waste, and the vacant leaves of the book, which will bear the mind's imprint; and this contrast is resumed and elaborated in the difference between the second quatrain and the third. What is committed to the empty white pages of the book, "children ... deliverd from thy braine," will successfully resist Time's encroachment, like the children of Sonnets 1-17.[34] His misreading of lines 9-10 is also conditioned by his stock response to "waste" in the second and tenth lines.[35] Waste blanks are simply vacant leaves (line 3), and there is no emphasis on the secondary meaning "*desert* or *uninhabited,*" supposedly reinforced by "waste" of line 2 (p. 60). In Shakespeare's temporal contexts "waste" signifies the passing, spending, or consuming of time, sometimes with an emphasis on destruction or decay (as in 12.10);[36]

it is seldom used as an adjective and perhaps never in the sense Winters alone finds in "waste bla[n]cks." In short, it is not the poem but the critic that "enters the realm of confusion instead of describing it."

VI

Both Ransom and Winters are good poets but eccentric and irresponsible critics. Their criticism of the Sonnets is vitiated by their tendency to take parts of poems and even whole poems out of context before subjecting them to the "scrutiny" of unenlightened common sense. The inevitable result is, at best, an oversimplification and distortion of the Sonnets; at worst, complete misinterpretation of them. If these critics do not get the basic "poetic facts" straight, we cannot expect them to succeed in more fundamental and more difficult critical endeavors. Ransom and Winters are linguistic rationalists who exalt denotation or sense over feeling, tone, attitude, and intention, the control of the referential functions of language over the influential.[37] To do this is to uphold the very reverse of what is the case in most poetry, including their own, and to ignore the fact that "there is a logic of the imagination as well as a logic of concepts," as T. S. Eliot once stated. Finally, our poet-critics would deny the elementary liberal principle that we must allow every competent poet his own style and method. If Shakespeare's sonnets consist mainly of a series of metaphorical variations on, or expansions of, relatively simple statements, as Leishman and I have pointed out, that is no cause for censure or regret. There is more than one poetically valid way of handling a subject, especially in the lyric where the associative process is strongest. We must not use Donne or Jonson or Shakespeare as the jawbone to slay the others, for the finest poetry of each is excellent in its own way and living proof that the Spirit blows where it wishes.

FRENCH TRANSLATIONS OF THE SONNETS

BY

MARSHALL LINDSAY

SINCE 1821 there have been some twenty-three partial or complete translations of Shakespeare's sonnets into French, and it is the purpose of this study to evaluate them. Questions of the theory and methods of translation, which have been discussed at some length during the past decade, will concern us only indirectly; the emphasis will be on actual accomplishment, that is, how successfully translators have rendered not only the literal meaning but also the tone, the attitude, and the diction. The success of a translation can be measured by comparing it both with the original text and with other translations of the same text, this in order to determine whether individual words and lines are adequately represented in French and whether the whole translation gives an impression analogous to the original. Since most of the translations are intended to stand on their own as poetry, our final concern is the poetic value of the translated sonnets without reference to the original text, according to whatever canons of aesthetic value may be applicable.

French translators seem, in general, since 1900, to be very serious about their task, and, with few exceptions, their modesty is evident. They give the impression of artisans working in a restricted medium according to strict rules and limitations. They seem to be humble servants of the original text, of the French language, and of certain ideals of art and perfection. They seldom adopt an attitude of superiority or even irony toward the original author, and they consider the text as something sacred, which, in theory, should be neither altered nor interpreted. We see them as infinitely patient, deriving satisfaction primarily from the perfection and polished quality of their handiwork. This attitude toward translation was extolled by Valéry in his tribute of 1941 to the self-effacing translator of Saint John of the Cross, the Père Cyprien, who, according to Valéry, created "une manière de chef-d'oeuvre en produisant des poèmes dont la substance n'est pas de lui."[1] His accomplishment was precisely this: he was faithful to the original text and at the same time he respected the demands of his own language: "C'est là véritablement *traduire,* qui est de reconstituer au plus près l'*effet* d'une certaine *cause,* —ici un texte de langue espagnole au moyen d'une *autre cause,* —un texte de langue française."[2] After such a feat, the humble Father simply disappeared from the history of French letters until his rediscovery by Valéry.

Translating all of Shakespeare's Sonnets is obviously a difficult and painstaking task. Each step, from the comprehension of the sonnets themselves to the finished version, presents separate and often insoluble problems. The first is perhaps the most difficult: to understand the language and meaning of the English text. Then there is the difficulty of transferring words and expressions from English to French, which includes several well-known traps. The questions of vocabulary—semantic evolution in English, false cognates, nonequivalence of connotative meaning—are compounded by the syntactical incompatibility of the two languages: the different uses in each of articles and prepositions, of singulars and plurals, of coordination and subordination, and so forth. Since the French reader is traditionally highly sensitive to these delicate aspects of style and grammar, the translator is expected to observe them with care. He must further choose a form suitable to render the Shakespearean sonnet, one he will be able to use consistently throughout the cycle, and which, if he is translating in verse, will be a convincing sonnet in French. The question of meter and versification has not proved particularly difficult, since nearly all of the verse translators chose the classical or a somewhat free Alexandrine as the most likely equivalent of the iambic pentameter line. But there is then the more subtle task of transferring, or rather re-creating, a poetic context. To the French mind the idiom of the Sonnets seems often unpoetic: the diction is rough, the movement abrupt and irregular; the conceits are complex and unclear, the metaphors lack nobility, and the sentiments are obscured by wit. It is the kind of poetry that causes contemporary readers to say: *ça ne chante pas,* as if speaking were less a function of poetry than singing. It is not that these elements are entirely absent from the French poetic tradition, for they can be found in Shakespeare's closest French contemporaries. Sponde, D'Aubigné, and La Ceppède, but these poets are considered *en marge,* Baroque, too irregular to be imitated. To render in French the poetic context of the Sonnets is a matter of finding not only the equivalent language but also analogous poetic conventions. Finally, one of the essential qualities of a translation—as it is of all careful writing in France — is its polished surface perfection: sonority in the choice and placement of words, balance in phrasing, clarity and logic, sometimes even in spite of the original text.

To isolate these problems and see how they have been met, I should like to compare several French versions of Sonnet 73. Since this is one of the best-known of the Sonnets even in France, and since its kind of lyricism can be expected to appeal to French readers of poetry, it is likely that translators have made an effort to render this sonnet with particular care:

> That time of year thou mayst in me behold
> When yellow leaves, or none, or few, do hang
> Upon those boughs which shake against the cold,
> 4 Bare ruined choirs where late the sweet birds sang.
> In me thou see'st the twilight of such day
> As after sunset fadeth in the west,
> Which by-and-by black night doth take away,
> 8 Death's second self, that seals up all in rest.
> In me thou see'st the glowing of such fire
> That on the ashes of his youth doth lie,
> As the deathbed whereon it must expire,
> 12 Consumed with that which it was nourished by.
>   This thou perceiv'st, which makes thy love more strong,
>   To love that well which thou must leave ere long.[3]

The first known translation is by Amédée Pichot, referred to as

"A. P., traducteur de Lord Byron," in the 1821 edition of Letourneur's translation of the *Œuvres complètes de Shakspeare;* six sonnets are translated.

> Tu peux voir en moi ce temps de l'année où quelques
> feuilles jaunies pendent encore peut-être aux rameaux que fait
> frémir le souffle glacé de l'hiver, et qui naguère servaient
> d'asile aux doux concerts des oiseaux. Tu vois en moi le cré-
> puscule d'un jour qui s'évanouit dans l'occident avec le soleil,
> et que la nuit efface peu à peu, telle que le symbole de la Mort
> apposant sur l'univers le sceau du silence. Tu vois en moi les
> étincelles mourantes d'un feu étendu sur les cendres comme
> sur une couche de mort et consumé par ce qui faisait son ali-
> ment. Voilà ce que tu reconnais en moi, et tu n'en aimes que
> davantage ce que tu dois perdre bientôt.

It is difficult to imagine anything more flat than the opening
words of this translation. *Tu peux voir en moi ce temps de l'année*;
the literal meaning of Shakespeare's first line is there, but nothing
else. In the translation of line 2, even the literal meaning is lost,
since *peut-être* says far less than the words "or none or few," not to
mention that it substitutes an abstraction for a concrete image.
"Which shake against the cold" is expanded and explained by *que
fait frémir le souffle glacé de l'hiver*; the translator probably felt
that "against the cold" was not explicit enough and that words
referring to winter and the wind had to be added to make the idea
clear. Half of line 4 is omitted to be replaced by an explanation
(*qui servaient d'asile*), and in the other half the literal image
becomes a classical cliché. It is evident that much of the poetry of
this first quatrain has been sacrificed to clarity, which was hardly
necessary since neither the images nor the syntax in the original
lines presented real difficulties. This reduction continues throughout the rest of Pichot's translation. It is worth noting only that lines
5 and 6 of the sonnet are almost unrecognizable in this French version and that *étincelles mourantes* is certainly the wrong way of
saying "glowing" in French—either *rutilement* or *lueur* would have
been preferable. It should be noted, finally, that the form adopted
by Pichot is the single paragraph.

Ernest Lafond's version (1856) is in verse:

> Je suis dans la saison par l'automne suprise
> Où, suspendue encor aux branches des ormeaux,
> Cloîtres abandonnés où chantaient les oiseaux,
> La feuille va tomber au souffle de la bise.
>
> Je suis au crépuscule, à l'heure où l'ombre grise
> Lentement se prolonge, et couvre les coteaux;
> A l'heure où vient la nuit, la nuit qui prophétise,
> Par le sommeil d'une heure, un éternel repos.
>
> Je suis d'un feu qui meurt la dernière étincelle
> Qui va se réunir à la cendre éternelle
> De tout ce qui vécut un instant pour mourir.
>
> Hâte-toi de m'aimer, hélas! le temps me presse;
> Dans ton amour pour moi mets toute ta jeunesse:
> Il faut aimer plus fort celui qui va partir.

The two quatrains are only a remote paraphrase of the original, and the relationship between the speaker and the person addressed is completely altered—the latter does not even appear until line 12. But Lafond's main difficulty seems to have been making Shakespeare's material fit the French sonnet form.[4] To do this he reduced Shakespeare's third quatrain to a tercet and expanded the couplet into a tercet. The result is that lines 10-13 are improvised and bear even less resemblance to the original than the octave. Furthermore, it seems that Lafond felt obliged to delineate the structure of his French sonnet with the artificial framework of *Je suis* at the beginning of each quatrain; *hélas!* in line 12 is sufficient to indicate to the French reader that the final tercet has arrived. In expanding Shakespeare's couplet to make a French tercet Lafond added a facile Epicureanism reminiscent of the popular Ronsard. Shakespeare asked to be loved well; Lafond would have it fast.

François-Victor Hugo's translation of the Sonnets was published in 1857. This was the first translation of all the sonnets, and it has been considered since its publication as one of the standard versions. For that reason it has been reprinted more than most, and when writers refer to the Sonnets it is often from the Hugo translation that they take their quotations. Later translators frequently

refer to it as "expressive and poetic." In a rhapsodic and pretentious sixty-four page introduction—in this the translator is not
unlike his father—Hugo explains that the Sonnets contain "tout un
drame," with exposition, complications, turns of fortune, and
dénouement. It is to give that drama a narrative progression that
Hugo has entirely rearranged the collection, beginning with the last
twenty-seven sonnets: "Dans le premier sonnet, au moment où
l'action commence, nous voyons Shakespeare amoureux." In this
scheme, Sonnet 73 is preceded by Sonnets 19 and 60 and followed
by Sonnets 37 and 22. In Hugo's collection it is numbered 141.

> Tu peux voir en moi ce temps de l'année où il ne
> pend plus que quelques rares feuilles jaunes aux
> branches qui tremblent sous le souffle de l'hiver,
> orchestres nus et ruinés où chantaient naguère les
> doux oiseaux.

> En moi tu vois le crépuscule du jour qui s'évanouit
> dans l'Occident avec le soleil couchant, entraîné peu
> à peu par la nuit noire, cet *alter ego* de la mort, qui
> scelle tout dans le repos.

> En moi tu vois la dernière étincelle d'un feu qui
> agonise sur les cendres de sa jeunesse, lit de mort où
> il doit expirer,

> Éteint par l'aliment dont il se nourrissait. Tu t'en
> aperçois, et c'est ce qui fait ton amour plus fort pour
> aimer ce que tu vas si tôt perdre.

Although the translation is done in prose, Hugo has obviously
attempted to make it look like a French sonnet by arranging the
paragraphs in a proportion similar to two quatrains and two tercets. This has the disadvantage of a run-on between the third and
fourth paragraphs and a definite stop within the fourth paragraph,
so that in none of Hugo's translations do form and content coincide. He has chosen to render Shakespeare in a periodic prose, with
one long, involved, and highly rhythmic sentence for each paragraph; unlike Pichot, Hugo rarely coordinated his sentences with
et.

In this version "do hang" of line 2 is made impersonal: *Il ne pend plus;* the "yellow leaves or none, or few" appears as *quelques rares feuilles jaunes.* The original is obviously attenuated in both of these expressions. Hugo may have been aware that *tremblent* is an inadequate rendering of "shake" (line 3), and it may have been to compensate that he translated "against the cold" as *sous le souffle de l'hiver,* as if the rich alliteration and the idea of wind would give to *tremblent* what it lacks in force. For one reason or another Hugo chose *orchestres* instead of *chœurs* or *chapelles* to translate "choirs" of line 4. Perhaps he meant the orchestra of a theater; at any rate, the image is lost. In attempting to give the intensity of Shakespeare's expression, sometimes he comes this side of an expression, at others he goes beyond; "consumed" in line 12 is reduced to *éteint* (called for metaphorically by *étincelle*), yet "lie" in line 10 is blown up into *agonise*. Here Hugo abandons Shakespeare's literal meaning but without gaining any of the connotative meaning. Much, then, is lost in this translation; however, read aloud it is not without a certain majesty and solemnity that somewhat compensates for all its inadequacies.

Emile Montégut's translation of the Sonnets (1873) has become, like Hugo's, a standard version.[5] It has been reprinted several times, most recently in 1945.[6] It is respected primarily for a supposed faithfulness to the original. It is a prose version and each sonnet is presented, as in r̄ ̇not's translations, as a single paragraph:

> Tu peux contempler en moi cette saison de l'année où les feuilles jaunies, rares quand elles ne sont pas tout à fait absentes, pendent à des rameaux qui tremblent sous les vents froids, chœurs ruinés et dépouillés où tout récemment chantaient les doux oiseaux. Tu vois en moi le crépuscule du jour quand après le coucher du soleil il se fond à l'occident, et que peu à peu il est enseveli par la nuit sombre, seconde mort qui scelle toutes choses du repos. Tu vois en moi le dernier éclat d'un feu qui gît sur les cendres de sa jeunesse, comme sur le lit de mort où il doit expirer consumé par cela même qui le nourrissait. C'est là ce que tu aperçois, et c'est ce qui rend

ton amour plus fort, parce que tu veux bien aimer ce
que tu seras obligé dc laisser avant longtemps.

It seems that Montégut has undertaken to explain whatever might
not be perfectly clear. "Yellow leaves or none, or few" becomes *les
feuilles jaunies, rares quand elles ne sont pas tout à fait absentes,*
and "shake against the cold" becomes *tremblent sous les vents
froids.* Similarly, the infinitive "to love" in line 14, which most of
the translators render as *pour aimer,* is explained by *parce que tu
veux bien aimer,* which does not account for the relationship
between the infinitive and "this" in line 13, but which has the advantage at least of making a coherent sentence in French. Yet, in
other lines Montégut does not explain; line 4 has no commentary,
and "with" in line 12 is merely translated as *par,* which eliminates
the meaning "at the same time as" with the consequence that the
line is unclear.[7] Perhaps it is when he understood an image that he
expanded on it, leaving the more difficult images in roughly literal
translations. This would explain why this version of the sonnet
appears lopsided, with some of its elements stressed and others
barely rendered.

But even when he translated literally, Montégut modified Shakespeare's meaning in one way or another. For "that seals up all in
rest," he wrote *qui scelle toutes choses du repos,* making obscure
by the use of the preposition *du* what had once been clear.[8] Furthermore, he added new metaphors: "fadeth" is given as *se fond*
(and the subject is not "sunset" but *crépuscule* or *jour*), which need
not be taken literally as "melt," but rather as a dead metaphor
meaning "disappear." "Take away" in line 7 becomes *enseveli,*
another dead metaphor meaning "hide" or "cover." Yet regardless
of the fact that the literal sense of such metaphors is no longer felt,
enseveli does have connotations concerning death, and these connotations give more weight to such expressions as "Death's second
self," "deathbed," and "expire." Also, "lie" in line 10 is in French
gît, which has markedly funereal associations. Montégut's translation, then, seems to change the emphasis of the poem to make it
speak of death rather than age. His so-called literal translation has
resulted in a poem whose general impact differs considerably from
the intent, as we understand it, of Shakespeare's sonnet, and the

difference is enough to modify the meaning.

The translation by Fernand Henry (1900) is of interest primarily for its weaknesses.

> Tu peux revoir en moi ce moment de l'année
> Où, tremblant sous les vents de l'hiver, les rameaux
> —Naguère tout remplis du doux chant des oiseaux—
> N'ont plus pour vêtements que des feuilles fanées.
>
> Tu contemples en moi la fin d'une journée,
> Lorsque, dans l'Occident, elle tombe en lambeaux
> Et qu'on la voit descendre au fond du noir tombeau
> Où par la Nuit elle est lentement entraînée.
>
> En moi tu vois encor la suprême lueur
> D'un feu qui se débat sur sa jeunesse en cendres,
> Lit funèbre où sa flamme a dû venir s'étendre,
>
> Détruite par cela qui faisait sa splendeur.
> C'est pourquoi ton amour est devenu plus tendre
> Pour celui dont bientôt tu devras te déprendre.

This series of undistinguished Alexandrines with commonplace rhymes is an example of the watering-down to be found in French translations of Shakespeare's plays. Henry's method seems to be to render not words or expressions but entire images which he paraphrases into French clichés (see especially lines 3, 4, and 12). Since each cliché corresponds only vaguely to the original image, the resulting French sonnet lacks coherence. Here the translator has made a simple poem without overtones or ambiguity out of a rather complex verbal structure. What might be disturbing in Shakespeare becomes simple décor.

In Charles-Marie Garnier's translation (1906–1907), each sonnet has a sense of unity that earlier versions did not have. Describing his translation in a subtitle as an "essai d'une interprétation en vers français," Garnier probably meant that this would not be a simple rendering but rather something like an explanation or commentary. His Alexandrines are correct (despite a false caesura in line 8), energetic, at times even distinguished:

> En moi tu vois l'automne où l'année agonise,
> Où la feuille jaunit et meurt sur les rameaux,

Pour tomber des arceaux qui tremblent sous la bise,
Chœurs nus et délabrés où chantaient les oiseaux.

En moi tu vois encor le mourant crépuscule
Qui, le soleil couché, s'attarde sur les eaux;
Et pas à pas la nuit le noircit et l'annule,
Sœur de la mort qui scelle tout au grand repos.

En moi tu vois encor la pâle et brève flamme
Qui sur la cendre meurt d'un feu qui s'est tari,
Berceau de sa clarté, lit de mort de son âme,
Consumé des ardeurs dont il s'était nourri.

Tu vois, et ton amour plus puissant vent m'étreindre,
Pressé d'aimer ce qui demain devra s'éteindre.

The superiority of this over earlier translations is evident. The expressions that had defeated previous attempts are either omitted ("or none or few," line 2) or are rendered with simplicity and directness while still remaining poetic, as is, for example, line 4: *Chœurs nus et délabrés où chantaient les oiseaux.* Since "late" can be understood in the tense of *chantaient,* and "sweet," in the meaning of *les oiseaux,* the two words are omitted; and while the line may be considered to have lost some of the poignancy given by "late" and "sweet," its meaning is still there. Perhaps the coherence of Garnier's translation is a result of his tendency to use expressions that all point in the same semantic direction. The following words have no equivalent in the English: *agonise, meurt* (lines 2 and 10), *arceaux* (reinforces *chœurs* in line 4), *mourant, sur lex eaux* (and since Poe the French know that water has to do with death), *annule, s'est tari, berceau, s'éteindre;* with the exception of *arceaux* and *berceau* these words refer explicitly to death. What in Shakespeare was implied or connoted by the imagery becomes in this translation part of the literal statement the poem makes. The translation refers throughout to death, and one can understand why the poet Francis Jammes, when he read Garnier's translation of the Sonnets, pointed out their "tristesse funéraire" and "indiscutable morbidesse."[9]

If Garnier's translation seems rather intellectual, it is because, as we have seen, he often omits expressions with a high charge of affectivity. Emile Le Brun (1927) restores that affectivity by his particular use of the speaker's voice:

> Tu peux la voir en moi, la saison que les feuilles
> Ou ne sont plus, ou bien, jaunes et rares, pendent,
> Pendent à des rameaux de froid tout frissonnants,
> Chœurs nus, chœurs ruineux, où les oiseaux chantaient;
> En me voyant, tu vois ce jour crépusculaire
> Qui, couché le soleil, pâlit à l'occident
> Et qu'emporte bientôt la nuit noire, autre mort,
> Enfermant sous le sceau du repos toutes choses;
> Et, me voyant, tu vois la lueur de la flamme
> Gisant là, parmi les cendres de sa jeunesse,
> Lit de mort où le feu doit enfin rendre l'âme,
> Consumé par cela dont il se nourrissait.
>   Ce que tu vois ainsi fait ton amour plus fort
>   Pour mieux aimer ce qu'il faudra quitter sous peu.

The familiar use of the article *la* in line 1, the repetition of *pendent* in lines 2 and 3 and of *chœurs* in line 4, and the tautology of *me voyant, tu vois* in lines 5 and 9 give to the poem a sense of immediacy and emotional intensity. This is emphasized further by the irregular rhythm of the lines with multiple accents and in the absence of any caesura in lines 10 and 14. The Alexandrines are strong, but the fact that they are in blank verse with irregular assonances keeps the translation from seeming erudite.

Giraud d'Uccle also translated in unrhymed Alexandrines (1942), and although his versions of other sonnets are quite uneven, he has succeeded in Sonnet 73 in maintaining a consistency of tone that is a good deal like that of the original, despite marked differences of diction.

> Tu reconnais en moi la saison de l'année
> où la froidure fait les branches frissonner.
> Une feuille jaunie ou quelques feuilles pendent
> aux rameaux dénudés où chantaient les oiseaux.
> Ce que tu vois en moi, c'est la chute du jour:
> par lents degrés l'obscure nuit, sœur de la mort,
> en son repos scellant le monde, ensevelit
> le coucher du soleil qui sombre à l'Occident.
> Ce que tu vois en moi, c'est l'éclat d'un brasier
> qui va s'éteindre sous la cendre de son âge:
> agonisante flamme et qui doit expirer

par ce qui lui servait d'aliment consumée.
Tout cela que tu vois rend ton amour plus fort
pour mieux aimer ce qu'il te faut quitter si vite.[10]

The liberties taken would seem to spoil the total effect: each quatrain is divided into two separate sentences, making the sonnet seem somewhat chopped up, and the order of the ideas in each quatrain is reversed. Furthermore, images have been altered; for example, in line 10, the fire is pictured as suffocated under the ashes of its age rather than lying on the ashes of its youth. Yet the total effect is markedly better than in most of the translations we have examined. There is a slightly archaic flavor that comes from the inversions in lines 2 and 12, and the effect is more appropriate than the pseudoclassical inversions used by Henry (above) and Baldensperger (below). In the first line, *Tu reconnais en moi* is a natural way to express Shakespeare's verb in French, much better than the *Tu peux voir en moi* of the literal translators. *La saison* is, once again, the most natural way of expressing "that time of year," despite the redundancy of *la saison de l'année. Sombre*—"to founder or sink"—is certainly a curious and original rendering of "fadeth," but it does not connote an effect of light unless one detects in it the influence of its homonym, the adjective *sombre.*

In these last two translations, the literal sense of Sonnet 73 has been, in a general way, retained—the translators have found equivalents for the basic elements of the original text, and they have not modified its sense by emphasizing one or another of those elements, as we have seen in the case of Garnier. Furthermore, Le Brun and d'Uccle have attempted to include in their versions elements of the sonnet's meaning that earlier translators did not concern themselves with.

Le Brun used a somewhat declamatory style to convey the speaker's attitude toward his listener, and he saw this attitude as an attempt to persuade. With an evocative use of language and with various recognized stylistic means of *mise en relief* such as repetition, placement in the sense group, inversion and alliteration, the speaker's voice seems to stress *saison, pendent, chœurs,* and *frissonnants.* Yet one may question the aptness of the stress in each case. Le Brun probably emphasized *saison* to compensate for its placement near the end rather than the beginning of the first line;

the repetition of *pendent* compensates for the verbal form *"do hang,"* nonexistent in French; and *chœurs* is stressed in order to convey the force of the juxtaposed adjectives "bare ruin'd," which in French had to be separated and postpositive.

D'Uccle's diction, on the other hand is less rhetorical. His accomplishment is that he has conveyed that part of the sonnet's meaning that I. A. Richards refers to as "feeling." By rearranging components of the images, he emphasized a negative attitude on the part of the speaker toward those images. In lines 1 and 2, it is not the yellow leaves that prevail but the ideas associated with cold; similarly, in the second and third quatrains, what stands out is the fact that the day is at its end (*chute du jour* means precisely that) and that the fire will soon go out (*va s'éteindre,* not in the English). In this way, d'Uccle plays down the spectacular, pictorial aspects of the imagery in favor of what is unpleasant about it. This, to be sure, constitutes an act of interpretation, but without it, translation of poetry tends to be vague or confused.

Fernand Baldensperger's translation was published in the United States in 1943, and although it is accompanied with considerable documentation and critical apparatus, it is clearly inadequate as a translation:

> Tu vois en moi ce temps de l'année où, peu sûre,
> La feuille jaune pend à l'arbre dépouillé,
> A des rameaux que fait se choquer la froidure
> —Bancs ruineux où hier chantait un chœur ailé.
>
> En moi tu vois alors un crépuscule, où dure
> Faiblement le Soleil, à l'Ouest en allé,
> Englouti peu à peu dans l'âpre Nuit obscure
> —Autre Mort où tout est d'un grand repos scellé.
>
> Tu vois en moi le rougeoiement de cette Flamme
> Qui succède aux tisons de la Jeunesse, quand
> Sur ce lit d'agonie il lui faut rendre l'âme
> Détruite par l'ardeur qui la nourrit pourtant.
>
> Tu vois là tout ce dont ton Amour se renforce:
> Car ce que tu vas perdre, il faut l'aimer—à force.

The diction is out of character with Shakespeare: Baldensperger adapts images of the original to neoclassical clichés (*un chœur ailé*) or faint echoes of a Verlaine-type impressionism (*un crépuscule, où dure / Faiblement le Soleil, à l'Ouest en allé*).

Maurice Blanchard's translation of twelve sonnets appeared in 1944. These prose versions are generally faithful and at the same time they are rendered with imagination:

> Tu vois en moi cette saison où des feuilles, et rares, et jaunies, pendent à ces branches qui s'agitent contre le froid, chœur nu et ruiné où naguère les oiseaux chantaient.
>
> Tu vois en moi le crépuscule d'un jour où le soleil couchant s'est effacé dans l'Ouest, soleil que pas à pas l'atroce nuit emporte, image de la mort posant son sceau sur le dernier repos.
>
> Tu vois en moi l'embrasement d'un feu étendu sur les cendres de sa jeunesse comme sur le lit de mort où il faut qu'il expire, consumé par cela même dont il s'était nourri.
>
> Tu vois cela qui fait ton amour plus fort pour aimer ce qui'il te faut quitter avant peu.

This is the most successful rendering of line 3 that we have seen so far, and it is because the word *s'agitent,* unlike *trembler* and *frissonner* chosen by earlier translators, does not explicitly refer to cold, a notion contained in the next word; Shakespeare wrote "shake against the cold," not "shiver." But Blanchard alters and interprets the original in line 4, where he makes *chœur* singular rather than plural; as he gives the image, the many branches form the rows of seats in a choir. He alters line 8 more radically: Shakespeare had night sealing up all in rest; in Blanchard it is night's image, death, that seals up all in an eternal rest, which gives the line an entirely new meaning.

Pierre-Jean Jouve, in his introduction to his translation of the Sonnets (1955), insisted, as Blanchard had, that they should be rendered in prose—in what he called "une prose intérieurement organisée." For the only adequate equivalent of "le vers anglais dur et rapide" is, for Jouve, "la prose française en sinuosité":[11]

Ce moment de l'année tu peux le voir en moi, quand des feuilles jaunes, ou aucune, ou quelques-unes, pendent, sur ces branchages frémissant contre le froid: voûte ruinée, où tout à l'heure l'oiseau chantait.

En moi tu vois le crépuscule de certain jour, quand après le couchant il s'éteint dans l'ouest, que petit à petit la nuit noire saisit, seconde de la mort qui met tout au repos.

En moi tu vois la lueur de ce feu qui sur les cendres de sa jeunesse est couché, comme au lit mortuaire où il va expirer, consumé de ceci par quoi il fut nourri.

Tu sais cela, qui fait ton amour plus puissant, aimer cela que tu devras quitter avant longtemps.

To the French reader, this is not a simple prose paraphrase like the translations of Pichot, F.-V. Hugo, Guizot, Montégut, and Legouis because it appears to belong to the recognized genre of the *poème en prose* in the tradition of Rimbaud, Eluard, Michaux, and Char, a form which Jouve himself had used in his *Histoires sanglantes* of 1932. But since this translation follows the original sonnet closely and the paragraphing is predetermined by the quatrains and couplet of the Shakespearean sonnet, the resemblance to a *poème en prose* is in its appearance on the page only. Nevertheless, Jouve's translation benefits from the resemblance because the strange, often surrealistic metaphors and extreme boldness in expression of the *poème en prose* serve to exempt it from some of the traditional rules of French prose. Shakespeare's words do not have to be touched up, and an expression like *des feuilles jaunes, ou aucune, ou quelques-unes,* which would otherwise be considered an awkward, literal translation, can be left as is, and the verb *aimer* in the last line can remain suspended, unattached syntactically to the rest of the sentence.

Of all the translations of Sonnet 73 so far considered, this is the most faithful; and among the faithful translations it manifests the most skill in finding apt equivalents. It is successful as a poem in French without betraying any one element of the original in favor of another, and without explaining it. It leaves mysterious what is mysterious in the English. And yet, it is in this seemingly most satisfactory translation of the sonnet that the basic weakness of all of the translations stands out most clearly: they lack depth. The words mean simply what they say; only one level of meaning can be drawn from the verbal context. The words fail to echo either among each other or in the reader's mind. It is a nice poem, not a great one. In this translation Shakespeare's sonnets as a whole provide easy reading. A French reader could read Jouve's translation in a few hours without being puzzled, without being challenged to participate in the creation of a work of art.

A verse translation like that of André Prudhommeaux (published in Switzerland, 1945) seems to give precisely that depth lacking in the Jouve translation but at the expense of resemblance to the original text. In a preface entitled "Trahir ou traduire?" Prudhommeaux states his principles: "... une traduction au sens littéral et vulgaire du mot serait ici une perte presque totale de substance." Most translators would agree, but they would find it difficult to go along with what follows. According to Prudhommeaux, Renaissance poetry employs Dante's four kinds of meaning, and, further, the anagogic meaning is the "poème du poème" or poem about poetic creation. Since this fourth level can be grasped and rendered only "dans l'imitation aussi complète que possible du geste créateur d'où sort le livre entier dans le cadre de l'œuvre," the translator need consider the details of the original only in relation to their function in the entire work. "Il nous paraît barbare," he continues, "de sacrifier le vers au mot, le poème au vers, le livre au poème, l'œuvre au livre." This is, of course, the old agrument that the spirit of the whole justifies whatever liberties are taken with the details. The spirit of the whole can hardly be measured objectively, but what happens to the details is quite clear in Prudhommeaux's translation of Sonnet 73:

> Regarde en moi: contemple une saison vieillie
>   Où la feuille jaunit s'isole et meurt de froid
>   Où sans oiseaux les arbres nus cabrés d'effroi
>   Agitent des arceaux ruinés d'abbaye!
> En moi vois d'un soir bas l'humble flamme accueillie
>   Crépuscule léchant la cendreuse paroi
>   Et sur quoi pas à pas la noire nuit s'accroît
>   Sœur de la mort scellant la parole inouïe.
> Tu vis brûler chez moi la gloire de ce feu
>   Qui sur les tisons gris palpite encore un peu

> Ainsi qu'au lit funèbre où ses restes expirent
> Et tu le vois mourir de ce qui l'a nourri—
> Et ton amour plus fort se rallume en esprit
> D'aimer ce qui bientôt quittera ces empires!

Without reference to the original, this French sonnet has definite qualities of its own as a poem, but as a translation it retains only the barest elements of Shakespeare's images and expands them in its own way. Lines 6 and 8 are typical: "As after sunset fadeth in the west" becomes a striking image, but it no longer means or even implies what the original says: *Crépuscule léchant la cendreuse paroi;* the tone is aggressive, the thought surrealistically illogical; the tenor and vehicle of the metaphor are so far apart as to be unrecognizable—*la cendreuse paroi* standing apparently for the darkening western sky. "Death's second self, that seals up all in rest" becomes *Sœur de la mort scellant la parole inouïe.* The expression in the first hemistich is the same as in some of the earliest translations of the sonnet, but the second hemistich abandons the original line to introduce the idea of incommunicability and the absolute Word, presumably bringing to the sonnet what Prudhommeaux called in his preface the anagogic.

In the two-volume edition of Shakespeare's complete works in the collection of the Bibliothèque de la Pléiade (1959), the Poems and Sonnets have been transplanted in verse by Jean Fuzier. Here the translator observed Shakespeare's rhyme structure, and it was his stated intention to retain all the elements in the Sonnets that are translatable. He accomplished this with remarkable technical virtuosity, and his Alexandrines are usually in a natural, flowing, modern French:

> Tu reconnais en moi ce moment de l'année
> Où pendent aux rameaux qui tremblent dans le froid,
> Chœurs nus et délabrés, quelques feuilles fanées,
> Où des oiseaux naguère on entendait la voix.
> En moi tu vois aussi le feu crépusculaire
> Qui décline à l'ouest au coucher du soleil
> Et que doit emporter bientôt la nuit austère,
> Autre mort qui sur tout pose un sceau de sommeil.
> En moi tu vois encor rougeoyer cette flamme
> Gisante sur la cendre où sa jeunesse a lui

> Comme en un lit de mort où elle rendra l'âme,
> Consumée à son tour par ce qui la nourrit.
> Ce voyant, ton amour grandit pour mieux aimer
> Tout ce qu'avant longtemps il te faudra quitter.

Unfortunately, these lines give the impression, common in second-rate French poetry, that the matter has been subordinated to concerns of prosody. For purposes of rhyme, components of the imagery in lines 2 and 3 have been rearranged, and line 4 has been given a classical inversion, which seems out of character with Shakespeare. In line 9, *Gisante sur la cendre où sa jeunesse a lui,* the second hemistich is an amplification of what Shakespeare had written and an obvious *cheville* to stuff the line and provide a rhyme.

The translation of twenty-six sonnets by Phelps Morand (1960) is hardly worth mentioning either as poetry or as a serious attempt to translate Shakespeare, but it does afford some variety in this long list of translations with little formal innovation. Morand has completely abandoned the sonnet form, and his poem, which is printed to look like free verse, is actually in stanzas of irregular length in mixed lines of six, eight, ten, or twelve syllables with frequently occurring interior rhymes and alliteration. The first line constitutes the title.

L'EPOQUE DE L'ANNEE

> Que tu peux voir en moi
> Est celle où les feuilles jaunissent
> Se plissent et tombent déjà
> Dans le vent qui glisse
>
> En moi tu vois le crépuscule de ce jour
> Qui se fane vers l'occident en teintes grises
> Et que la nuit atteint de son pas lent
> La nuit qui ressemble à la mort et pose
> Son sceau
> Sur le parchemin fané par les ans
>
> En moi tu vois les cendres d'un tel feu
> Frémir en étincelle où la jeunesse expire
> Cendres d'un lit de mort qui se consume
> Rouges charbons déjà teintés de blanc

De les voir donne-t-il encore à ton amour
La force d'aimer ce qui meurt ce jour

Although a respected poet and novelist of the recent generation, Henri Thomas seems to have made little attempt to translate the Sonnets into poems that could stand on their own as poetry. He has given us, rather, reflections of the original in unrhymed, very free Alexandrines (1961).

> Tu contemples en moi ce moment de l'année
> Où des feuilles jaunies, quelques à peine, pendent
> A ces branches tremblant devers le froid, ruines
> Des chapelles où chantèrent les doux oiseaux.
>
> Tu vois en moi la fin du jour, soleil couché,
> Dont l'ultime clarté s'éteint à l'occident,
> Et peu à peu la nuit noire vient l'emporter,
> Seconde mort qui met le sceau sur toutes choses.
>
> Tu vois en moi la lueur dernière du feu
> Qui se couche sur les cendres de sa jeunesse,
> Lit de mort sur lequel il lui faut expirer
> Se consumant avec ce qui le nourrissait.
>
> Tu vois, et ton amour est plus fort, pour chérir
> Mieux encore ce que bientôt to devras perdre.

Perhaps the most remarkable innovation, if it can be called such, of this version is the literal translation of "with" in line 12 into *avec;* almost without exception earlier translators had used *par* or *de* to introduce the agent of the action, i.e., the fire was consumed *by* that which nourished it. Thomas was apparently the first to see that "with" could mean along with or at the same time as, which the French *avec* can denote. However, *contemples* in line 1, meaning to be absorbed in the observation of something, is certainly wrong, since the context makes it clear that by "behold" Shakespeare meant "discern." Otherwise this version lacks a unified tone because it is a conglomeration of heterogeneous material: the obsolete preposition *devers* (meaning "toward" or "in the direction of" —certainly not the right word for "against"), such modern and familiar locutions as *soleil couché* and the *Tu vois* without an object in line 13, and the ellipsis *quelques à peine* for *quelques-unes à peine.*

The following translation of Sonnet 73 (published in England in 1964) is given here mainly as a curiosity. Dikran Garabedian has done all of the Sonnets in the so-called *sonnet régulier* (*abba abba ccd ede*), which is used in France not so much by poets as by purists. Although the words are French this translation scarcely seems to be written in French; the translator has abandoned normal syntax for obsolete constructions (often incorrectly used), Anglicisms, and other bizarre forms.

> De l'an tu peux en moi contempler ce temps faire,
> Où feuilles jaunes, riens ou rares, vont pendant
> A ces branches vers la froidure grelottant,
> Chœurs nus, ruine, où doux oiseaux chantaient naguère.
>   En moi tu vois tel jour qui va crépusculaire,
> Dès le soleil couché, devers l'ouest se fadant,
> Pris tout de suite en la nuit noire l'emportant,
> Second soi de la Mort, qui tout au repos serre.
>   En moi tu vois tel feu, qui d'y luire en rougi
> Sur les cendres de la jeunesse sienne gît,
> Lit de mort sur lequel il faudra qu'il expire,
>   Consumé par ce dont s'était nourri ce feu.
> Ce tu perçois, dont ton amour plus fort se tire,
> A bien l'aimer, ce qu'il te faut laisser sous peu.

The most recent translation, by Armel Guerne (1965), illustrates a fault which, although it occurs in earlier translations as well, is most blatant here.

> En moi tu peux la voir, la saison de l'année
> Où, rare ou nul, se suspend un feuillage jaune
> À la branche des arbres frémissants de froid,
> Chœurs désertés, où naguère chantaient les doux oiseaux.
>
> En moi tu vois le crépuscule de ce jour
> Qui tombe à l'occident, après le coucher du soleil,
> Et que la noire nuit emporte peu à peu,
> Cette sœur de la mort, enfermant tout dans le repos.
>
> Ce que tu vois en moi, c'est la lueur du feu
> Qui gît, couché sur les cendres de sa jeunesse

Comme en ce lit de mort où il doit expirer,
Se consumant avec ce qui le nourrissait.

Tu le perçois, cela, qui fait ton sentiment plus fort,
Pour bien aimer ce que tu dois perdre bientôt.[12]

Here certain grammatical relationships are changed, which in turn changes the meaning of the lines in what is otherwise a fairly faithful rendering. In line 2, "yellow leaves" is made into the collective *feuillage jaune,* which stands in contradiction to *rare ou nul* at the beginning of the line. In line 3 *branche* is made singular, the plural *arbres* is added, and it is to the trees that the "Bare ruined choirs" are in apposition; it is no longer the boughs which shake against the cold, but the trees, which are trembling *with* rather than against the cold. A more substantial change in the meaning comes in lines 6 and 8. In the first of these, the elements of the image are reversed to make it clear that it is the twilight and not the sunset that fades in the west, but the image loses all sense of duration in the substitution of *qui* for "as" and *tombe* for "fadeth." In line 8 a relative clause is replaced by a participle clause: "that seals up all in rest" becomes *enfermant tout dans le repos.* What was in English a definition or a characterization of night as it always is becomes in the French version an action taking place at a particular time. In this way two syntactical alterations change the connotations of the entire quatrain from the general to the particular, from the eternal to the temporal.

One may safely conclude that no one translation of Sonnet 73 is fully satisfactory. Although some versions are more successful than others in one respect or another, and although certain of the more recent translators have solved difficulties that in the last century seemed insurmountable, the modern French reader who cannot read English does not have available to him an experience analogous to the one we meet when we read Shakespeare's Sonnets. By and large, the other sonnets are translated relatively less well than Sonnet 73, with, of course, certain exceptions. I should like now to examine in more detail and with references to several different sonnets the principal single weakness of the French translations, namely the inability of translators to account for and convey an entire complex of meaning. (The same could certainly be said, with some modification, of translations into any language.) A French translation of a sonnet always says both less and more than the original, that is, it fails to convey all the relevant connotations of the original lines and it inevitably adds irrelevant ones. Whether this is the fault of the translator or of the French language is still debatable, and it is not my intention to make judgments of this sort but to indicate the general areas in which the particular translations under consideration insufficiently transmit meaning and relevant connotations.

That the Sonnets are translated not only from one language to another but also from one form to another presupposes an alteration of content. In its broadest sense, Shakespeare's meaning undergoes a change, and in most cases it is a reduction, when it is shifted to French prose or molded to fit into Alexandrines. This is most apparent when one of his lines or images lends itself readily to conventional diction or versification in French. Some lines seem to demand an Alexandrine typical of Racine or even Baudelaire, and when they are cast into one of these molds they seem lost in foreign territory, uprooted from their own cultural context.

Line 4 of Sonnet 64, "And brass eternal slave to mortal rage," is one of those lines that cry out by virtue of their vocabulary for a classical, heroic Alexandrine reminiscent of Boileau and Corneille. The words suggest the noble, elevated poetic style in French, and the idea had been a classical commonplace since Du Bellay. It is perhaps for these reasons that it is rendered so often even by recent translators into the most banal and symmetric kind of Alexandrine:

Et la mort s'asservir jusqu'au bronze éternel   (Garnier)

Et le bronze éternel par la Mort asservi   (Le Brun)

Et l'airain éternel par la rage entravé   (Baldensperger)

Et l'airain obéir à la rage mortelle   (d'Uccle)

Et le bronze immortel à la mort asservi   (Fuzier)

It is curious that there is a certain variety in the words chosen by the different translators and that no two lines are exactly the same; yet the rhythm is as identical in these lines as poetic rhythm can be. They must all be scanned in the rigid 3-3-3-3. What is at fault here is not that a regular iambic pentameter has been transposed into a similarly regular Alexandrine but that the French Alexandrine is, under any circumstances, an improper vehicle for the Shakespearean line, and this point is made several times, in particular in the prefaces of those translators who work in prose; but since no other traditional French line is as versatile, the Alexandrine is the only possible compromise other than prose. Each compromise has its own particular insufficiency, of which the translators were undoubtedly aware. This one example, although an extreme one, serves to show at what disadvantage translators in verse find themselves at the outset. That Shakespeare's meaning should be altered or reduced when forced into a form that is incompatible to it is only natural.

It would seem that all of the translators considered here were aware of the difficulties presented by Shakespeare's ambiguity. Some of them mention it in the prefaces to their translations, and others refer to it in footnotes in which they give some of the possible meanings for particular words.[13] The difficulty becomes acute in the case of puns, and translators point out the impossibility of rendering such a word as "lie" in Sonnet 138. But, as anyone who has read the Sonnets closely knows, the most common problem of ambiguity in them is less spectacular; it involves an expression that may be understood in two or more ways which are permitted by the context and all of which say something that is essential to our understanding of the sonnet. Traditionally, French critics are less inclined to discern ambiguity in French poetry than English-speaking critics do in English poetry. Whether such a phenomenon derives from the characteristics of the language, of the poetry, or of the critics is difficult to ascertain, but the fact remains that the ambiguity of Shakespeare's language is somewhat, though of course not altogether, foreign to the French concept of poetry, and some translators seem to regard the inclusion of all possible meanings for a given expression of secondary importance to other considerations.

The eighth line of Sonnet 15, "And wear their brave state out of memory," is typical of the kind of ambiguity that appears so often in the Sonnets, yet it is not overly complex and its ambiguity is obvious because the line cannot be taken literally. Without attempting to exhaust the semantic possibilities of this line, it is clear that "wear" can mean to wear as clothes, or to wear out; "brave" has a number of relevant connotations: courageous, daring, gaudy, defiant, bold, or excellent; "state" refers to everything that concerns external or physical conditions; "out of memory" can be taken as analogous to the expression "out of sight," but it can also be analogous to the expression "out of habit." This last expression, "out of memory," can refer either to a period during one's life or after death. All of these possible meanings are relevant, and their sum constitutes the total meaning of the line. The French translators, almost without exception, accept only "wear out" for the verb and treat "out of memory" as meaning that it is forgotten. I give as an example only the best translation of the line: *effaçant leur éclat orgueilleux des mémoires* (d'Uccle).[14] *Eclat orgueilleux* comes about as close to including everything "brave state" suggests that we could expect, but since "wear" and "out of memory" have been reduced to one possibility for each, the French line is only a ghost of Shakespeare's original. Even in prose translations, where the translator is supposedly free to expand and elaborate in order to capture connotations that one or two French words cannot hope to convey, little attempt is made to do what is necessary; Jouve's prose line says no more than d'Uccle's Alexandrine: *puis effaçant leur valeureux éclat de la mémoire.* The weakening of this line is all the more striking because many of the translators exercised great ingenuity in their translation of the rest of the sonnet in order to include most if not all of the entangled conceits that make up Sonnet 15—often with considerable success (in particular, Fuzier and Le Brun).

The opposite phenomenon occasionally occurs, however: that is, when an English word is capable of several meanings most which are irrelevant to the context, and the French translator either includes some of these connotations or gives only one of the incorrect possibilities, as happens in the translation of the word "rack" in line 6 of Sonnet 33. In Shakespeare's line the word is used to denote a path of storm clouds or a driving mist or fog. Some translators use words that approach this: *amas, exhalaisons, brouillard,* and *vapeurs.* Two translators introduce a new metaphor: *rideaux.* In three translations, a horse's gait, a possible reading of "rack," is used, perhaps because it picks up the implications of "to ride" in line 5; thus Garnier, Legouis, and Guerne substitute *chevauchée*. Le Brun and Jouve translate "rack" as *traînée*, i.e., a trace or vestige. Less relevant are the following: F.-V. Hugo chooses the machine of torture, *roue;* Garabedian, *monture,* referring either to a mount or a framework (rack in the sense of clothes-rack). D'Uccle, on the other hand, translated not "rack" but "rake" (*râteaux!*). Other translators—Baldensperger, Prudhommeaux — avoid the word altogether.

In the example taken from Sonnet 15, the possible meanings ascribed to the words were important but not central to a reading of the entire sonnet. It occurs, however, that the translation of one ambiguous term can make or break the translation of a sonnet. The meaning of Sonnet 110 depends to a large extent on the value given to the word "truth" in line 5, and since no one French word can embrace the meanings given to the word "truth" by its context, the sonnet is virtually untranslatable unless the translator resorts to lengthy commentary or paraphrase. The sonnet resembles a set of variations on the theme of truth: lines 1 and 5 include the adjective "true," and "truth" in line 5 is set into strong relief by the enjambment. In line 1, "I have gone here and there" implies untruth in the sense of inconstancy. However one understands "motley" in line 2, the line declares that the speaker has been masked or inauthentic in one way or another in the eyes of others. Moreover, "motley" stands in opposition to "pure" in line 14, which implies "true" in the sense of "unmixed." "Proved" (line 8) and "proof" (line 11) connote the establishment of the truth of a statement. The statement "I have looked on truth / Askance and strangely" (1) sums up the kinds of untruth mentioned earlier in the sonnet and in the preceding sonnet, and (2) prepares for the oath in line 6, "but, by all above," which attests the truth of whatever the speaker is saying now as opposed to whatever untruths he may have said or lived in the past.

The main difficulty here is that the French word *vérité* does not mean "constancy" as well as "conformity to fact." Following are some of the solutions the translators have proposed. Ernest Lafond simply omits lines 5 and 6. Hugo and Henry translate "truth" as *bonne foi,* that is, sincerity, honesty, or a conviction that what one says is true. Some of the recent translators use *constance,* that is, a kind of perseverance in the same sentiments but without necessarily a commitment to them: *J'ai pu étrangement regarder la constance* (Fuzier). Others prefer *fidélité,* which implies a persevering observation of a duty and connotes a sense of dependence. Further from the original are those translations that do not describe the speaker's attitude toward truth but simply state that he has been unfaithful: *C'est bien vrai, je fus étrangement / déloyal, infidèle* (d'Uccle). The result in all of the translations where "truth" is taken as constancy or fidelity only is that the whole sonnet is reduced to a description of the return of the unfaithful lover and his request for forgiveness from the loved one.

While the majority of the translators render "truth" literally as *vérité,* the semantic insufficiency of this term is compounded by the unnecessary modification of the word's context. In the translations of Guizot, Montégut, and Guerne, the context of *vérité* is altered because the phrase that follows is weakened: "by all above," becomes *à tout prendre* or *après tout,* so that one of the main reasons for using the word "truth" in line 5 is left out, since it is not followed by an attestation of truth. That they have looked on *la vérité* strangely and with "discontent" has little bearing on the rest of the sonnet. Even though they retain the word *vérité,* Baldensperger, Prudhommeaux, and Morand translate these lines so freely that their meaning is entirely new: *Il est très vrai que de la vérité / J'ai fait mensonges* (Morand).

Two versions deserve special attention. Garnier is quite far from capturing the complexity of the quatrain, but he does establish a relationship between truth and fidelity. His translation makes clear that in abandoning his friend, the speaker is somehow foregoing truth as a fact and truth as an ideal. But this relative success is counteracted by the two flat and prosaic lines that follow:

> C'est trop vrai, j'ai tourné loin de la vérité
> Mes yeux indifférents; mais aux cieux j'en appelle,
> L'orage m'a rendu comme un deuxième été:
> Des feux plus violents l'amour sort plus fidèle.   (Garnier)

Jouve sacrificed the rest of the quatrain to relate "look askance on" and "blenches":

> Il est vrai que j'ai regardé ce qui est vrai, étrangement
> de travers, mais après tout, ces faux regards ont donné
> une autre jeunesse à mon coeur, et les pires essais te
> montrent le meilleur.   (Jouve)

Jouve has re-created the quatrain into an almost Shakespearean complexity with his play on *j'ai regardé ce qui est vrai ... de travers ... faux regards,* but it is a different kind of complexity and it no longer concerns either the truth of what the speaker is saying or his attitude toward constancy. One is tempted to conclude that Sonnet 110 is untranslatable, since the sixteen French translations considered here are so far from being satisfactory. Each one omits at least one essential part, each is like an incomplete poem, one that is missing a few lines. No one translation is able to say that constancy and truth to fact or to an ideal are the same or that in the end Truth and the Friend are one.

In some sonnets there are syntactical rather than semantic obstacles to a full rendering of the meaning. To illustrate this I should like to examine the French attempts to translate the optative at the beginning of Sonnet 116:

> Let me not to the marriage of true minds
> Admit impediments.

The vocabulary here presents no insurmountable difficulties; *admettre* is a good equivalent for "admit," *mariage* or *union* serve well in rendering "marriage."[15] The majority of translators use *fidèles* for "true," *âmes* for "minds," and *obstacles* for "impediments"; these last three are arguable, of course, and the equivalent legal term for "impediments" is *empêchements* (used in two translations), but it is a heavy, unpoetic word. Of nineteen translations of this sonnet, only two retained the optative in its normal French form, that is, a present subjunctive with future value, either introduced by *que* or with inversion of subject and verb:[16]

> Ah! puissé-je ne jamais apporter d'entraves au
> mariage de nos âmes fidèles!   (Hugo)

> Ne soit admise opposition au mariage des vrais esprits.
> (Jouve)

It is curious that although the same grammatical form is used, the tone in these sentences is entirely different. Hugo's version is exclamative and affective because of the addition of *Ah!* and *jamais;* Jouve's, on the other hand, is distant and almost legal in feeling, which derives from the initial *Ne soit,* the omission of the article before *opposition,* and the absence of any personal pronoun, which is an unjustifiable departure from the original. In four translations the exclamative rather than the optative form is used; the first line begins with the word *non,* and the verb is indicative present or future: *Non, je n'admettrai pas d'obstacles au mariage / Des cœurs sincères.* (Thomas; same form but different word order in Arnaud, Lafond, Garnier.) This is much stronger than an optative; it expresses a conviction rather than a hope. What is more serious, the *non* placed at the beginning of the first line implies a denial of the statement made in Sonnet 115, which in reality Sonnet 116, far from contradicting, amplifies and develops. This illustrates a tendency of some translators to consider individual sonnets in isolation rather than in the context of the sonnets immediately preceding and following them. The optative of Sonnet 116 is also rendered as the negative indicative, present or future, of *admettre,* with no exclamation: *je n'admets pas* or *point* (Guizot, d'Uccle, Fuzier, Mélot du Dy), or the negative indicative of some other verb (Henry, Morand). In other translations the verb is in the first-person plural imperative (Baldensperger, Guerne), which changes the "me" to "us," an obvious modification of the intent of the line. Other attempts to render the optative: *Je ne saurais admettre d'obstacle au mariage des âmes fidèles* (Montégut)—the auxiliary verb implies the negation of a possibility; *Je ne crois pas qu'il soit d'entrave aux unions / Des esprits vrais!* (Prudhommeaux)—a subjunctive of uncertainty. Le Brun tries to suggest the optative by means of a familiar syntax: *Aucun obstacle à l'union des cœurs fidèles! /En admettre un? non pas!* But the statement is categorical, and the sentence is without an explicit subject. Once again it seems that no translation of these two lines is satisfactory: in all of the French versions, the magnificent opening of this sonnet is either weakened or exaggerated.

Another aspect of the Sonnets that is rarely fully transmitted into French is the full impact of the images. A good example is the

first quatrain of Sonnet 33, not only because it is a well-known sonnet but also because of the frequency of the sunrise motif in French
Renaissance poetry:

> Full many a glorious morning have I seen
> Flatter the mountain tops with sovereign eye,
> Kissing with golden face the meadows green,
> Gilding pale streams with heavenly alchemy;

A tone of plenitude is established for the entire quatrain by the
first word, "Full." Unfortunately French syntax will not support
Shakespeare's word order, and even Garabedian, who follows
Shakespeare quite closely by disregarding French syntax, hits
below the mark because of the long, heavy, adverbial form of his
first word: *Pleinement maints matins glorieux ai-je vus.* Other
translators can only approximate the energy of the original: *Com-
bien de fois j'ai vu le matin glorieux* (Le Brun). In Shakespeare the
word "morning" serves as the object of "seen" and the subject of
"flatter," and it also has an adverbial sense in that it tells when the
action takes place. Thomas is one of the few translators to use
matin in the same way: *J'ai vu plus d'un matin radieux caresser /
Le haut des monts,* but compared to Shakespeare's lines or, in the
French tradition, to the opening lines of some of Scève's *dizains,* it
is inexpressive. Most of the other translators use *matin* in its adverbial sense only and use the sun or dawn as the center of the
image: *Bien des matins j'ai vu la gloire de l'aurore / Caresser les
sommets de ses regards royaux* (Garnier; the diction and rhythm
here compensate somewhat for the weak translation of "morning").

   Line 3, "Kissing with golden face the meadows green" is of particular interest because "with golden face" is not explicitly related
to the morning, the sun, kissing, or the meadows, with the result
that it refers to the whole morning, to the entire landscape
described by the speaker. It is not just that the sun has a golden
face as it kisses the meadows, but also the morning with its kiss
imprints on everything a golden, laughing face. Almost without
exception, the French translators associate "with golden face" exclusively with the sun: *De son visage d'or baisant l'herbe des prés*
(Fuzier). The only satisfactory French translation here is Le Brun's:
Posant sa face d'or sur les prés verts qu'il baise.

Miscomprehension on the part of the translator is another reason French translations of the Sonnets often seem dull and uninspired. A difficult poem like Sonnet 94 illustrates what happens when a translator does not understand the original text.

> They that have pow'r to hurt and will do none,
> That do not do the thing they most do show,
> Who, moving others, are themselves as stone,
> 4   Unmovèd, cold, and to temptation slow—
> They rightly do inherit heaven's graces
> And husband nature's riches from expense;
> They are the lords and owners of their faces,
> Others but stewards of their excellence.
> The summer's flow'r is to the summer sweet,
> Though to itself it only live and die;
> But if that flow'r with base infection meet,
> 12   The basest weed outbraves his dignity:
>   For sweetest things turn sourest by their deeds;
>   Lilies that fester smell far worse than weeds.

The difficulty seems to be mainly in the second quatrain, where the ambivalent and ironic attitude of the speaker toward the "unmoved mover" is missed, and the translators tend to give the entire description as favorable.

> Ceux-là héritent légitimement des grâces du ciel et économisent les richesses de la nature. Ils sont les seigneurs et maîtres de leur visage, et les autres ne sont que les intendants de leur excellence.   (Hugo)

> Ceux-là des dons du ciel sont les vrais légataires:
> La Nature les voit conserver ses trésors;
> —Seuls ils sont les seigneurs et maîtres de leurs corps
> Quand les autres n'en sont que les valets précaires.
>   (Henry)

The translators proceed more or less literally without attempting to set right the contradiction in their lines or to give consistency to the rest of the sonnet, with the result that the octave and the sestet make two irrelevant and even contradictory statements. Even in the later, more subtle translations the important distinctions are not made; unless "faces" (line 7) and "excellence" (line 8) are set in opposition, the distinction between "lords and owners" and "stewards" loses its meaning:

> Ceux-là sont, à bon droit, les favoris des Cieux,
> Car ils sont ménagers de leur magnificence
> Et maîtres souverains de leurs biens copieux;—
> Les autres, moins heureux, n'en ont que l'intendance.
>
> (Garnier)

Here "faces" have become fortunes, and the "stewards" are stewards of the same fortunes; this rules out Shakespeare's opposition between outward show and real quality, which is essential to the meaning of the quatrain. The same error appears in the translations of Baldensperger, Mélot du Dy, and Fuzier. Thomas renders the second quatrain ironically, but his irony becomes inappropriately sarcastic when he translates "stewards" with the often pejorative *commis:*

> Ceux-là sont justes possesseurs des dons célestes
> Et ne dissipent pas les trésors de nature;
> Ils sont les maîtres et seigneurs de leur visage,
> D'autres ne sont que les commis de leur beauté.

The best version of the octave is the following prose translation by Blanchard; it should be noted that the entire octave is made into one paragraph, which indicates that the object of the speaker's apparent admiration and later scorn is one and the same.

> Ceux qui peuvent tout le mal et ne le font point, ceux qui sont autres qu'ils ne paraissent, ceux qui, entraînant les hommes, sont comme la pierre, impassibles, froids et sourds à la tentation, ceux-là, comme il convient, recueillent les grâces du ciel, épargnent les richesses de la nature magnificente. Ils sont seigneurs et propriétaires de leurs grimaces. Les autres ne sont qu'intendants de leur grandeur.

It can be argued that *grimaces* is too strong a word for "faces" and that *grandeur* misses the point of "excellence" in that it might imply something put on rather than something real. Nevertheless,

Blanchard's emphasis interprets the lines correctly, and the values of his words, although they make the irony more explicit than Shakespeare may have intended, are at least relevant. Unfortunately, in translating the couplet Blanchard commits an error that is common to most of the translations:

> Les plus douces choses deviennent les plus amères et
> les lis qui pourrissent sentent beaucoup plus mauvais
> que les herbes.

The word "deeds" from the original has been omitted, and we are not told why "sweetest things" turn sour. It is by virtue of the word "deeds" that the couplet is related to the rest of the sonnet, for it is deeds inconsistent with sweetness that make the sweetest things turn sour. Some translators, aware that they are working with moral poetry, relate the sonnet to the nonpoetic French tradition of the moralists and turn the couplet into a maxim: *Si doux qu'il soit, tout bien par l'abus est gâté* (Henry). Thus line 13 becomes a kind of eternal truth independent of daily contingencies, of time, and, in this particular case, of the rest of the sonnet. Like Blanchard and Henry, most translators omit "deeds" in their translation, and they add other reasons to explain why the sweetest things turn sour. For Baldensperger it is when they are used: *Les plus grandes douceurs à l'usage s'aigrissent;* for Le Brun if they happen to turn sour, they are very bad: *Les plus douces douceurs, s'aigrissant, sont les pires;* for others, it is simply in the nature of sweetest things to turn sour: *Rien ne s'aigrit si bien que la suavité,* Mélot du Dy (similarly, Garnier, d'Uccle, and Fuzier). This, of course, makes the sonnet fall apart, for the word "deeds" is essential to the meaning of line 13, and it is line 13 that explains why the "unmoved movers" and the "owners of their faces" can be like the summer flower that meets with infection. Jouve and Thomas attempt to clarify the line:

> Car la plus douce chose en acte devient aigre (Jouve)

> Le plus doux s'il déchoit devient le plus amer (Thomas)

But Jouve's *en acte* wrongly suggests actions consistent with *la plus douce chose,* and Thomas's *s'il déchoit* leaves the cause of decline unexplained.[17]

None of the translations of Sonnet 94 is faithful enough to the subtle texture of the original to convey its meaning. The same might be said of the French translations of the rest of the Sonnets, for although they seem by-and-large less difficult, most of them are either too subtle or too complex (or even too simple) to be transmitted accurately. That the French translations of the Sonnets are not satisfactory was, to be sure, predictable, but are we to conclude that they are untranslatable? Le Brun, d'Uccle, Blanchard, and Jouve did render a number of lines without losing the meaning and tone of the original. Furthermore, it is undeniable that the translations have improved since the last century, and with the increasing frequency with which translations of the Sonnets are being published in France, it is likely that their quality will continue to improve and that one day an acceptable version will exist.

Yet it is also undeniable that the French translations already published impress English-speaking readers as being, with the exceptions noted above, inaccurate, insipid, and generally lacking in what makes Shakespeare a great poet. Are we to conclude, then, that the effort of French translators has been wasted? The effect of the translations on French poets or even on the literate public could not be measured without considerable documentation. But from the above analyses, it is safe to conclude that the French translations do give, with varying success, a kind of pale reflection of the original; they can suggest what the Sonnets are like, and perhaps this is all that can be justly expected of them.

French Translations of Shakespeare's Sonnets

A Bibliography

There have no doubt been a number of translations of the Sonnets in private printings and strictly limited editions that are not in the collections of the Paris libraries, and they are not included here. This bibliography also omits mention of anthologies of

English poetry in translation and translations of individual sonnets published in reviews or included in the collected poetry of the translators. A number of well-known translations of Shakespeare's works (e.g., those of Benjamin Laroche, Francisque Michel) do not include the Sonnets.

Arnaud, Simone, trans. "Les Sonnets de Shakespeare." *La Nouvelle Revue,* LXXI (July–August, 1891), 537-555. (Translation of 24 Sonnets with commentary.)

Baldensperger, Fernand, trans. *Les Sonnets de Shakespeare.* Berkeley and Los Angeles: University of California Press, 1943. (English text included; "Key to the Sonnets as Rearranged.")

Blanchard, Maurice, trans. *William Shakespeare. Douze Sonnets.* Paris: Editions des Quatre Vents, 1944.

Copin, Alfred, trans. *Les Sonnets de Shakespeare.* Paris: A. Dupret, 1888.

Fuzier, Jean. Translation of Sonnets in *Shakespeare. Œuvres complètes.* Edited by Henri Fluchère, Preface by André Gide. Vol. I. Paris: Gallimard, 1959.

Garabedian, Dikran, trans. *The Sonnets of Shakespeare: Translated into French "Regular" Sonnets.* Oxford: University Press, 1964. (English text included.)

Garnier, Charles-Marie, trans. *Les Sonnets de Shakespeare: Essai d'une interprétation en vers français.* Cahiers de la Quinzaine, vol. 8, cahiers 7 and 15. Paris, 1906 and 1907.

Guerne, Armel, trans. *William Shakespeare: Poèmes et sonnets.* Edited by José Axelrad, with introduction and notes by Patrick Rafroidi and Jean-Paul Hulin. Paris: Desclée de Brouwer, 1964. (Volume IV of *Œuvres complètes de William Shakespeare.* English text included.)

Guizot, François, trans. *Œuvres complètes de Shakspeare,* 8 Vols. Rev. ed. Paris: Didier, 1862. (Sonnets in Vol. VIII.)

Henry, Fernand, trans. *Les Sonnets de Shakspeare, traduits en sonnets français.* Paris: Ollendorff, 1900. (English text included.)

Hugo, François-Victor, trans. *Les Sonnets de William Shakespeare, traduits pour la première fois en entier.* Paris: Michel Lévy, 1857. (With a concordance of French and English editions.)

Jouve, Pierre Jean, trans. *Shakespeare: Sonnets.* Paris: Le Sagittaire, 1955.

Lafond, Ernest, trans. *Poëmes et sonnets de William Shakespere.* Paris: Lahure, 1856. (Translation of 48 Sonnets.)

Le Brun, Emile, trans. *Shakespeare: Les Sonnets.* Introduction by Valery Larbaud. Paris: J. Schiffrin, 1927. (English text included.)

Legouis, Emile, trans. *Shakespeare.* Pages choisies des grands écrivains, Vol. XLVI. Paris: Armand Colin, 1899. (Includes translation of 31 Sonnets.)

Mélot du Dy, Robert, trans. *XXV Sonnets de Shakespeare.* Brussels: Editions du Cercle d'Art, 1943.

Montégut, Emile, trans. *Œuvres complètes de Shakespeare,* 10 Vols. Paris: Hachette, 1867–1873. (Sonnets in Vol. X, 1873.)

Morand, Phelps, trans. *Elisabethains: Le roman d'un mistère.* Paris: Editions Sésame, 1960. (Translation of 26 Sonnets in whole or in part.)

Pichot, Amédée. Translation of "Choix de sonnets" in *Œuvres Complètes de Shakspeare.* Translated by Letourneur. New ed. revised by François Guizot and Amédée Pichot, 12 Vols. Paris: Ladvocat, 1821. (No Sonnets included in earlier Letourneur translations; Sonnets 25, 29, 37, 71, 73, and 102 are translated in Vol. I of this edition.)

Prudhommeaux, André, trans. *Les Sonnets de Shakespeare: Essai d'interprétation poétique française.* Porrentruy, Switzerland: Editions des Portes de France, 1945.

Roth, Georges, trans. *Œuvres choisies de Shakespeare,* 5 Vols. Paris: Larousse, 1924-1926. (Sonnets in Vol. V.)

Thomas, Henri, trans. *Sonnets de Shakespeare, suivis de le Phoenix et la colombe.* Paris: Union Générale d'Editions, 1965. (First printed in *Shakespeare: Œuvres complètes.* Edited by P. Leyris and H. Evans. Paris:, Club Français du Livre, 1961, Vol. VII.)

Uccle, Giraud d', trans. *William Shakespeare. Sonnets.* Algiers: Edmond Charlot, 1942. (Sonnets 1-126 only.)

Since the completion of this bibliography, the following French translations of the Sonnets have been published:

Astrow, Igor, trans. *Shakespeare. Cent Sonnets en vers français.* Geneva: Perret-Gentil, 1968.

Jouve, Pierre Jean, trans. *William Shakespeare. Sonnets.* Paris: Mercure de France, 1969. (First published 1955.)

Mansat, André, trans. *Shakespeare. Sonnets.* Paris: Marcel Didier, 1970.

Rousselot, Jean, trans. *Les Sonnets de Shakespeare.* Paris: Seghers, 1969.

THE SYLLABLES OF SHAKESPEARE'S SONNETS

BY

PAUL RAMSEY

===

SOME PRELIMINARY ARGUMENTS

THE purpose of this essay, a preliminary study to both a critical study and an edition of Shakespeare's Sonnets,[1] is to try to answer a minor but vexing question, "How many syllables occur in each foot of Shakespeare's sonnets?" The answer given is "two." Put differently, the question is, "How deal with the apparent extra syllables in these poems?" I exclude the feminine endings, which are genuine extra syllables and not relevant to this discussion, except in a freakish instance discussed later (in note 43). The question admits of three answers, each corresponding to a position held by scholars: (1) that they are simply syllables, to be sounded and counted metrically; (2) that they are light (or semi-) syllables, lightly sounded and not counted metrically; (3) that they do not exist: "they" are neither pronounced nor counted metrically.

The first position has been held by George Saintsbury, and by Laura Riding and Robert Graves,[2] who hold that the Sonnets include anapests. The second is the prevalent view, and held by an impressive array of scholars, including Jakob Schipper, Norman Ault, and A. W. Partridge, for Elizabethan poetry generally; C. H. Herford and others, for Ben Jonson;[3] and W. G. Ingram and Theodore Redpath, for the sonnets of Shakespeare in their recent edition, in which they state that in the 1609 edition of the Sonnets the apostrophe indicates "a lightening or semi-elision of a syllable" and believe that to take, for instance, "th'expence" as "disyllabic" is "entirely false" and destructive of "many delicate rhythms."[4] Their view for "th'expence" is, I believe, demonstrably false, as I shall attempt to show. They also concern themselves only rarely with the apparent syllables where no apostrophe is involved, a lack that further weakens the text of an edition in most respects highly admirable. The third position has been held by B. A. P. van Dam and Cornelis Stoffel (for Elizabethan poetry generally). and by Helge Kökeritz (for Shakespeare generally):[5] namely, that two syllables metrically are two syllables linguistically and that no anapests or semi-elisions occur in the Sonnets. This essay supports the third position, for the Sonnets, and strictly only for them, even though a good deal of the evidence goes beyond. One of the frustrations of trying to settle such questions is that finally one has to decide the question for a particular text by separate scrutiny; I offer that sort of scrutiny only to one book.

The positions are not so discrete as my summary suggests. The semi-elision theory is really a special case of the anapest theory, and could more simply be described as the "light anapest theory." What is claimed is that light extra syllables are allowed, and to say that they occasion light anapests would explain them without severing metrical and linguistic reality. The very severance is telling. The semi-elisionist, presumably recognizing that Elizabethan prosody is strict, and not wishing to admit certain reductions, has recourse to a theory that oddly separates meter and sound.

Positions (2) and (3) are not sharply divided because syllables in our speech are not always neatly countable: borderline instances occur. Position (3), however, explains such instances more logically than (2). To say that certain syllables are borderline instances, but counted by Elizabethans sonally and metrically as one, makes better sense than (again) to divide meter and sound. The burden of proof is on those who divide practice from theory. What must be explained as genuinely extra? In Shakespeare's sonnets, nothing. Further, the problem arose largely because of gaps between Elizabethan orthography and nineteenth- and twentieth-century linguistic and aesthetic understanding. To show that there is no such gap in many instances of Elizabethan practice is to dissolve much of the need for a semi-elision theory.

Nonetheless, some variety of practice may have occurred. It is hard to show that it did not. One can show that reductions we would not expect often happened and were by prosodists and some poets deliberately intended. One cannot very well show that in the reading of poems light extra syllables were never pronounced. Unless a reader is deliberately and unremittingly careful of metrical demands (and actors are not typically the most pedantic people in the world), he would tend to pronounce variant forms variously without precise regard to the meter. If readers were as careless as spellers (poets, scribes, editors, and compositors) in showing metrical forms, then there was inconsistency in practice.

At least four considerations, however, suggest that the inconsistency was infrequent in practice and that the disyllabism was formally and deliberately made plain in reading. First, the variant doublets discussed in a section below were clearly meant to exhibit sharp difference of pronunciation. Second, the figures discussed by rhetoricians of the period included deliberate distortions, including syllabic change for the sake of meter (e.g., aphaeresis, syncope, apocope) and for the sake of rhyme (antisthecon).[6] Third, there is the rather artificial rhyme of such instances as "perpetuall." and "thrall" of Sonnet 154, line 10, and 154.12, which likewise suggests some forcing of pronunciation to make two syllables of "-uall." Fourth, there is an interesting passage in Campion not immediately concerned with syllabic count. He writes, objecting to pyrrhic substitutions in English poems, that such substitutions curtail the "verse, which they [the poets] supply in reading with a ridiculous, and vnapt drawing of their speech. As for example: *Was it my desteny, or dismall chaunce?'*"[7] That is, it was the practice of poets in reading their verse to pronounce sometimes such words as "destiny" as three syllables, with the third syllable artificially drawn out. Poets pronounced their lines to fit the meters.

Van Dam and Stoffel damage their case by many of their ruthless and linguistically implausible reductions (Kökeritz himself objects to these), and by their scornful refusal to admit the existence of borderline syllables. Kökeritz hurts his case by the aesthetic circularity I shall shortly discuss, and by the following considerable admission (his eyes were at the moment on another target than the semi-elisionists): "In fact, we have no means of determining today the quantity of the sounds used in *I'm* and *I am;* the former might have been emotionally prolonged to [aˈɪmː] and the latter uttered very rapidly, perhaps [aɪam]."[8] If so far, then a little further or shorter to syllabic inconsistency. "We have no means of determining" with certainty.

Some inconsistency of practice probably occurred; that does not mean that apparent extra syllables were regularly lightly pronounced or so pronounced by deliberate aesthetic choice or semi-elision theory. The evidence is that a strict disyllabism was intended in the Sonnets (and probably in much other poetry).

THE AESTHETIC ARGUMENT

The danger of circularity in discussing these questions is manifest. Kökeritz brings a wide and subtle linguistic knowledge to bear on Shakespeare's pronunciation, but is plainly circular when he discusses the matter theoretically, offering the dubious aesthetic premise that "Shakespeare was an accomplished metrist and that consequently his verse was intrinsically regular."[9] Once one assumes this, the matter is settled, and each apparent extra syllable has to be explained away. In actual practice, however, Kökeritz handles his evidence more flexibly and sensibly than do van Dam and Stoffel.

Circularity exists on the other (semi-elisionist) side, as when A. C. Partridge writes that Kökeritz shows an "insensibility to Shakespeare's skill in modulating . . . for dramatic purposes—an aesthetic gift to which systems of typography could hardly do justice."[10] Pushed to the end of its logic, that position would mean that one could ignore any evidence for disyllabism, since Shakespeare was on presumption too fine an artist to submit to such an aesthetically narrow system. In practice, Partridge is a careful observer of orthographic niceties, but the pressure of the assumption is there.

The aesthetic argument on either side is unconvincing because (1) modern rather than Elizabethan aesthetic assumptions intrude (of course Elizabethan and modern aesthetics overlap greatly, but the differences are for this issue crucial); and (2) the difference is *not aesthetically important enough* to be conclusive. Kökeritz seems to be saying that rigor is the essence of good metrics; Partridge is saying that subtle modulation is essential. He speaks of "Shakespeare's subtly modulated accentual rhythms" in the later plays, as opposed to the "old Marlovian pattern," and says that the "English ideal was not metrical regularity."[11]

The trouble is that both are right—that is, when exclusive, wrong. The aesthetic truth is that a firm base which allows for subtle rhythmical variety makes for a sound and beautiful poetry, and that Shakespeare's poetry achieves this whether or not his "elisions" are reductions or slurs. He had at his disposal the firm base of the iambic pentameter, with allowable trochaic, pyrrhic, and spondaic substitutions, with a great range of actual stress within the pattern of relative stress, with more variant syllabic forms than in modern English, with great freedom of syntax, and with no rules except the idioms of the language governing the variety of quantity, timbre, speed, phrasing, and pausing. Such a metrical system is a magnificent instrument, and we know how magnificently he used it, with or without light extra syllables. Certainly he could have used the choice of sometime-elision, sometime-semi-elision for delicate rhythmical effects, as Ingram and Redpath and others would have. Wallace Stevens in "Sunday Morning" uses a similar metrical system with profound and exquisite success. The question is, whether Shakespeare did, on the available evidence.

The simplest, and perhaps the most sensible and generous course, would be to say with Abbott that "it is impossible to tell" whether some syllables are lightened or omitted, and go on to more interesting matters.[12] But the problem vexes, and sometimes one can tell.

I was persuaded of the semi-elision theory, and I have changed my mind on the evidence I have encountered. That in itself proves nothing—one can change and become wrong—but at least it should suggest I have not merely trundled the evidence to the tune of a prior theory. I felt that the strict disyllabic theory was crude aesthetically and unnatural linguistically, and thus perhaps I am in fair position to explain the objection, having shared it.

The modern feeling that elision is crude and unnatural is at least threefold. First, forms or reductions not in present English sound unnatural to us—but the evidence is clear that such forms and reductions often did exist in Elizabethan speech and poetry. Second, we object to poetic license, to changing or distorting speech forms for metrical purposes—but Tudor and Elizabethan poets availed themselves of a good many licenses overtly recognized in works on prosody and rhetoric. This modern objection, which is called "naturalistic" by Chatman,[13] is accompanied by a curious companion, not mentioned by Chatman, not very consistent with "naturalism": third, the feeling that poetry should be formal and not indulge in colloquial contractions and reductions—but Elizabethan poetry uses them high and low.[14] Poetry must be like speech, we tend to think, but it must not be like actual speech. All poetry, by its nature, combines the natural and the artificial, but our notion of what of artifice and nature is allowed blocks our view of Elizabethan practice.

All three of these feelings, in strong combination, work for the semi-elision theory and against disyllabism; and, whatever else may or may not be concluded, it is certain that Elizabethan theory and practice contradict all three. This does not automatically mean that Shakespeare's sonnets use no extra syllables or glides, but it shows that when modern critics feel that Elizabethan poetry must have used such glides they are being manifestly unhistorical.

Some Metrical Fundamentals

Since tacit metrical assumptions can be variously confusing or question-begging, I shall—before looking at the specific evidence —offer some general ideas about meter.

Verse is language in meter. Meter means measure. Various features of language can be made into metrical framings. Accentual-syllabic verse, the most important and widespread verse in England and America from the late sixteenth to the twentieth century (it was also much used in the Middle Ages, and is still widely used), consists of certain patternings of stress, or accent, with syllables.

Stress is whatever gives prominence to a syllable, involving loudness, pitch, length, and quality, with loudness and pitch predominant. Metrical stress, or ictus, is relative. All syllables have some stress (or would be silences), and many actual degrees of stress exist. In meter, a syllable is stressed if it has more prominence than the other syllable or syllables in the foot. Feet do not represent a rhythmical shape (phrasing and pausing in a line being independent of the feet), but divide a line metrically according to the principle of simplicity to show fundamental patterns of stressed and unstressed syllables.

What a syllable is, is (if possible!) even less clear than what a stress is (a mild handicap to writers about iambic meters). English vowels tend to diphthongization, with even such a nearly pure vowel as the "i" of "it" admitting a little glide. Hence, if one seeks a pure vowel per syllable, there are no pure syllables in English. There is no clear line between a vowel and diphthong or a diphthong and two syllables. Some words occupy a borderline between one and two syllables. Words of the -our series (hour, power, flower, and such) include in present English either a very complex diphthong or are two syllables, and have been counted as one or two syllables metrically for over three centuries. Words with light final -n (heaven, even, and such) can also represent one or two syllables, and can represent four distinct stages: hevn [hevn], flatly one syllable; hevn [hevn̠], with syllabic n; hevun [hɛvən], two syllables with reduced vowel; heven [héven], two syllables with full vowel. The first and fourth probably do not occur in speech, but could occur in verse, since meter puts some pressure on pronunciation. This uncertainty of boundary has been recognized for some centuries. Alexander Hume wrote in a seventeenth-century manuscript, "we in manye places soe absorb l and n behynd a consonant . . . that the ear can hardlie judge quhither their intervenes a voual or noe."[15]

Further, syllabification in English is moderately fluid. Words often lose syllables historically and much less often add them, and many simultaneous variant forms exist, words with medial -r or -er being one of the strongest examples. Hatred is two syllables in present English; mystery can be clearly two or three syllables, or something in between. Even greater freedom of syllabification existed in Elizabethan English.

An important principle in metrics, as elsewhere, is Occam's Razor, the principle "Do not multiply entities without necessity." It involves two points, both important: (1) one should use the simplest explanation that covers all the evidence; (2) one should not simplify: the explanation should cover all the evidence. One should be careful not to reduce everything to one of two alternative explanations, when both may occasionally have applied, even when one is predominant. A lion cage is occupied some of the time by people, or sparrows. Thus in the present discussion one should realize that, even though disyllabism seems to account for all the evidence, something like semi-elision may also have occasionally occurred: it did at least for a moment in the mind of George Puttenham. A danger of the Razor is that it tends to exclude the unusual just because it is unusual: it requires some imagination not to tidy up the untidy too nicely. But the Razor is, after cautions, a very valuable principle. It is essential in describing feet, since without it any wild description that fits the facts would be allowable: for instance, scanning—in a Pickwickian sense correctly—a regular iambic pentametric line as anacrusis amphimacer amphibrach trochee truncated foot [x/x/ x/x /x l].[16] Five iambs make better sense. It is by the Razor that the Riding and Graves view can be called "anapestic." For any extra unstressed syllable within a line (feminine endings work differently) can be described using the anapest as the only trisyllabic foot. Thus /xxx/x/x/x/ is *diiii,* but also *taiii,* x/xx/x/x/x/ is *biiii,* but also *iaiii,* and so forth.

Substitution is the use of a different kind of foot than the predominant one. Thus trochees (and pyrrhics and spondees) frequently appear in iambic lines. Strict iambics I shall define, stipulatively but not randomly, as iambics that never (or only rarely) allow trisyllabic substitutions. Thus, by these definitions, the Riding and Graves position implies that Shakespeare wrote loose iambics, Kökeritz's position, that Shakespeare wrote strict iambics; and the semi-elision position sits a tricky fence between.

THE EVIDENCE

What is the evidence? First, a statement by contemporaries about Shakespeare's metrical intent. Second, the more or less contemporary prosodists. Third, certain features of the 1609 text.

HEMINGE AND CONDELL

Heminge and Condell, in their preface to the First Folio—"To the Great Variety of Readers"—claim to offer texts as "absolute in their numbers, as he [Shakespeare] conceiued them."[17] They were actors who had worked with Shakespeare and who had read verse on the stage; they were Shakespeare's contemporaries and friends.

Partridge, who takes them to be supporting strict disyllabism, goes to some pains to attempt to discredit their testimony.[18] The testimony is hard to discredit, but it may be merely a general praise of Shakespeare's rhythmical powers and a claim that Heminge and Condell represent accurately his metrical intent without specifying what his metrical intent exactly is. Still, the suggestion of strict syllabic count is strong. Uncountable numbers are hardly "absolute."

THE PROSODISTS

The evidence of the prosodists has its frustrations. It is troublesome to cite what a prosodist says about an issue when in the same passage he is making bad prosodical mistakes. Late sixteenth- and early seventeenth-century prosodists were seriously confused about a number of issues, most notoriously but not exclusively about the relation of accent to quantity. None of them seem to understand the Razor.

Further, "contemporary" is not always contemporary. 1575 or even 1580 is a long, long way from the 1590s, metrically speaking. The transition from Gascoigne, with his great talent but over-strict prosody (no substitutions in theory and few in practice, strongly reinforced lines, and a pause normally after the fourth syllable), to Sidney and Marlowe and Shakespeare shows an astonishing change of practice, one of the greatest triumphs of the poetic spirit in any nation. Consequently, the casual lumping together of even two decades of prosodists can mislead.

Nonetheless, the evidence of the prosodists is, I feel, after making what I hope are sufficient allowances for the slipperiness of some of the evidence, strongly on the side of disyllabism rather than semi-elisionism or trisyllabic substitution.

The controversy I deal with is an old one: it goes back to the 1580s when *The Arte of English Poesie* was published. Puttenham seems at moments to support in a muddled way both the anapestic and the semi-elision positions. In Book 2, chapter 14, he quotes several lines of poetry, including the following from Wyatt:

$$- \;\smile\smile$$
The furi ous gone in his most raging ire. [sigla his]

Then he writes:

> And many moe which if ye would not allow for *dactils*
> [by my scanning, anapests] the verse would halt vnless
> ye would seeme to kepe it contracting a sillable by ver-
> tue of the figure *Syneresis* which I think was neuer their
> meaning, nor in deede would haue bred any pleasure to
> the eare, but hindred the flowing of the verse.[19]

Like Ingram and Redpath, Partridge, Ault, and the others, Puttenham objects on aesthetic grounds to cutting out a syllable. But
he does admit the possibility of the reduction and even seems to
feel it as the ordinary explanation.

Elsewhere he wanders, for a moment, into the semi-elision position, or something like it:

> [Our] odde [i.e., extra] sillable . . . is in a maner
> drownd and supprest by the flat accent [i.e., is a light
> unaccented syllable], and shrinks away as it were inau-
> dible and by that meane the odde verse comes almost to
> be an euen in euery mans hearing.[20]

Van Dam and Stoffel cite this passage and dismiss it as "absolutely
worthless."[21] Such a statement is extravagant and eristic. Yet, as
the following five points show, the evidence of Puttenham, while
something, is not very much.

First, he is thinking quantitatively (about verse that was not
written quantitatively!), and his position exemplifies anapestism or
semi-elisionism only in so far as he gets quantitative and accentual
confused. Remove that confusion, and what he says would be simply irrelevant, since, among other things, quantitative verse allows
the mixing of trisyllabic and disyllabic feet.

Second, he is puzzled and conscious that he offers an unusual
explanation, rejecting the more normal explanation (syneresis).

Third, none of his examples require a semi-elisionist or anapestic explanation; each fits a disyllabic explanation as well or
better. In the immediate contexts of the two quotations I have discussed, he quotes nine lines that involve one or more extra syllables. Some have feminine endings. Some are either hexameters or
feminine lines with contractions. The others admit obvious contractions, as in the three following.

Shed Caesars teares vpon Pompeius hed

The furious gone in his most raging ire

So is my painefull life the burden of ire.

The first two can be examples of synizesis (the consonantization of a vowel resulting in syllabic reduction): Pompa'yus [pompéjas] and fur'yus [fyú:ʎjas]. Light final *en* in words such as burd*en* is frequently nonsyllabic in the period.

His explanation is aimed at explaining all such syllables and makes absolutely no sense whatever for the feminine lines or the hexameters. So, in several of his examples he is plainly, even wildly, wrong; and in the remaining examples he has at the very best only an equal chance of offering a correct explanation. Which is to thin the odds considerably.

Fourth, he is talking about an earlier poetry before iambic disyllabism was settled on, and is trying to explain that poetry in terms that make sense with the disyllabism of Gascoigne and others in the late 1570s and early 1580s. That is, he is committing an anachronism similar to that of the modern semi-elisionists.

Fifth, he is confused about scansion, and is inconsistent even for an Elizabethan prosodist in many of his metrical positions.

Put the other way, his evidence, if not much, is something. The main point is simply that all the other evidence cuts precisely across his momentary views.

THE COUNT OF SYLLABLES

King James writes, "zour first syllabe in the lyne be short, the second lang, the thrid short, the fourt lang, . . . and sa furth to the end of the lyne."[22] This is strictly disyllabic, and, despite his use of "short" and "lang," in its context essentially accentual.

George Gascoigne says "we [English versifiers] use none other order but a foote of two sillables. . . ."[23] Thomas Campion says ". . . when we speake of a Poeme written in number, we consider . . . distinct number of the sillables. . . ."[24] Samuel Daniel says that "Iambique verse in our language . . . [is] the plaine ancient verse consisting of ten sillables or fiue feete," elsewhere admitting the one exception, "our verse of eleuen sillables, in feminine Ryme."[25] Abraham Fraunce says that "Rime [i.e., rhymed verse] containeth a certaine number of sillables ending alike."[26] William Webbe speakes of verse as "measurable Speeche . . . framed in wordes contayning numbers or proportions of iust syllables. . . ."[27]

THE ACTUAL REDUCTION OF SYLLABLES

What applies to Latin verse does not necessarily apply to English verse, but the terms "elision" and "synaloepha" derive from Latin prosody, where the terms clearly refer to the actual dropping of a syllable. Thus John Palsgrave in his translation of *Acolastus* (1540) says that "Synaloepha" means that a vowel shall be "lefte unscanned or sounded," that is, not counted metrically or pronounced.[28]

In English verse the omission or reduction of syllables comes sometimes from the actual speech habits of Elizabethans, as Kökeritz, Dobson,[29] Partridge, and others have clearly shown. Other reductions come from the "metaplasms" discussed by the rhetoricians: changes of letter or syllables for metrical purposes. Similar changes are called "poeticall license" by Gascoigne, who gives many examples, including such examples as *"orecome* for *ouercome"* and *"tane* for *taken,"* in which the spelling makes certain that an actual syllabic reduction is involved.[30]

In the very passage cited in Puttenham that attacks a strict disyllabism, a sturdy piece of evidence occurs against one sort of semi-elision favored by Ingram and Redpath. Puttenham gives "Th'enemie" as a "dactil," thus:

Th'enemie

That is, he assumed no syllabic problem whatever in "Th'en-". It was just pronounced as one syllable.

Peacham says that in *Synalaepha,* one vowel "is cut of[f]" and gives as an example "t'aske for to aske."[31] No glide, but a cutting. We are very apt to feel that a contraction we still use, such as "it's," was a contraction, but that where we relax a vowel and glide, as in "The enemy" or "To ask," that the Elizabethans did *not* contract. But the firm evidence is that they did.

Campion includes among examples of *elision* "t'inchaunt," "th'inchaunter," along with "let's," "hee's," and others.[32] All are treated as contractions without a difference in pronunciation: they are simply shortened.

Ingram and Redpath, as I noted above,[33] feel that it is "entirely false" to think of "th'expense" as actually "disyllabic," an assertion contradicted by Puttenham, Sidney, and Campion, and by the statement that follows about the nature of "apostrophus."

Jonson, in *The English Grammar,* speaks plainly: "*Apostrophus* is the rejecting of a Vowell from the beginning, or ending of a Word." He gives among his examples "th'outward" and "th'inward," saying that in such cases the vowel is "cast away."[34] Jonson speaks with some authority, as poet and observer (and as Shakespeare's friend), and "rejecting" and "cast away" are metaphors impossible to square with lightening or semi-elision. Either his theory and practice were radically inconsistent, or Herford and Simpson, and Partridge, are in error in believing that his pronunciation in *Sejanus* and elsewhere indicates semi-elision. My present opinion is that such a form in Jonson as "you 'are" means "you're" (or "y'are") though the question is worth some further study.

VARIANT FORMS

The existence of words with variant syllabic forms in Elizabethan English is unmistakable on all sorts of evidence. It will be abundantly exemplified in my discussion of the 1609 edition, and is not contested. Ingram and Redpath themselves point out correctly in a footnote that "spatious" and "gracious" are trisyllabic in Sonnet 135, lines 5 and 7, implicitly recognizing that the *-cious* ending is normally monosyllabic in the Sonnets.

The existence of such forms does not as such disprove the semi-elision theory, but it tilts strongly against it. Time and time again, forms that seem to us irreducible are in fact reducible by a full syllable in Elizabethan speech and poetry. As the discussion that precedes and follows should show, the cases that seem strongly to work against disyllabism vanish when we look carefully at the text and at Elizabethan practice.

In any instance of variant syllabic forms for a word, it is possible that the poet intended for the longer nonmetrical form to be sounded for (speculative) aesthetic reasons; hence one cannot refute the semi-elisionists by showing forms with actual syllabic reductions. But the semi-elision theory for such instances offends against the Razor, and is anachronistic: no one balks at forms with actual syllabic reductions in present English being reduced to the metrical requirements in Elizabethan poems; it is the forms which lack reductions now that call forth the imagined need for light extra syllables or glides. Consequently, the existence of variant forms in each relevant instance shows that the semi-elision theory is for that instance most probably false. But the relevant instances in the 1609 text are all the instances.

THE TEXT

The 1609 edition of Shakespeare's Sonnets is virtually the only authority we have for these poems except for the two sonnets printed earlier in the unauthorized *The Passionate Pilgrim,* which have no independent metrical value for my purposes. The 1609 edition has some fifty errors and (this it shares with a good many other books and with manuscripts) many metrical inconsistencies.[35] In my judgment, it was unauthorized but came from a fairly good manuscript. I have no doubt that all, or almost all, of the 154 sonnets are authentic. The carelessness of the printing, combined with the metrical inconsistencies common in Elizabethan books and manuscripts, actually works against the anapestic theory and semi-elisionism. If the text were rigorously reliable on metrical matters, then it would be likely that such lines as 142.9, "Be it lawfull I loue thee as thou lou'st those," and 17.9, "So should my papers (yellowed with their age)," would represent extra syllables or glides in "Be it" and "yellowed," instead of being inconsistent renderings of the contraction "Be't" and the reduced form "yellow'd."

Here are some examples of apparent extra syllables in the Sonnets, representing important classes. I underline the relevant "syllables."

16.7   With vertuous wish would beare your liuing flowers

17.3   Though yet heaven knowes it is but as a tombe

52.14 Being had to tryumph, being lackt to hope

82.8 Some fresher stampe of the time bettering dayes

86.5 Was it his spirit, by spirits taught to write

124.4 Weeds among weeds, or flowers with flowers gatherd

Since there are only a hundred or so examples of such apparent extra syllables, which is not very many out of over 10,000 feet and over 20,000 syllables, one can safely say that at the most Shakespeare uses anapests sparingly in the Sonnets. One can add, from these examples and all others, that the apparent anapests are all light. The theory that Shakespeare simply allowed anapestic substitutions is out of court. The question remains, did he intend occasional light anapests, or semi-elisions?

THE CASE OF *BEING*

The word *being* is in normal pronunciation a light two syllables to begin with. In the Sonnets it occurs (spelled indifferently *beeing* or *being,* usually the latter, with no metrical significance to the spellings) in contexts where (1) by a light anapest theory, it sometimes occasions light anapests and sometimes does not; or (2) by a semi-elision theory, it is sometimes pronounced and counted as two syllables, sometimes pronounced as two syllables (or as one syllable plus a glide or slur) but counted as one; or (3) by the disyllabic theory, it is sometimes two syllables and sometimes one.

Henceforth I shall normally discuss examples in terms of disyllabism, not for polemical suasion but to avoid such verbosities as the previous sentence. The supporter of anapests or semi-elision may interpret the evidence in his own terms. I do not think they will prove satisfactory.

I find fourteen examples of monosyllabic "being" in the Sonnets, each of them occurring in an unstressed position. Similar words, such as "greeing" (aphaeretic form of "agreeing") and "seeing," are in each instance disyllabic. Even though a stressed "being" or a "seeing" or similar word is occasionally monosyllabic in Elizabethan poetry, the fourteen unstressed forms can hardly occur by chance. The odds against mere chance are over 16,000 to 1. But, if the anapestic theory were true, those occurrences would be by chance. A semi-elisionist could claim that they represent lessened but still glided forms as opposed to the stressed forms. The problem though, is that "being" is sufficiently light so that any reduction makes it one syllable. These considerations, in conjunction with the truth that one "being" occurs in the variant doublet in 52.14 (quoted above—variant doublets are discussed shortly), yield about as pure a certainty as one can achieve in such matters that there was a monosyllabic form of "being" and that meter and actual syllabification concur.

THE CASE OF *SPIRIT*

My first exhibit is from *Zepheria* (1594), a sonnet sequence whose authority history has charitably left unknown.

> Loue then the spirit of a generous sprite
>
> . . . .
>
> The summe of life that Chaos did vnnight
> (IV.9,11)

This example is really enough to show that there were two forms of *spirit,* one monosyllabic and one disyllabic and quite distinct. We hesitate, by a modern sense of idiom, to think of "sprite" as a full synonym for (i.e., a monosyllabic form of) "spirit," since nowadays "sprite" has a much narrower band of meaning than "spirit." But that was clearly not so in Elizabethan English. References, for instance, to the Holy Sprite are frequent. The evidence on this word is too conclusive to need much drumming. Yet in their edition Ingram and Redpath give monosyllabic "spirit" without reduced form, slur mark, or note. Claes Schaar says of 86.5 (quoted above) that "*Spirit* can hardly be anything but disyllabic in this line."[36] No, it is once monosyllabic, once disyllabic, and, since the two forms occur together, the difference was intended to be elegantly exhibited in the reading of the line, as in the passage in *Zepheria* and in the following examples.

VARIANT DOUBLETS

The two forms of *being* and *spirit* in 52.14 and 86.5 respectively, quoted above, are examples of variant doublets—two forms of a word in the same line or near context. Several other examples occur in the Sonnets. One, which does not happen to involve a syllabic change, is unambiguous evidence that (1) such doublets were considered an aesthetic nicety, and (2) that they were to be pronounced with a distinct difference:

> From this vile world with vildest wormes to dwell
> (71.4)

The two forms are plainly pronounced differently. Henry Peacham in *The Garden of Eloquence* (1577) gives *vilde* for *vile* as an example of the orthographical scheme "paragoge" (addition of a letter or syllable).[37] Such orthographical schemes ("metaplasmus" is his generic term), he tells us, exist for meter "or else to make the verse more fine."[38] Shakespeare and other poets obviously felt it made the verse even finer to offer the two pronunciations of a word as companions.[39]

Other examples in the sonnets are *flattery* as three syllables in 114.2 and as two syllables in 114.9 (these may be too far apart to be consciously felt as a doublet), "ti's" as monosyllabic in 24.3 and "it is" as disyllabic in 24.4, and the monosyllabic and disyllabic *flowers* in 124.4, quoted above. Another example of a probable doublet is 59.11 and 59.12:

> Whether |whe'r| we are mended, or where better they,
> Or whether reuolution be the same.

The "where" in 59.11 is the common contraction for "whether," and the first "whether" is probably intended to be the same contraction.

The Suffixes -st-est, -ed

The greater freedom in Elizabethan English for syllabic choice over modern usage is extended considerably by the syllabic and non-syllabic forms of *-st* or *-est,* and *-ed/-d/or-t.* The suffix [*-st/ -est*] had differing syllabic values both for the verb ending, now lost, and for the superlative, for which we retain the form but not the syllabic choice. The distinction between *-st* and *-est* is kept with consistency by the 1609 text with only a few problematic instances

(136.14, "And then thou louest me for my name is *Will*," should possibly read "And then thou louèst me for my name's *Will*" rather than "And then thou lov'st me for my name is *Will*"); and some examples are like 82.2, monosyllabic "maiest," which was probably felt as *maie-* and *-st* rather than *mai-* and *-est*.

The syllabic distinction for past participial endings is also observed(the apostrophe is sometimes used with the shortened spelling, sometimes not—a mere inconsistency), but with some errors, and with a metrically significant class of possible errors.

In well over two hundred instances (I count 239, but with enough problematic instances for the count to be trustworthy only in bulk), syllabic value is correctly indicated. Four instances are plain mistakes. In twelve instances, the full form is given when the -*ed* is either extra-metrical or not pronounced: 17.9, 26.11, 85.6, 97.8, 97.10, 108.8, 117.12, 120.4, 120.8, 129.7, 138.14, and 143.2. I once believed that these were aesthetic niceties, with a pleasant extra glide not used in the shortened examples, for instance, these:

So should my papers (yellow͡ed with their age)
                                        (17.9)
Vnlesse my Nerues were brasse or hammer͡ed steele
                                        (120.4)
Past reason hated as a swollow͡ed bayt
                        (129.7)

A glide sounds well and the sound fits the sense nicely in these three and some other examples. But the actual explanation is, I now believe, more homely and more disyllabic.

In the text the non-syllabic endings for the past participle outnumber the syllabic endings by over three to one (over 180 to just over 50, with a few ambiguous or uncertain instances). In these twelve instances, the longer form represents the shorter pronunciation; but in almost no instance does the shortened form represent the longer pronunciation (the only exception, in 74.12, is discussed later). These truths concur to suggest that Elizabethan usage was already strongly tending toward the modern situation where the participial endings are non-syllabic but represented by -*ed*. Thus in prose the spelling "hallowed" would normally represent the pronunciation "hallow'd." A spelling such as "totter'd" or "askt" was a deliberate indication of metrical choice, and it was a very easy and natural mistake for a poet, scribe, or compositor to write "hallowed" when the pronunciation "hallow'd" was intended.

The Classes of Apparent Extra Syllables

The following list of classes of words in the Sonnets apparently having an extra syllable is in intent exhaustive. The order has no meaning except that the first seven groups have instances with reduced spellings, and the last six groups do not. The classes overlap somewhat, a fact that is not relevant to my purposes.

1. Words in which -e- appears to but does not represent a syllable: e.g., "maicst" (82.2), "alaied" (56.3) rhyming with "said" (56.1). *Maiest* is presumably felt as *maie-* and *-st* rather than *mai-* and *-est,* as I noted earlier, and similarly for *alaied.*

2. Words with -en or -n endings: *even, heaven, given.* These are pronounced as one syllable or two, usually as one. No reduced form of spelling occurs except in "stolne," (31.6 and elsewhere), which is always one syllable.

3. Words with a medial -r- sound. Spellings with -er- can represent full or reduced syllabic count—the spelling "flattery" is three syllables in 114.2, two syllables in 42.14. Reduced spellings occur: "watry" (64.7), "robb'rie" (40.9). Many of these have variant syllabic forms in present English.

4. The -our, -ower group, spelled as one syllable or two, usually pronounced as one syllable: "houre" (33.11), "hower" (52.3), "howers" (5.1). These words count as one or two syllables in present English. Kökeritz suggests that some of these words may have had a shorter pronunciation in Elizabethan English than now.[40]

5. Words with medial -n- sound. Full forms can represent full or reduced pronunciation: "gluttoning" (75.14), "prisoner" (5.10), respectively. Reduced forms occur: "Darkning" (100.4). Some forms come out right in syllabic count but are misleading, e.g., "sharpned" (56.4), possibly pronounced *sharpn'd* rather than *sharp'ned.* Most of these words have variant syllabic forms in present English.

6. Words with -air or -ayer. Both syllabic spellings occur: "prayers" (108.5), "ayre" (21.8), "ayer" (21.12). All such words are monosyllabic in the Sonnets.

7. Contractions. These are real contractions. Contractions of

two words usually appear in reduced form: "Wer't" (125.1), "Tis" (121.1), but examples of unreduced forms that should be reduced occur: "Were it" (39.10), "Be it" (142.9), and possibly "name is" (136.14). Contracted forms of one word also occur: "greeing" (114.11 for *agreeing*), "ore" (107.12, for *over*), "where" (59.11, for *whether*).

8. The word (or words?) *toward, towards,* always monosyllabic: "toward" (9.13), "Towards" (51.14). This word can be monosyllabic in present English.

9. The word *spirit,* discussed above.

10. The word *being,* discussed above.

11. Words with medial -*u*- before a vowel as in two-syllabled "influence" (15.4) and "vertuous" (16.7), and three-syllabled "influence" (78.10). Syncopation in such words is common in Elizabethan practice (i.e., *influ'nce*), and even without syncopation, the two vowels may virtually or actually constitute a diphthong. In trisyllabic "influence" the -*e*- [ɛ] is a full vowel distinctly pronounced. The suffix -*ual* is always monosyllabic in the sonnets ("perpetual," 56.8) except once ("perpetuall," 154.10, rhyming with "thrall," 154.12).

12. Words with medial -*i*- or -*y*- before a vowel. The -*i*- can be syllabic (happier) or non-syllabic (gracious) in present English. It is virtually always non-syllabic in the Sonnets. Occasionally it is merely a spelling error or freak: "vnstayined" (70.8) for *vnstayned* or *vnstained*. It occurs between words in "many a" (33.1) [menja], a combination that is commonly disyllabic in Elizabethan poetry. Other examples of non-syllabic medial -*i*- are "happier" (6.8), "gratious" (62.5). "misprision" (87.11), "ouer-partiall" (137.5). They can represent syncope or synizesis, e.g., [mɪsprɪzan] or [mɪsprɪzjan] respectively. Examples of rare syllabic medial -*i*- are "viall" (6.3) where the *i* is tense, and "spatious" (135.5) which is an archaism and a joke. He is saying that the brunette woman's will (vagina) is "large and spatious" and the joke requires a spacious pronunciation.

13. Final non-syllabic -*er*. There are many examples of final syllabic -*er*: "neuer" (5.5), "whether" (59.12), "either" (47.9) and over two dozen others. The only examples of non-syllabic final -*er* are "Whether" (59.11) and "Either" (70.10). "Whether" solves easily

one of two ways: as an uncontracted form of the contraction "where" (used in the same line, discussed above) or as disyllabic followed by the contracted form of "we are"—*Whether we're mended*. "Either" may be an example of end curtailment,[41] or a shortened form, *e'r*,[42] or a natural error for "Or," since *either . . . or* and *or . . . or* are exact synonyms, both common and both used elsewhere in the Sonnets: 47.9 and 81.1-2 respectively. Textual emendation should be the last resort of the beset theorist, since thereby hangs the noose of circularity; but since there are, not counting this possible error, three errors and a spelling unique for the Sonnets in a run of eight lines, the suspicion of a weary compositor is not irrational. But I confess that I am not sure, and semi-elisionists may take any glimmer of joy they can find at my perplexity. But it is the only example in the Sonnets that at all bothers me, and *eith'r* with a nonvocalic, tapped *r* can be mono-syllabic.

The above list attempts to show that all the examples of appar-ent extra syllables vanish on inspection.[43] Nor do I think I am forcing their departure to suit a theory. When I began to examine these examples I held the semi-elision theory; when I finished I was a disyllabist.

THE SPELLING "ERRORS" GO ONE WAY

I have attempted to discuss every class of instances in which spelling seems to indicate an extra syllable. The following are the only five examples I find in the Sonnets in which the spelling seems to indicate one syllable too few: "guil'st th'eauen" (28.12); "disa-bled" (66.8); "remembred" (74.12); "th'East" (132.6); "t'haue" (138.12). The first, fourth, and fifth are patent errors, and in the other two instances the *-l-* and *-r-* are syllabic, but misleadingly spelled.

The fact that the longer spellings represent the shorter pronun-ciations much more often than vice versa indicates that the shorter spellings are deliberate means of showing shorter pronunciations to fit the meter. However, since the longer form as in present English frequently represents a shorter pronunciation in prose, it was easy to leave the longer spelling. The very fact that spellings fairly often seem to represent extra syllables happens precisely *because* these spellings do *not* represent extra syllables but, as in prose, represent shortened forms. That is, the evidence that appears to require anapests or semi-elisions (without that evidence, there would be virtually no case whatever for either), turns out to be potent evidence for disyllabism.

SUMMARY AND CONCLUSION

The case for light anapests or semi-elision consists in (1) the belief that certain spellings in Elizabethan texts seem to indicate extra syllables, combined with (2) a complex modern prejudice against (a) demonstrable Elizabethan pronunciations that happen to exist no longer, (b) poetic license, and (c) colloquial forms. I have tried to show that, at least for the Sonnets, the first point is evidence for disyllabism, and that the second is contrary in all three instances to what can be established as Elizabethan practice.

In addition, Heminge and Condell possibly speak for Shakespeare's disyllabic intent; the contemporary prosodists overwhelmingly support disyllabism; and the 1609 text offers no instance that requires a semi-elisionist or anapestic explanation and only one instance ("Either" in 70.10) that is even problematical.

The aesthetic arguments on either side are inconclusive and the semi-elisionist side vitiated by non-Elizabethan assumptions. Though there may have been mild inconsistency in practice, disyllabism was probably the prevailing practice and theory. It is famously hard to prove the nonexistence of the nonexistent; it is hard to show conclusively that no Elizabethan poets adopted semi-elisionism on aesthetic grounds. But no evidence (except a moment in Puttenham) exists to show that they did; and the burden of proof is surely on the semi-elisionist.

More strictly, no claim here solidly extends beyond the Sonnets: to settle particular problems one has to look at (decidedly!) minute particulars, and I have done that only for the Sonnets. Whether in Jonson's *Sejanus* and other works, whether in Donne, whether in Shakespeare's plays, whether elsewhere the disyllabism is as strict as I find it in the Sonnets, are other questions that must be answered, if they are to be answered, by particular scrutiny of a good many texts. But my concern is not there, but with establishing one basis for a more exact text and more informed aesthetic criticism of the sonnets of Shakespeare. I have argued, and I hope shown, that in those poems the metrical and actual disyllabism is strict.

THE PUNCTUATION
OF SHAKESPEARE'S SONNETS

BY

THEODORE REDPATH

In this study I want to discuss some aspects of two topics: (1) the punctuation of the 1609 Quarto, and (2) how the Sonnets should be punctuated in a modern edition.

The punctuation of Shakespearean texts has, of course, received fair attention during the present century; but scholars and critics have usually either discussed it in general terms, or concentrated on texts of the plays. General discussions of Shakespearean punctuation have sometimes referred to examples from the Sonnets, and critics have, on occasion, scrutinized the punctuation of particular sonnets in some detail; but no rigorous or careful study has been devoted specifically to the punctuation of the Sonnets. On the other hand, there has been a fair amount of loose (though sometimes ingenious) writing on the subject, and various facile and dangerous generalizations have been made, which need to be countered in the interests of sound scholarship. The present study is offered as a step in the required direction.

THE PUNCTUATION OF THE 1609 QUARTO

How authoritative is the punctuation of the 1609 Quarto? How likely is it to be Shakespeare's? How likely is it to be the editor's, or the publisher's, or the printer's, or the compositor's? And, if more than one mind was brought to bear on it, how large a role is each mind likely to have played? Again, does the Quarto punctuation show any signs of system, and, if so, what? And in what relation does the Quarto punctuation stand to other examples of punctuation in printed editions of poetry in the late sixteenth and early seventeenth centuries? In this connexion, moreover, what were the prevalent conventions of punctuation? Furthermore, regardless of the question who was responsible for the Quarto punctuation, did that punctuation probably express subtleties of sense, movement, and tone which would have been lost if it had been different?

A number of these questions have been raised and discussed by scholars and critics during the present century; and there has been considerable disagreement on the right answers. This in itself is good ground for reconsidering the questions; but there is also the additional ground that the discussions themselves have often been far too perfunctory. Let us start by reviewing a few features of the Quarto punctuation, relating these, where it seems significant to do so, to prevalent practice at that time.

One striking fact is that there are a very great number of commas in the Quarto, and very few semicolons. There are actually some 1900 commas (i.e., twelve or thirteen per poem), and only about thirty semicolons (i.e., less than one in every five poems). Now, in Bush and Harbage's meticulous modern text of the Sonnets published in 1961,[1] whose punctuation could hardly be accused of heaviness, we find about eight times as many semicolons. When we examine the Quarto text in detail we see that it often prints a comma where modern punctuation would require a heavier stop, often a semicolon. In its sparing use of the semicolon, however, the Quarto was by no means eccentric for a book of its period. If we look at other books of poems printed in England between, say, 1560 and 1610, we encounter a similar dearth of semicolons. The explanation is that the semicolon was only gradually coming into vogue as a printed stop. It is possible that it was introduced by Aldus Manutius the Elder in his book of printing-house rules published in Venice in 1561.[2] If so, it was a fairly recent introduction in any case. It seems, moreover, to have taken some time to catch on in England. Puttenham, writing in 1589, does not even mention the semicolon in his discussion of punctuation.[3] In the first half of the seventeenth century, however, semicolons became far more frequent in printed books of poems. They are already used more freely, though not very freely, in the 1633 edition of Donne's Poems.

Another interesting feature of the Quarto punctuation is that there are many more colons than semicolons—more than five times as many. This again was in entire accord with current printing practice, and probably also with the prevalent practice of writers attentive to such matters. (Puttenham wrote of three marks of punctuation: the comma, the colon, and the full stop.) At all events, as generally in printed books of poetry at that time, the comma and the colon virtually do duty for all pauses or breaks in sense less than a period. The only other exception, besides the few semicolons, is the parenthesis, of which there are just over forty instances in the whole collection.

Yet, even though there are in the Quarto more than five times as many colons as semicolons, they only amount to about 160, an average of one per poem, as contrasted with about 1900 commas. It is therefore the commas that represent the great majority of all pauses and breaks less than those represented by full stops. This is already a heavy duty, but the duty can be seen to be still heavier when we realize another important fact: that commas are frequently printed in the Quarto where a modern text would print no stop at all. If we take the Bush and Harbage text again for comparison we shall find that there are nearly four hundred cases in which the Quarto has a stop and the modern text does not (the Quarto stop being almost always a comma). About seven-eighths of the cases occur at the ends of lines. The ever-recurring commas of the Quarto therefore not only do duty to mark a considerable range of pauses and breaks, but also stand firmly at many points (especially at the ends of lines) where a good modern text might well have no stop at all. In the Quarto, indeed, there are only about two hundred lines which have no end stop whatever, whereas in the Bush and Harbage text there are about five hundred such lines.

An examination of the approximately two hundred lines not end-stopped in the Quarto is instructive. There seems to have been some attempt at system, since well over 150 of the cases fall into six fairly well defined groups. The largest of these (accounting for about sixty cases) consists of instances where a subject occurs in one line, and its verb, generally in the indicative, in the next line, e.g., Sonnet 3, lines 9-10:

> Thou art thy mothers glasse and she in thee
> Calls back the louely Aprill of her prime,

Another large group comprises cases (about thirty) where a verb occurs in one line and its object in the next line, e.g., 4.7-8:

> Profitles vserer why doost thou vse
> So great a summe of summes yet can'st not liue?

There is also a small group (about half a dozen cases) where a comparison is started in one line, and the second leg (introduced by "As" or "Than") occurs in the following line, e.g., 55.3-4:

> But you shall shine more bright in these contents
> Than vnswept stone, besmeer'd with sluttish time,

A far larger group (over forty cases) is formed by instances where the first of two lines leads to a preposition at the start of the second line, e.g., 49.9-10:

> Against that time do I insconce me here
> Within the knowledge of mine owne desart,

There are also a dozen or so cases where the first of two lines leads to a relative at the beginning of the second line, e.g., 116.5-6:

> O no, it is an euer fixed marke
> That lookes on tempests and is neuer shaken;

There is also a small group (about half a dozen) whose members all involve inversion, e.g., 55.9-10:

> Gainst death, and all obliuious emnity [sic]
> Shall you pace forth, . . .

There are a few instances of various other kinds of case; but the above form the bulk, and they enough for our purpose. They might seem to provide evidence that the Quarto punctuation is, as some scholars and critics have believed, intelligently systematic. But careful scrutiny of the text reveals that in each of these six kinds of case the Quarto quite often prints one of its importunate terminal commas. Indeed, in one type of case (the comparisons), it prints a comma more frequently than not. Now such inconsistent punctuation may have its appeal for some scholars; but at least it cannot justifiably be called "systematic" without considerable qualification. Moreover, it is hard to see any real advantage in the inconsistencies. On the contrary, it would have been a distinct improvement if the Quarto had followed out such system as can be traced in those lines which it does print without an end stop. For the result would have been well over a hundred additional unstopped lines; and this would have differentiated between lines of those types and lines requiring more of a pause or break, and so would have relieved the overworked comma at the end of its wide range of duties.

Surely we must regard as primitive a form of punctuation which used the same sign for such an extensive range of pauses and breaks? Surely the introduction and wider use of the semicolon were steps in the right direction? And surely Shakespeare's printer would have done well to make more use of it, as well as rigorously to relinquish stopping where this was unnecessary? This is not, however, to imply that George Eld, who printed the 1609 Quarto, was either exceptionally conservative or exceptionally unsystematic. Richard Field, the printer of Shakespeare's *Venus and Adonis* in 1593, and one of the very best printers in London, had only used the semicolon about twenty times in almost 1200 lines, and the colon about seventy times; and only a couple of dozen lines were not end-stopped. The comma was thus even more grievously overworked there than in the 1609 Quarto of the Sonnets. As to the unstopped lines, they seem to fall into roughly the same groups as those in the Sonnets; but there are many more instances where lines falling under the respective principles are nevertheless end-stopped.

The question naturally arises whether the Quarto punctuation is likely to be Shakespeare's own, or that of an editor, or printer, or compositor. It is certainly quite unscholarly to assume that it is Shakespeare's own, and then to "discover" in it subtleties which may really be the invention of ingenious critics rather than anything emanating from the poet himself. The classic example of this kind of criticism is the discussion of Sonnet 129 ("Th'expence of Spirit in a waste of shame") by Laura Riding and Robert Graves.[4] I shall scrutinize this critique later in this study. Even writers who start by being more cautious than Riding and Graves, however, can only too easily slip into the habit of writing or speaking of the Quarto's punctuation as "Shakespeare's punctuation." Such an inclination should be circumspectly resisted.

Enough, however, of warnings! What is the evidence, external and internal? First, then, we do not know from what copy Eld printed. To those familiar with manuscripts of that time, however, it seems likely that the copy was very close to the original; and it may, indeed, have been either wholly or partly the original itself. There are certainly comparatively few actual words in the Quarto which seem likely to be mistakes of a manuscript copyist rather than mistakes of an editor, printer, or compositor. If any of Eld's copy was transcript, however, it would have been a good deal less likely to have carried what punctuation there may have been in Shakespeare's original, than the original itself. Many copyists were very negligent about punctuation. On the other hand, even if the copy from which Eld printed was wholly Shakespeare's original, it would not *follow* that the printed punctuation is either wholly, or for the most part, or even in any instance, Shakespeare's own. It seems probable that some of Shakespeare's own punctuation would be preserved; but it would be hard to say how much. Unfortunately, very little Elizabethan or Jacobean copy from which an extant printed book is known to have been set up is known to survive.

There is, however, a manuscript in the British Museum (Add. 18920) which provides important evidence as to the treatment of manuscript punctuation by an Elizabethan printer; and it has been studied by several scholars including the late Sir Walter Greg.[5] The manuscript is of thirty or so cantos of Sir John Harington's translation of the *Orlando Furioso,* and it was used by Richard Field for the first printed edition published in 1591. As Greg observed,

Harington's own punctuation is very mechanical. In every one of a sample of seven successive stanzas Harington puts a colon at the end of the fourth line of the *ottava rima,* and a full stop at the end of each stanza, regardless of the sense. Practically all his lines end with a comma; and there is often at least one comma in the course of a line, marking a pause, sometimes grammatically required, sometimes not. The printer makes considerable changes. He replaces some of the central colons by commas, and for terminal commas substitutes full stops, colons, or, occasionally, semicolons, where the sense seemed to require it. (It still seems to.) He discards quite a number of the commas Harington wrote in the course of lines. Field is not completely consistent; but the result is very different from the punctuation of Harington's manuscript. Yet Harington was a highly educated man, and a punctilious man, who evidently bothered about punctuation even if he did not punctuate very satisfactorily.

If Harington's punctuation was so radically modified by his printer, is it not probable that Shakespeare's punctuation would be not a little transformed in the printing house? The sound answer seems to me to be "Yes" rather than "No." We need to be cautious, though. Sir Walter Greg concluded from the Harington case that in such a printing house as Field's the compositors had a recognized standard of their own for spelling and to a lesser extent for punctuation, and that they adhered to that standard fairly consistently. He also asserted that their work was certainly more uniform and more modern than that of any save a very few of the most punctilious writers of their day; but that when they were puzzled by a word in the manuscript, or whenever their attention relaxed, peculiarities of spelling and punctuation in the copy tended to be transferred to the printed text. How do Greg's observations bear upon the case of the 1609 Quarto? Greg himself warns us to be careful how we generalize from the practice of an office of such high quality as Field's. He holds it reasonable to suppose that inferior craftsmen would have a less rigorous standard, and that while they would make more mistakes and introduce more anomalies they would also be more influenced by the manuscript.

Now, if we accept this principle, which seems to ring sound, it becomes relevant to ask at this point : How good a printing house was Eld's? And it also becomes relevant to ask: Is there any external evidence as to Eld's competence at printing poetry, and as to the care with which the Sonnets were printed? How competent does the printing itself seem to be?

The answer to the first of these questions is that Eld's printing house seems to have been a good one. He appears to have generally printed well,[6] and he attained a high position in the trade. Six years later, in 1615, he was named in a document among fourteen of the Master Printers of London allowed to have two presses.[7] That list includes the names of such eminent printers as Masters Dawson, Field, and Lownes. But there is more to be said. Eld had been admitted to the Freedom of the Stationers' Company in 1600 (II, 725), but he had not started printing on his own account until 1604 (V, 233). He went on printing for twenty years (V, 233), but at the time when he printed the Sonnets he had not been running a printing house for very long. He had, however, already printed a fair amount of verse: for instance, in *The Retourne from Pernassus,* published in 1606, which he had printed for John Wright (III, 304) (one of the two booksellers commissioned to sell the Sonnets); in Marston's *What you will,* published in 1607, which he had printed for Thomas Thorpe (III, 358), the publisher of the Sonnets; and in *The Revengers Tragedie,* which he published himself in 1607 (III, 360).

On the other hand, Eld's printing house was pretty busy in 1609. He printed at least twelve books published in that year.[8] He also printed a very large folio volume (921 pages plus preliminaries) published in 1610, which he had actually entered at Stationers' Hall as his own copy on 3 May 1608, but which finally bore the imprint "for T. Thorp." This volume was Healey's translation of Augustine's *De civitate Dei,* with the commentary by Ludovicus Vives (III, 377). It was a major undertaking, and we may reasonably suppose that it occupied a good deal of setting and printing time in Eld's printing house during 1609. One of the works published in 1609 was also sizable (303 pages in quarto), namely J. F. Le Petit's *Low Country Commonwealth,* which Eld had entered on 6 August 1607 (III, 357). A number of the other books Eld printed in 1609 were slenderer, e.g., Shakespeare's *Troilus and Cressida,* which he printed for two young publishers, Richard Bonian and

Henry Walley (III, 400), and a reprint of Marlowe's *Dr. Faustus,* which he executed for John Wright;[9] but another of the books, Thomas Draxe's *Worldes resurrection* (III, 383) (124 pages plus preliminaries) is quite densely printed. The total bulk of work is certainly great. Now, even the Sonnets, which was among the shorter works undertaken, would have required at least a fortnight's work by one compositor at what was probably the average speed of typesetting at the time.[10] There is, moreover, further evidence that business was brisk that year, namely that Eld himself only entered one book at Stationers' Hall between 15 June 1609 and 2 April 1610,[11] and that only one other book known to have been printed by Eld was entered for any other publisher between those dates.[12]

It is naturally important to consider what labor Eld had at his disposal to deal with this heavy assignment. Tentatively, I should regard the most probable answer as: his own, and that of one journeyman and two apprentices.[13] The journeyman may have been Thomas Watkins, who had been freed by Eld in 1605; and the apprentices were probably Luke Norton, who had been bound to Eld for seven years from 3 December 1604, and Pursivant (Pursivaul?) Morgan, who had been bound to Eld for seven years from 15 December 1608.[14] Neither of these two apprentices had a distinguished subsequent career as printers, though Norton was admitted to the Freedom of the Stationers' Company in 1612.[15]

Now, during a hectic period of business we can imagine that what may have seemed the comparatively easy task of setting the Sonnets could have been assigned to one of the apprentices, and even perhaps to the inexperienced Morgan. In any case, the pressure of work could have resulted in undue hurry by the typesetter, whoever he may have been. Moreover, the job may well have been regarded as an urgent one, especially if, as seems likely, publication was unauthorized by Shakespeare.[16] Thorpe had commissioned two booksellers (William Aspley and John Wright, who had had previous connexions with Thorpe and Eld),[17] and the intention may quite possibly have been to unload very quickly what was probably regarded as a scoop. It may well be objected that if the book was regarded as a scoop, then the printer, so far from entrusting it to inferior craftsmen, would be likely to lavish on it special care. That objection cannot be dismissed out of hand; but it does not take into account the distinct possibility that Eld and his assistants were too busy with other work which from a technical point of view demanded more attention. Furthermore, speed of publication and sale may have counted in this case for more than typographical accuracy.

At all events, the Sonnets cannot be described as a really well-printed book. It compares unfavorably, for instance, with the Quarto of *Troilus and Cressida* and with the translation of Augustine, which the house was engaged on during the same year. Making all allowances for the variety of current spellings of words at the time, there are a considerable number of definite misprints. There are even a number of clear mistakes in punctuation, e.g., the commas or lack of stops at the ends of Sonnets 2, 16, 18, 26, 28, 35, 43, 62, 75, 79, 108, 117.

This of itself suggests that Eld, though a good printer in general, did not give this particular piece of work his usual care and attention. Indeed, the late Professor Tucker Brooke may well have been right in believing that the Quarto was taken on as a piece of job-printing. Tucker Brooke thought, moreover, that Eld's compositor was probably following the copy without attempting to reduce it to the style of the house.[18] This is what we should expect, according to Greg's principle, if the craftsman (or craftsmen) were inferior. Tucker Brooke made this inference, however, from the spellings of words, not from the punctuation.[19] Apart from clear mistakes, the punctuation does not differ perceptibly, in general, from that of Field's printing house, or that of other competent printing houses of the period. It remains quite possible that in this respect the compositor was making some attempt to set up according to house rules. He may, moreover, have asked for advice from time to time—from Eld (assuming that Eld did not himself set the book up), or even from Thorpe or some editor employed to prepare the manuscript for press. We simply do not know. It would not follow, on the other hand, that the resultant punctuation was always very different from that in the copy, or that there are not passages where some special punctuation of Shakespeare's own survives. What one can say is that, in general, there is little, if anything, that we have any good ground for considering specifically Shakespearean about it. It follows the general customs of printers at that time; and it follows them with much the same consistency or inconsistency.

Nevertheless, partly in the belief that the Quarto punctuation is certainly, or pretty certainly, Shakespeare's own, great claims for it have been made by some modern critics, particularly during the present century; and varying degrees of opprobrium have been heaped on the practice of scholars, greater and lesser, thoughtful or merely traditionalist, from Malone onwards, who have dared to alter substantially the Quarto punctuation, and so to "put a barrier between readers and the real Shakespeare."

Especially influential on readers of the Sonnets, and on certain subsequent critics and editors, has been the comparison made by Laura Riding and Robert Graves[20] of the version of Sonnet 129 printed in *The Oxford Book of English Verse* with that in the 1609 Quarto. I have already mentioned this critique; and I now want to examine it in some detail. It will be convenient to reprint the two versions (as quoted by Riding and Graves)[21] here:

The Oxford Book Version

Th'expense of Spirit in a waste of shame
Is lust in action; and till action, lust
Is perjured, murderous, bloody, full of blame,
4   Savage, extreme, rude, cruel, not to trust;
Enjoy'd no sooner but despisèd straight;
Past reason hunted; and, no sooner had,
Past reason hated, as a swallow'd bait
8   On purpose laid to make the taker mad:
Mad in pursuit and in possession so;
Had, having, and in quest to have, extreme;
A bliss in proof, and proved, a very woe;
12   Before, a joy proposed; behind, a dream.
    All this the world well knows; but none knows well
    To shun the heaven that leads men to this hell.

The Quarto Version

Th'expence of Spirit in a waste of shame
Is lust in action, and till action, lust
Is periurd, murdrous, blouddy full of blame,
4   Sauage, extreame, rude, cruell, not to trust,
Injoyd no sooner but dispised straight,
Past reason hunted, and no sooner had

> Past reason hated as a swollowed bayt,
> 8 On purpose layd to make the taker mad.
> Made In pursut and in possession so,
> Had, hauing, and in quest, to have extreame,
> A blisse in proofe and proud and very wo,
> 12 Before a ioy proposd behind a dreame,
> All this the world well knowes yet none knowes well,
> To shun the heauen that leads men to this hell.

Riding and Graves start somewhat hazardously by telling us that the 1609 version was "apparently, though pirated, printed from Shakespeare's original manuscript" (page 63). On the very next page the 1609 version is already called "Shakespeare's original sonnet" (a powerful piece of rhetorical false coinage which adds much apparent plausibility to the subsequent argument). At the same time, the often extremely thoughtful work of scholars is dismissed as irresponsible by dubbing it "the juggling of punctuation marks." We are then told how much of the original atmosphere of the poem is lost by modernizing the spelling.

But the writers consider that it is the editorial changes of punctuation that do the most damage (page 66). Writing of line 2, our critics allege that "a semicolon after the first *action* instead of a comma gives a longer rest than Shakespeare gave; but it also cuts off the idea at *action* instead of keeping *in action* and *till action* together as well as the two *lust*'s" (page 67). Now, first, we do not know whether Shakespeare himself wrote a comma after the first "action" or not. Secondly, we do know that commas in the Quarto cover a very wide range of pauses, and that the book was printed at a time when semicolons for longer pauses were only gradually coming into use. Thirdly, the value of "keeping *in action* and *till action* together as well as the two *lust*'s" any more closely than the Oxford Book punctuation does is far from evident.

The next point is better, though I for one do not accept it. It is that the Quarto punctuation of the latter half of line 3, "blouddy full of blame" is superior to the Oxford Book's "bloody, full of blame" because "blouddy" and "full" really form a single word meaning "full as with blood." The whole phrase would then presumably mean "full of sin (or crime) as with blood." The image is attractive; but there is a linguistic objection to the phrase: Shakespeare

nowhere else uses "bloody" adverbially. He uses "bloodily." This is
not conclusive, but it is a factor. Moreover, Shakespeare does frequently use "bloody" as an adjective meaning "bloodthirsty"; and
this sense would follow very readily from "murd'rous."

Our critics go on to complain at the substitution of semicolons
for commas in lines 4-6 of the Oxford Book version. They say that
"if Shakespeare had wanted such pauses he would have used semicolons as he does elsewhere" (page 67). This statement is very
obscure. What do they mean by "elsewhere"? In the Quarto text of
the Sonnets? In some of his other writings? We cannot say. But
what we can say is that once again the two critics are illegitimately
assuming that this Quarto punctuation is Shakespeare's own; and
that once again they show no sign of awareness of the use of
commas in contemporary printing, or of the historical position of
the semicolon at the time. And are we really to believe that no
greater pauses are called for after, at all events, "trust" and
"straight" than after any of the other words succeeded by commas
in the Quarto version of line 4?

Riding and Graves find "particularly serious," however, "the
interpolation of a comma after *no sooner had,*" arguing that "this
confines the phrase to a special meaning, *i.e.* 'lust no sooner had is
hated past reason,' whereas it also means 'lust no sooner had *past
reason* is hated past reason.'" They add that "the comma might as
as well have been put between *reason* and *hated;* it would have
limited the meaning but no more than has been done." And what
are we to say about this? My own answer is that I do not believe
their assertion that the clause also means "lust no sooner had
past reason is hated past reason." I believe that the contrast is
between "past reason hunted" and "no sooner had, past reason
hated," and that any attempt to intrude that further meaning
would be illegitimately blurring the contrast. If it be argued that
there is no comma in the Quarto after "had" and that this needs
explanation, the answer is that a comma there (given that there was
simply a comma after "hunted") could have interfered with the forward reference required to give the real meaning, "lust no sooner
had is hated past reason."

We are next asked to consider lines 7 and 8. As we might by now
have expected, we are informed that "Shakespeare" put a comma
after "bayt." This is supposed to have the effect of taking us back

"to the original idea of *lust,*" whereas without the comma "On purpose layd" "merely carries out the figure of *bayt.*" We have every right to be skeptical about this supposed subtlety, and about Shakespeare's having intended anything of the kind.

Our critics' next objection is that "in the original there is a full stop at *mad,* closing the octave"; whereas "in the revised version" there is a colon "making the next line run right on" (pages 67-68). The colon is also said to have the effect of "causing the unpardonable change from *Made* to *Mad.*" It is interesting to note that even those stout supporters of the Quarto text, Mr. Martin Seymour-Smith and Professor Dover Wilson, print "Mad," which is often, as Professor Dover Wilson notes, printed as "Made" in the plays.[22] "Made" is, however, by no means an impossible reading here; but it would cohere better with a colon or even with a Quarto comma than with a full stop, for our critics' idea (page 68) that the word "so" at the end of line 9 can refer forward to line 10 or even beyond is surely unacceptable? Line 9 itself limits the scope of "so" to pursuit and possession, whereas line 10 refers to three phases, pursuit, possession, and past possession. If we were to read "Made" in line 9, the word could therefore only refer back, not forward. The reading "Mad," however, seems to be on the whole preferable. "Made" would divert attention from the power of lust, which is of the essence of the poem. As to our critics' certainty that the capital *I* of "In" was in the manuscript, and that "Shakespeare undoubtedly first wrote the line without *Made,* but probably deciding that such an irregular line was too bold, added *Made* without changing the capital *I* to a small one," the idea is ingenious enough, but one can only wonder at their capacity for imagining mythical hypotheses to be rocklike verities.

Our critics' *pièce de résistance,* however, is probably their complaint at the editorial shift of the comma after "quest" (line 10) to its new position after "have" (pages 68-70). They maintain that "Had, having, and in quest" "might have been written in parentheses if Shakespeare had used parentheses." (Since there are over forty instances of parentheses in the Quarto text one wonders why they did not say that he does use them!) The resultant meaning (only one of several) is said to be "that lust comprises all the stages of lust ... and that the extremes of lust are felt in all these stages" ("to have extreame" meaning "to have extremes" or "to have in extreme degrees"). Now this interpretation of "to have extreame" is downright nonsense for which no authority can be cited in Shakespeare or in Elizabethan usage. Our critics go on to say quite rightly, however, that one meaning of the line is that "one stage in lust is like the others, as extreme as the others"; but when they suggest that *"Had, hauing, and in quest* [sic] is the summing up of this fact" they are not offering any substantial support for their view about the right position of the comma, for one could equally well say that "Had, having, and in quest to have" is the summing up of the fact described. Indeed, nothing else that they say gives any substantial support to their opinion about that comma. They urge (of course) that "Shakespeare" put the comma after "quest," and so the modern version changes the rhythm (page 70. They never even consider the possibility that a stumbling compositor may have mistakenly thought that "Had," "hauing," and "in quest" were coordinate; and so comma'd off "in quest" like "Had" and "hauing." They argue that with the modern punctuation line 10 becomes a mere repetition. This is incorrect, since *three* phases are now mentioned as "extreme," whereas only *two* (before and during) were called "mad" in line 9; and this naturally leads to the contrast in line 11 between during and after, and then to the contrast in line 12 between before and after, Shakespeare finally emphasizing *contrast* (and these contrasts in particular) as the most important aspect of lust.

Riding and Graves next tell us that line 11 "should explain *to have extreame"* (page 70). Why should it? Because there is only a comma in the Quarto after "extreame"? We know by now that that could be no valid reason. But Riding and Graves do attempt to give us a reason, and the one they adduce is very curious: "To fulfil the paradox implied in *extreame* it [line 11] should mean that lust is a bliss during the proof and after the proof, and also *very wo* (real woe) during and after the proof. The altered line only means that lust is a bliss during the proof but a woe after the proof, denying what Shakespeare has been at pains to show all along, that lust is all things at all times" (page 71). But has Shakespeare been at pains to show this all along? Where in the sonnet has he said, or will he say, that *after* lust has had possession it gives satisfaction?

Have Riding and Graves forgotten the start of the poem, and line 5, and (even on their own interpretation) "Past reason hated" (line 7)? Their *goût du paradoxe* seems to have run away with them. They have crucially misunderstood the poem. Shakespeare has *not* been at pains all along to show "that lust is all things at all times," whatever meaning we attach to that loose phrase.

Yet our critics peg away: "Once the editors tried to repunctuate the line they had to tamper with words themselves in the text. A comma after *proof* demanded a comma after *proved.* A comma after *proved* made it necessary to change *and very wo* to apply to *provd* only [sic]" (page 71). This account of the editorial process is not a convincing one. It seems more likely that editors started by trying to make sense of what must have seemed a very odd line. Shakespeare has nowhere in this poem suggested that the aftermath of lust is bliss—quite the contrary. So an editor might justifiably believe that to take "in proofe and proud [prov'd]" as a key phrase would not make good sense here. Some stop after "proofe" was therefore advisable. Now the phrase "and proud [prov'd] and very wo" does not seem to make good sense either, and, in view of what Shakespeare has so far said in the sonnet about the aftermath of lust, the substitution of "a" for "and" would appear very reasonable, especially if one realized that the letter *a* could easily be read by a compositor as an ampersand, and that, alternatively, a compositor could easily have caught the "and" after "proofe" and mistakenly repeated it after "proud." (Our critics never mention such technical matters.)

We have still three lines to consider. Our critics object to isolating line 12 by printing a semicolon at the end of line 11 (page 71). They contend that this makes it a mere repetition of "the sense of a bliss during proof as against a woe after proof." They seem to have failed to see that the contrast Shakespeare is now drawing is between what the experience seemed in prospect, and what it seems in retrospect, whereas in line 11 the contrast was between the full flood of lust in consummation and the aftermath. Moreover, in line 12 the contrast is between the prospect of joy and its vanishing insubstantiality; whereas in line 11 the contrast was between the actual joy and the subsequent pain and sorrow. The critics' preoccupation with their own ingenuities seems to have blinded them to

Shakespeare's own subtle shifts and distinctions. Their account of the various meanings with which they suppose line 12 to be "inlaid" is too much of a strain on credulity to be worth discussion. I shall confine attention to what they take to be "the final meaning" (page 72). This is that "even when consummated, lust still stands before an unconsummated joy, a proposed joy, and proposed not as a joy possible of consummation but one only to be desired through the dream by which lust leads itself on, the dream behind which this proposed joy, this love, seems to lie." This seems to be completely off beam. Riding and Graves are taking "before" and "behind" as adverbs of place instead of adverbs of time. Yet "behind" is certainly, I believe, here being used as "in the time which one has lived beyond, in the past" (*OED,* 1c), and Schmidt rightly glosses the word here as "when past."[23] The meaning is simple and strong; not complex, fussy, and diffused. It is a development of Tarquin's still simpler thought in *Lucrece* (211-212):

> What win I, if I gain the things I seek?
> A dream, a breath, a froth of fleeting joy.

The meaning is, in fact, that lust promises a joy, but when the experience is looked back on it is a mere insubstantial fantasy. Now our critics allow this as "a possible contributory meaning," but they hold that if it were the *only* meaning it would make the theme of the poem that lust is impossible of satisfaction, "whereas the theme is, as carried on by the next line, that lust as lust *is* satisfiable but that satisfied lust is in conflict with itself" (page 73). Both these contentions deserve to be challenged. Just because Shakespeare asserts that the experience of coitus seems a mere nothing in retrospect it does not follow that he is asserting that lust achieves no satisfaction at all. In this sonnet he is reflecting on various aspects of lust, and he has allowed in line 11 that the actual experience of physical lovemaking is intensely pleasurable. Again, our critics' attempt to sum up the central theme is not satisfactory. That part of the theme is that lust is satisfiable (in a limited sense) is true, but the theme is larger than this, and more various and specific than the idea that satisfied lust is in conflict with itself. The poem explores a number of aspects of lust: Lust is a shameful squandering of vital energy. To gain satisfaction, it will use all manner of crookedness and violence. After its momentary satisfaction it causes remorse and loathing. It even seems like a trap. It is furious in chase, and the fury continues once it clasps its quarry. Indeed, it is violent in all its moods, including the negative reaction after satisfaction. Yet physical lovemaking is an exquisite pleasure; but also, once over, its results are painful. Lust gives great promise of joy; but once the experience of sexual intercourse is over it seems a mere nothing. Actually, then, there is not one overall theme such as Riding and Graves attempt to summarize, but a number of sharp insights into lust. That Shakespeare thinks he has made a number of points, and not one general point, is borne out by the start of line 13:

> All this the world well knows . . .

But let us see what Riding and Graves have to say about the final couplet (pages 73-74). They maintain that line 13, "if unpunctuated except for the comma Shakespeare put at the end," is a general statement of the conflict of lust with itself. If only they had had a little less faith in the significance of the Quarto's terminal commas, and in their own interpretation of that significance! If only they had looked just at the sonnet before, and noticed another instance of a terminal comma before a similar infinitive:

> . . . those Iackes that nimble leape,
> To kisse the tender inward of thy hand,   (128.5-6)

They might have saved themselves a further "expense" of fruitless and even positively misleading ingenuity. What Shakespeare seems to be doing in this couplet is contrasting the general knowledge which everybody has about lust with the apparent impossibility of finding any way of escaping lust's attractions. Riding and Graves, however, believe that line 13 means both "'All this the world well knows yet none knows well' (*i.e.* the character of lust), and 'All this the world well knows yet none knows well' the moral to be drawn from the character of lust (*i.e. to shun the heaven that leads man to this hell*)." They sum up their interpretation as follows: "The character and the moral of lust the whole world well knows, but no one knows the character and the moral really well unless he disregards the moral warning and engages in "lust"; no one knows lust well enough to shun it because, though he knows it is both heavenly and hellish, lust can never be recognized until it has proved itself lust by turning heaven into hell" (page 74). Surely this is unnecessarily complicated? From where in the sonnet do our critics derive their last clause? It is simply not there. But what (apart from their belief that the punctuation of line 13 is Shakespeare's) are their objections to putting a semicolon after "well knows" and removing the comma at the end of the line? First, they urge that this would destroy the direct opposition between "world" and "none" and between "well knows" and "knows well," as well as the whole point of the wordplay between "well knows" and "knows well." All this is quite untrue. The oppostion between "world" and "none" remains as strong as ever, and that between "well knows" and "knows well" can be seen as an opposition between theoretical and practical knowledge (cf. Ovid's *Video meliora, proboque; / Deteriora sequor*).[24] As to the wordplay, it is just as vibrant as on the other interpretation. Secondly, they object that the repunctuation "robs *All this* of its real significance, as it refers not only to all that has gone before but to the last line as well." But what is the evidence that "All this" does refer also to the last line? I see none; and I do not believe that it does. To try to make it do so seems to me to run the danger of smudging Shakespeare's clearly drawn poem.

I have spent a good deal of time examining the Riding and Graves comparison because it has been very influential. It has been accepted uncritically by many readers, and it has been considerably overrated even by certain discerning scholars and critics who might have known better. It has contributed to what has become, in some quarters, a strong tendency to make a fetish of the Quarto punctuation. Other influences have, however, helped to create this tendency. Some of these have derived ultimately from Percy Simpson's little book, *Shakespearian Punctuation.*[25] This book was designed primarily to show that the printers of the First Folio and of the Sonnets had a system of punctuation and knew what they were doing. Simpson's book was useful; but it was less systematic than it appeared to be to some readers at the time, and its conclusions were highly vulnerable, so that it came under heavy fire from a number of scholars.[26] Nevertheless, it can still be put to good use. Unfortunately, however, Simpson himself started to misuse his findings to discredit modern editors of Shakespeare, from the eighteenth century onwards, for their repunctuation of Shakespearean texts. A number of critics and scholars have since taken up the cry, and it has become quite fashionable in some circles to berate generations of editors for not knowing *their* job, and "playing old Harry" with the punctuation.

I shall return to Simpson's book, and make a little use of it in the second part of this study. Meanwhile I want, in concluding this first part, to mention a typical loose misconception which is current about the Quarto punctuation. It is often said that the Quarto punctuation, in contrast to that of typically modern texts, is "fluid." As a corollary, moreover, it has been alleged from time to time, and even "demonstrated" with some dexterity, that this "fluid" punctuation enables a reader to connect lines and phrases both backwards and forwards, thereby greatly increasing the number of meanings packed into the poem. If, however, we bear in mind the data adduced earlier in the present study, we shall tend to adopt an attitude of salty skepticism toward such interpretive *tours de force.* For we shall feel little confidence that the Quarto punctuation can properly be described as "fluid." Those 1300 terminal commas, representing pauses of various lengths; those 400 cases where the Quarto has a stop and Bush and Harbage none; the small number (200) of un-endstopped lines as contrasted with Bush and Harbage's 500—is "fluid" the right contrasting adjective for the Quarto punctuation? Nor is the position substantially modified by the further fact that there are somewhat less that seven hundred stops of any kind in the course of lines in the Quarto text, whereas there are over nine hundred in Bush and Harbage. For some 850 of these stops in Bush and Harbage are commas of light value. If we keep these facts within mental reach we shall feel chary of accepting as Shakespeare's meanings at least some of the extravagant acrobatics of creative interpretation.

It is now high time, however, to pass to our second topic.

How Should the Sonnets Be Punctuated in a Modern Edition?

No less an authority than the late Professor Dover Wilson writes in the preface to his 1966 edition of the Sonnets that "the only safe thing, the only scholarly thing" is to leave the Quarto punctuation virtually unchanged, on the hypothesis that at best it may be Shakespeare's, and at worst will pretty certainly be Thorpe's, when it is not palpably compositorial.[27] Despite the distinction of its propounder, I find it impossible to accept this exclusive view, which not only runs counter to the general practice of scholars from Malone onwards, but also to the explicit opinion of such eminent authorities as Beeching, Alden (the editor of the 1916 Variorum edition), and the late Sir Edmund Chambers.[28] Moreover, such a view would involve condemning as "unscholarly" in this respect the texts printed by a number of editors during the present century, who were probably well aware of what such scholars as Simpson, Pollard, and Dover Wilson himself, had had to say about the punctuation of Shakespearean texts. These editors include scholars of distinction, such as Pooler, Tucker, Tucker Brooke, and Professors Bush and Harbage. It is, incidentally, gratifying to find that Dover Wilson himself makes well over a hundred changes from the Quarto punctuation in his own edition; though I could wish he had made more.

A more reasonable view on this matter would seem to be that while we ought to be grateful to those scholars who have brought to our notice common practices in Elizabethan and Jacobean punctuation, and also specific instances in Shakespearean texts where the punctuation may well have a special significance which deserves to be taken account of by a modern editor, we should resist any temptation to antiquarian exclusiveness, and leave the editors of each period, present and to come, free to exercise their judgment as to the best way of rendering most faithfully, in modern punctuation which makes use of all the resources and accords with the best usage of their own time, the meanings, feelings, tones, and movement of the poem concerned. For it is surely the poem which matters, in all its life and in all the refinement and subtlety it may have; and this may well be very imperfectly represented to a modern reader by punctuation of a generally most primitive kind, such as that found in English books of the Elizabethan and Jacobean periods. It is not the old marks that are sacrosanct, but the poem. In the case of Shakespeare's Sonnets, modern readers of poetry might naturally be inclined to accord more authority to the

Quarto punctuation if it were known to be that of the poet's autograph manuscript. Yet they might not be right to do so, for Shakespeare's punctuation might, for all we know, not have been so
good, on the whole, as that of Thorpe or of Eld's printing house.
Even, however, if every single punctuation mark in the Quarto were
Shakespeare's own, it would not follow that that would be the only
right way, or even the best way, of punctuating a modern edition. It
is hard to know how much trouble that old primitive punctuation
caused to readers at the time. Its inadequacy was almost certainly
felt, and punctuation was much developed during the next hundred
years. For a modern reader, on the other hand, it is quite certain
that that old punctuation very often, far from enabling him to
regain contact with the real Shakespeare, distracts by its obsolete
stopping (or lack of stopping), and even, in certain cases, tends to
mislead as to movement and meaning. Scholars conversant with the
methods of punctuation of over three-and-a-half centuries ago may
not have great difficulty in responding readily to the poems in their
old punctuation, but the vast majority of readers of the Sonnets are
not, and cannot reasonably be expected to be, on familiar terms
with those old ways; and they have every right to have the difficult
work of satisfactory punctuation done for them by a modern editor
conversant both with the old forms of punctuation and with those
of the twentieth century. (To retain the Quarto punctuation, correcting "obvious misprints"—though there might be some dispute
as to exactly which these are—is, of course, for the editor himself a
far easier task; more like copying out a printed book in a foreign
language and correcting obvious misprints, as contrasted with
translating it into English.)

Several objections have, however, been raised against the use of
modern punctuation. It has been objected, for instance, that an
editor using it is forced to make up his mind about the meaning of
the original, and that this means that the sense of the poem is nar-
rowed down, robbing it of a multiplicity of meaning which may be
an inherent part of it. This objection involves more than one point.
Presumably, if the original has some definite meaning, it will be no
bad thing for an editor to make up his mind what it is. The objection would therefore only lie where the original text has not one
definite meaning but several. Even in such cases, however, we

surely cannot be justified in simply *assuming* that modern punctuation must be less capable of expressing the multiplicity of meaning than the Quarto punctuation would be? (In any case, in certain specific instances the two might be precisely the same.) If a particular instance of modern punctuation obliterates a multiplicity of meaning which is really there, then a mistake has been made; and that should be debited not to "modern punctuation" but to a bad use of it in that specific case.

Another objection sometimes made is that modern punctuation "interferes with the rhythm of the original." But is this bound to happen? And, in any case, what *is* "the original"? It is surely not any particular set of marks on a page, but what those marks ought to express—Shakespeare's poem? And are modern marks less likely to express Shakespeare's poem to a modern reader than the old marks are? It is certainly not justifiable to assume this; and I hope to offer evidence against it.

It has also been objected, in more general terms, that a modern edition which uses modern punctuation will represent a subjective impression of the original text. If this simply means that a modern editor will make decisions as to what he believes to be the real meanings, feelings, and tones of the poems, or of lines, phrases, or words; and decisions as to what he believes to be the true movement of the poems, or of parts of them, it can readily be accepted. His specific decisions may, in certain cases, be open to objection; but that is no good reason why he should not make such decisions. To allow such decisions to be made is not to open the gates and accord equal validity to any editorial decisions, including those by individuals ignorant of Elizabethan language and punctuation, and of Shakespeare's own modes of thought, feeling, and perception, his use of language, and his characteristic kinds of verse movement. Every specific case of deviation from the Quarto punctuation needs to be considered on its merits. Equally, however, in any modern edition, except a faithful reprint or facsimile of the Quarto text or an edition intended for historical purposes or for specialists in Elizabethan and Jacobean punctuation, every specific decision to adhere to the Quarto punctuation is open to challenge. The criterion in both cases should be whether the punctuation adopted expresses, for the modern general reader, the meaning (or meanings) and the feelings, tones, and movement of the poem.

Let us consider a few miscellaneous instances of Quarto and of modern punctuation.

Lines 9-12 of Sonnet 44 in the Quarto read:

> But ah, thought kills me that I am not thought
> To leape large lengths of miles when thou art gone,
> But that so much of earth and water wrought,
> I must attend, times leasure with my mone.

Bush and Harbage print this as follows:

> But, ah, thought kills me that I am not thought,
> To leap large lengths of miles when thou art gone,
> But that, so much of earth and water wrought,
> I must attend time's leisure with my moan.

Apart from the comma after "But" (line 9), is not the modern punctuation distinctly superior for modern readers? The lack of a stop after "thought' (line 9) could actually yield a wrong meaning. The modern comma after "that" (line 11) helps to indicate the sense. The comma in the Quarto's line 12 between the verb and its object is one of a number of such instances of obsolete stopping in the Sonnets. What possible advantage would there be in retaining it here in a modern edition?

Another kind of case where in a modern edition the Quarto punctuation would seem to need modification is where the total structure of the sonnet would not be properly represented by it. An interesting case is Sonnet 15, which is printed in the Quarto as follows:

> When I consider euery thing that growes
> Holds in perfection but a little moment.
> That this huge stage presenteth nought but showes
> 4 Whereon the Stars in secret influence comment.
> When I perceiue that men as plants increase,
> Cheared and checkt euen by the selfe-same skie:
> Vaunt in their youthfull sap, at height decrease,
> 8 And were their braue state out of memory.
> Then the conceit of this inconstant stay,

> Sets you most rich in youth before my sight,
> Where wastfull time debateth with decay
> 12 To change your day of youth to sullied night,
> And all in war with Time for loue of you
> As he takes from you, I ingraft you new.

Would the full stops at the ends of lines 2, 4, and 8, the colon at the end of line 6, and the comma at the end of line 12 properly express the structure of this sonnet to a modern reader? It might be urged that the full stops represent the depth of the pondering, or the discreteness of the individual thoughts as they occur. It is certainly possible that this was what was intended by whoever was responsible for this punctuation; though if we compare the punctuation of Sonnet 12, which has a similar structure, but has a comma at the end of line 2, and colons at the ends of lines 4 and 8, we can reasonably surmise that in Sonnet 15 colons might have seemed to the punctuator himself just as good as full stops, if only he had thought of using a semicolon or a comma instead of a colon at the end of line 6! For the modern reader I suggest that a less distracting and more satisfactorily expressive punctuation here than the Quarto's would be a comma at the end of line 2, a semicolon at the end of line 4, a comma at the end of line 6, a full colon at the end of line 8 (marking the transition from the "When" clauses to the "Then" clause), and a semicolon at the end of line 12 to mark the transition from the oppressive perceptions of lines 9-12 to the retaliatory action of the final couplet. (This is, in fact, the stopping printed by Bush and Harbage, as I found after writing these suggestions.)

Such cases of the need for modification adequately to express total structure are by no means rare; but there are still more cases where the Quarto punctuation would be inadequate to express local movement. In the great meditative Sonnet 64, for instance, we find lines 11 and 12 printed in the Quarto thus:

> Ruine hath taught me thus to ruminate
> That Time will come and take my loue away.

Is it not at least arguable that the dash first printed by Malone at the end of line 11 better represents the apprehensive feeling in the sonnet at that point, which must surely be marked by a pause?

> Ruin hath taught me thus to ruminate—
> That Time will come and take my love away.

It certainly seems to me to cohere much more satisfactorily with line 13's announcement that "This thought is as a death." And the result of rumination is, in any case, not properly to be thought of as immediate. Malone makes a few other effective uses of the dash, either alone or with a comma or semicolon. A particularly apt use occurs in his printing of lines 11-12 of Sonnet 130:

> I grant I never saw a goddess go,—
> My mistress, when she walks, treads on the ground:

This surely brings out Shakespeare's satiric flash far more vividly than the tame (and all-too-unusual) comma that we find in the Quarto.

There are, indeed, several hundred cases in which a modified pointing seems to express the meaning and movement of the poems definitely better than the Quarto pointing would do. It may now be worth indicating more systematically some of the typical kinds of case.

There are not all that many cases (apart from clear misprints) where the Quarto punctuation could definitely mislead a modern reader into misunderstanding the sense of the words; but there are some such cases. Take, for instance, 128.1-4, which appear in the Quarto thus:

> How oft when thou my musike musike playst,
> Vpon that blessed wood whose motion sounds
> With thy sweet fingers when thou gently swayst,
> The wiry concord that mine eare confounds,

The comma after "swayst" might easily mislead a modern reader into thinking that the reference was to the motion of the player's body. Another instance occurs at 137.11-12. Lines 9-12 of that sonnet appear in the Quarto thus:

Why should my heart thinke that a seuerall plot,
Which my heart knowes the wide worlds common place?
Or mine eyes seeing this, say this is not
To put faire truth vpon so foule a face,

The lack of a comma after "not" at the end of line 11 is not
regarded as a misprint by the most recent modern editors favoring
the Quarto punctuation;[29] but most modern readers would be likely
either to take "say ... face" as one clause, and so to misunder-
stand the sense, or at least to be extremely confused. An even
clearer case is 144.1, which the Quarto prints as

Two loues I haue of comfort and dispaire,

What advantage is there in not printing a comma after "haue"?
Without the comma the line could easily mean that each "love"
had elements of comfort and of despair. Admittedly, the impression that this is the meaning would be counteracted for a reader as
he continued to read the poem; but why should he be started off on
a wrong trail? Jaggard had printed the line better in 1599 in *The
Passionate Pilgrim:*

Two Loues I haue, of Comfort, and Despaire,

There are a certain number of other instances where the Quarto
punctuation could well positively mislead as to sense, e.g., 117.10,
where the Quarto comma after "surmise" would suggest that
"surmise" is a verb, whereas it is a noun. There are more, however,
where its effect is muddling rather than positively misleading. It is
more than questionable whether, for instance, a modern reader can
be expected to respond readily to Shakespeare's lines if what he
encounters on the printed page is this:

Thus can my loue excuse the slow offence,
Of my dull bearer, when from thee I speed,
From where thou art, why shoulld I hast me thence,
Till I returne of posting is noe need.   (51.1-4)

Space precludes what might, in any case, be a tedious recital of
comparable cases. I therefore simply ask the reader to consider in

the Quarto text the following passages or lines, and judge for himself whether the punctuation would be likely to confuse a modern general reader: 52.6-7, 58.10-11, 84.1-5, 86.14, 87.13-14, 93.1, 99.1-5, 109.5, 119.10, 131.9, 137.5, 140.5-6.

Still more often, however, the unfamiliar character of the Quarto punctuation would be likely to distract or irritate a modern reader. This is especially so with the Quarto's commas, many of which would seem to him utterly needless. The following may serve as examples: the terminal commas in 5.1, 6.1, 33.1, 38.5, 67.7, 71.5, 74.1, 74.5, 77.7, 82.7, 82.9, 83.3, 93.2, 100.1, 100.5, 101.10, 107.9, 109.9, 118.7, 128.9, 139.1, 140.3, 143.1, 143.6, 144.5, 147.1, 151.7, 151.9, 151.13, 153.5; and the medial commas in 31.13, 61.1, 77.4, and 94.2.

It is, indeed, with respect to this matter of Quarto commas that I wish to make a little use of Percy Simpson's researches. Simpson devotes nearly a third of his book to Elizabethan and Jacobean uses of the comma which differ from those current in modern times. He enumerated and exemplified twenty such uses. One such use Simpson describes as "Comma equivalent to a dash."[30] We might justifiably conclude that where a Quarto comma is really "equivalent to a dash" the proper way of representing it in a modern edition is by a dash. Such a case occurs in 54.9-11. Here the Quarto has:

> But for their virtue only is their show,
> They liue vnwoo'd, and vnrespected fade,
> Die to themselues.

I suggest that the comma after "fade" is really equivalent to a modern dash, and that if we print a dash we shall represent the movement and tone of the poem better for modern readers.

Another use indicated by Simpson is to mark the logical subject (page 34). Among the examples he gives is a line from *A Midsummer Night's Dream:*

> For beasts that meete me, runne away for feare,   (II.ii.95)

Simpson's point is that this use differs from modern usage, in which there would be no comma after "me." He is quite right; but

I submit that there is therefore nothing to be gained, in such a case, by printing a comma after "me" in a modern edition. There are parallel cases in the Sonnets, e.g., 69.1-2, where the Quarto has:

> Those parts of thee that the worlds eye doth view,
> Want nothing that the thought of hearts can mend:

The comma after "view" marks off the logical subject; but in modern usage logical subjects are not marked off in this way, so that it will be proper to drop that comma.

Another heading in Simpson is "Comma before a noun clause" (page 41). The Quarto itself does not adhere to such a practice consistently (e.g., 56.1-2), but there is a good instance at 57.9-10:

> Nor dare I question with my iealious thought,
> Where you may be, or your affaires suppose,

In modern practice there would be no comma after "thought,"; and so, clearly recognizing the difference in practice, we can reasonably keep to our own.

Similar considerations apply to a number of Simpson's other categories, such as "Comma before the 'defining' relative"; "Comma before 'as'"; "Comma before 'then'." We have, indeed, already considered cases of these kinds in the first part of this study, and found that the Quarto is not consistent with regard to them. Even were it consistent, however, since the practices mentioned would differ from modern practice there is no good reason why we should adopt them. All those practices were merely conventions for the sake of indicating grammatical structure, not for the sake of indicating pauses,[31] and those conventions for indicating grammatical structure are no longer used.

On the other hand, Simpson does include two kinds of use which present a different problem: "Comma marking a metrical pause" and "The emphasizing comma" (pages 29 and 26). Fortunately, he includes a number of examples from the Sonnets of the first use, and one example of the second.

One or two of the examples Simpson gives of commas marking a metrical pause are well worth serious consideration. For instance, he contends perceptively that the rhythm is spoiled by the pointing of 12.13-14 often found in modern editions:

> And nothing 'gainst Time's scythe can make defence
> Save breed, to brave him when he takes thee hence.

Yet it does not follow that we should adopt his suggestion and simply reproduce the Quarto pointing:

> And nothing gainst Times sieth can make defence
> Saue breed to braue him, when he takes thee hence.

Such pointing in a modern edition could even suggest the absurd idea that the child would be born simultaneously with the death of its father! Indeed, in this case the best course for a modern editor may be to drop the comma altogether. With regard to some of Simpson's other examples, e.g.,

> Or who is he so fond will be the tombe,
> Of his selfe loue to stop posterity?   (3.7-8)

and also 4.1-2, 6.1-4, 7.1-2, 151.7-8, I can only agree with Alden in finding Simpson's defense of the Quarto punctuation quite unconvincing.[32] In each of these instances I feel quite sure that a modern editor who drops the comma is right in doing so.

Simpson's solitary example from the Sonnets of "The emphasizing comma" is equally lacking in cogency:

> And when a woman woes, what womans sonne,
> Will sourely leaue her till he haue preuailed.   (41.7-8)

We do not know why a comma was written or printed after "sonne." For all we know it may not have been for anything to do with emphasis. In any case, even if that was the whole reason, it would be useless for the modern editor to try to convey the emphasis by the same means. To do so he would need to use italics for the last three words of line 7, and drop the terminal comma.

Indeed, we may, I believe, truly say in general terms that if Simpson were right in holding that the Elizabethan and Jacobean

printers printed systematically but that their conventions of punctuation were in many cases very different from our own, it would by
no means follow that these conventions should be adopted in
modern editions of such books as Shakespeare's Sonnets; but, on
the contrary, the true implication would be that a modern editor, in
order to represent the poems accurately to a modern reader, would
often need to depart from the old punctuation. Thus Simpson's
work (though Simpson himself would not have liked the idea) can
be used in support of the general practice followed by modern editors of the Sonnets, of modernizing the punctuation.

There is, however, one particular punctuational feature noted by
Simpson which calls for special mention here, though, strangely
enough, he does not insist upon it. It is a curious use of the colon
(pages 67-71). Simpson quotes several examples of it from the Sonnets. These are:

> If thou suruiue my well contented daie,
> When that churle death my bones with dust shall couer
> And shalt by fortune once more re-suruay:
> These poore rude lines of thy deceased Louer: (32.1-4)

> That by this seperation I may giue:
> That due to thee which thou deseru'st alone: (39.7-8)

> Nor *Mars* his sword, nor warres quick fire shall burne:
> The liuing record of your memory.   (55.7-8)[33]

Simpson considers that the colon was in each case intended to
mark an emphatic pause, but he comments that in these cases,
unlike some others he had quoted from the plays, "the sense hardly
seems to justify so strong a pause" and that "the check to the
rhythm could be given equally well by the emphasizing comma."
Simpson's last point seems to be a slip, since "the emphasizing
comma" was, according to him, intended to emphasize the words
preceding it, not those following it. His first point is also rather
doubtful, for these cases are puzzling. I should not be greatly surprised if here we do have instances of Shakespeare's own punctuation surviving in the printed text, and if the intention was, in each
case, to give strong emphasis to the following line. There are occasional instances of the same phenomenon in the work of other

sonneteers, e.g., in Constable's *Diana* (1592 or 1594):

> shee knowes the richnes of that perfect place:
> hath yet such health as it my life can saue.[34]

The "perfect place" there being the mistress's face, the colon precedes what is clearly intended as a striking conceit. In the cases from the Sonnets I cannot agree with Simpson that a comma would have done as well as a colon, for who could have told that it was an "emphasizing comma" and not some other kind? On the other hand, how should a modern editor represent the emphasis, if it was intended? Three courses seem possible: (1) to drop the colon, and print the emphasized line in italics; (2) to keep the colon, and explain what function it may have been intended to fulfill (as Dover Wilson does); or (3) simply to drop the colon and rely on the power of the emphasized line to come over to the reader without any special device of punctuation. For (3) as against (2) it could be argued that the power of the line itself is essential evidence for the intention of the old punctuation, and that therefore the meaning might well be clear to a reader without the colon. But (1) might possibly be the best course.

I must now leave Simpson, however, and continue indicating some of the typical kinds of case where modified pointing seems to express the meaning and movement of the poems better than the Quarto pointing would do.

One very large class of cases is where the Quarto punctuation would involve a mistaken proportion between pauses. Can one credibly maintain that the Quarto punctuation of 35.9-14 indicates accurately the proportion between the pauses in the poem? The lines in the Quarto stand thus:

> For to thy sensuall fault I bring in sence,
> Thy aduerse party is thy Aduocate,
> And gainst my selfe a lawfull plea commence,
> Such ciuill war is in my loue and hate,
>   That I an accessary needs must be,
>   To that sweet theefe which sourely robs from me, [sic]

The reader may care to consider a number of other instances (terminal except where otherwise indicated), for which, in the case of references to single lines, I indicate in parentheses what would seem preferable pointing in a modern edition: 7.4 (;), 38.9-12, 41.1 (: or .), 74.6 (:), 74.12 (: or .), 79.2 (;), 79.10 (medial) (;), 81.6 (;), 83.8 (.), 85.12 (., 91.6 (;), 97.10 (;), 109.14 (medial) (; or :), 110.8 (.), 110.9 (:), 111.7 (: or .), 117.4 (;), 117.6 (;), 118.2 (;), 120.13 (: or ;), 121.10 (; or :), 122.10 (;), 130.1-4, 133.10 (;), 133.13 (medial) (;), 136.3 (; or :), 138.7 (: or ;), 151.1-2, 151.10 (medial) (. or at least ;). These are all cases where a heavier stop than the Quarto's seems to be required. There are also cases, though fewer, where a lighter stop than the Quarto's would be preferable. For instance, something lighter than the Quarto's full stops seems advisable at 49.8, 63.8, 64.4, 64.8, 75.4, 93.8, 118.4, 122.4, 141.4, 147.12. We must also remember (so as not to fall again into the habit of feeling confident that the Quarto punctuation is "light" or "fluid") that a modern edition should often drop the Quarto's commas.

The last type of case I want to mention is where punctuational devices not used or rarely used in the Quarto would bring out the sense, feeling, tone, or movement more vividly for modern readers. Quotation marks would be helpful in, e.g., 2.10-11, 32.10-14, 51.13-14, 105.9-10, 139.9-12, 145.2, 145.13, 145.14, 151.14. Dashes, either alone or after a comma, semicolon, or colon would express the life of the poem well in certain cases, e.g., 65.13 (—), 80.14 (:—), 90.12 (;—), 93.10 (,—), 97.5 (,—), 110.11 (—), 132.1-2 (,——), 140.6 (;—), 142.1 (—), 142.7 (—), 143.10 (;—), 149.14 (—), 153.14 (—). Exclamation marks, which are used in the Quarto, but not often, would help in, e.g., 65.9, 93.14, 96.10, 96.12, 109.2, 125.13, 128.8, 133.2, 142.14.

I have been concerned in this study to defend the traditional practice of editors since the middle of the eighteenth century, who have altered the Quarto punctuation so as to represent more fully to readers of the Sonnets in their time the sense, feeling, tone, and movement of the poems. In the course of my defense I have attacked the Quarto punctuation for its inconsistencies and inadequacies, and certain modern critics for their superstitious beliefs or "certainties" about its authenticity, and for their hypersubtle "discoveries" of the nonexistent. It is important, on the other hand, not to fall into exaggeration in one's turn. One must admit that it is possible that some at least of Shakespeare's own punctuation survives in the Quarto text. One must allow to the Quarto text some attempt at system. One must also admit that even in a modern text designed to fulfill the functions described, the Quarto punctuation of a fair number of lines could be kept. Indeed, the maximum number of lines for emending whose punctuation a good case could be made seems to me to be about 1250. (Pooler in his third Arden edition [1943] repunctuates about that number.) Thus approximately 900 lines definitely need no alteration; and possibly about 150-200 more could be allowed to stand without seriously derogating from the ideal of expressing the poems as accurately as possible to modern general readers. All the same, this does mean that to attain that ideal it is advisable to repunctuate half, or somewhat more than half, the total number of lines. This is not to say, however, that it is not also useful for modern editors to issue editions altering the Quarto punctuation very little. Such editions, which purge the Quarto only of gross errors, also have their value. This is partly a historical value (to show how the Sonnets might have been punctuated in Shakespeare's time if they had been correctly printed), and partly a criticial value (to help to check any really wild tendencies in repunctuation, and to enable specialists familiar with the ways of Elizabethan and Jacobean punctuation to form their own interpretations). I cannot believe, however, that they have any considerable value as a means of revealing to the general reader significances which could not be better represented by forms of punctuation current in our own time. Good facsimile Quartos also have a historical and critical value; and scholarly and critical annotation of them, both textual and interpretative, is a service to Shakespearean scholarship. Again, however, the general reader should not expect to "get closer to Shakespeare's meanings" in virtue of their punctuation than he would by using editions in which the obsolete items of punctuation have been discriminatingly discarded. We need to resist the very natural tendency of editors who issue editions preserving the Quarto punctuation with few or no changes, to try to persuade us that such editions are the only right kind, and that a long line of modern editors have been ,on the wrong track. These modern editors may well have been a good deal more lucidly mindful of the transmission of Shakespeare's poems as living works of art than champions of exclusive antiquarianism could ever be.

NOTES

NOTES TO POISSON

[1]Laurens J. Mills, *One Soul in Bodies Twain: Friendship in Tudor Literature and Stuart Drama* (Bloomington, Ind.: Principia Press, 1937). See Ch. IV. Five pages of this chapter identify a number of classical commonplaces relating to the Sonnets.

[2]In Barnfield's twenty sonnets the youth, Ganymede, appears simply to be a substitute for the usual mistress of the sonnet convention. The poet does not develop the theme but abandons it for conventional love in the odes which follow immediately in the 1595 edition. See *Cynthia. With Certaine Sonnets and the Legend of Cassandra* (London: Humphrey Lownes, 1595).

[3]"Of Friendship," *Essays of Michael Lord of Montaigne*, trans. John Florio (1603), World's Classics (London, 1904), I, 218.

[4]*De Amicitia*, VI, 22 (p. 132). This and all subsequent references to the original are in the Loeb edition (London: Heineman, 1959). In all cases the English is cited from the translation of Thomas Newton, *Fowre severall treatises of M. Tullius Cicero Conteyninge discourses of Frendshipe: Oldage: Paradoxes and Scipio his Dreame* (London: Thomas Marshe, 1577), STC 5274. The reference here is to folio 10 verso.

[5]*De Amicitia*, XXVII, 100 (p. 206). Newton, fol. 42^r.

[6]This essay follows the text of Irving Ribner's revised *The Sonnets*, ed. George Lyman Kittredge, (Toronto, (1968).

[7]*De Amicitia*, XXI, 80 (p. 188). Newton, fol. 34^v

[8]*De Amicitia,* XXI, 81 (p. 188). Newton, fol. 35ʳ.

[9]*De Amicitia,* XIV, 50 (p. 160). Newton, fol. 22ᵛ.

[10]Montaigne, ed. cit. (above, n. 3), p. 218.

[11]Montaigne, pp. 219-220.

[12]Montaigne, pp. 216-217.

[13]Montaigne, p. 220.

[14]*Symposium,* 183, in *Plato,* trans. Lane Cooper (New York, 1955), p. 229.

[15]*Marsilio Ficino's Commentary on Plato's Symposium,* trans. Sears Jayne, Univ. of Mo. Stud., XIX, 1 (Columbia, Mo., 1944), pp. 146-147.

[16]Montaigne, p. 222.

[17]*De Amicitia,* VII, 23 (p. 132). Newton, fol. 10ᵛ, 11ʳ.

[18]Marginalia upon Ficino's *Epistolae* (Venice, 1495), xviiᵛ, ll. 34-36, in Sears Jayne, *John Colet and Marsilio Ficino* (London, 1963), p. 96.

[19]Montaigne, p. 222.

[20]*Symposium,* 196 (p. 244).

[21]Loc. cit.: ". . . once Eros fastens upon him everyone becomes a poet," says Agathon.

[22]Ficino spells out the basis of this conceit: "But when the loved one loves in return the lover leads his life in him. Here surely, is a remarkable circumstance that whenever two people are brought together in mutual affection, one lives in the other and the other lives in him. In this way they mutually exchange identities." *Commentary* (above, n. 15), p. 144.

[23]See above, n. 15.

[24]*De Amicitia,* XIX, 69(p. 178). Newton, fol. 30ᵛ.

[25]Montaigne, p. 224.

[26]Loc. cit. Cf. "Friendship based on utility is for the commercially minded"—Aristotle, *Nichomachean Ethics,* trans. W.D. Ross (Oxford, 1925), 1158a.

[27]*De Amicitia,* XXV, 91 (p. 198). Newton, fol. 39ʳ.

[28]Aristotle, op. cit. (above, n. 26), 1159a.

[29]Menander, cited by Plutarch, "Of Large Acquaintance,"

Essays and Miscellanies, ed. A.H. Clough and William W. Good-win (Boston, 1909), p. 470.

[30]Aristotle, 1157b.

[31]*De Amicitia,* IX, 32 (p. 144). Newton, fol. 15ᵛ.

[32]See Hilton Landry, "The Marriage of True Minds: Truth and Error in Sonnet 116," *Shakespeare Studies,* III (1967), 98-110.

[33]Plutarch, ed. cit. (above, n. 29), p. 474.

[34]Some years later Shakespeare reworked the fine gesture to per-fection and gave it to Antony: stripped of the pearl conceit it becomes the master stroke of the poet who could touch the heart of his characters alive: "Fall not a tear, I say; one of them rates / All that is won and lost." (*Antony* III.ix.69-70.)

[35]*De Amicitia,* XXIV, 88-89 (p. 196). Newton, fol. 38ʳ.

[36]*The Sonnets* (above, n. 6), p. 40. See also Sonnet 42.6.

[37]Edward Jenynges, *The Notable History of Two Faithfull Lovers Named Alfagus and Archelaus* (London, 1574), Dii. The story shares another feature with the Sonnets. One of the young princes is reluctant to marry despite the entreaties of his counselors.

[38]*De Amicitia,* XVI, 59 (p. 166). Newton, fol. 26ʳ.

NOTES TO INGRAM

[1]See, e.g., the following works of Caroline Spurgeon: *Leading Motives in the Imagery of Shakespeare's Tragedies* (London, 1930); *Shakespeare's Iterative Imagery* (London, 1931); *Shakespeare's Imagery and What It Tells Us* (Cambridge, 1935).

[2]E. A. Armstrong, *Shakespeare's Imagination* (London, 1946).

[3]G. Wilson Knight, *Myth and Miracle* (London, 1929) and sub-sequent studies.

[4]M. M. Morozov in *Shakespeare Survey,* II (1949); Wolfgang H. Clemen, *The Development of Shakespeare's Imagery* (London, 1951).

[5]T. W. Baldwin, *Shakespeare's Small Latin and Lesse Greeke*

(Chicago, 1944); Sister Miriam Joseph, *Shakespeare's Use of the Arts of Language* (New York, 1947).

[6]G. Wilson Knight, *The Mutual Flame* (London, 1955).

[7]J. W. Lever, *The Elizabethan Love Sonnet* (London, 1956).

[8]T. W. Baldwin, *The Literary Genetics of Shakespeare's Poems and Sonnets* (Urbana, (1956).

[9]H. W. Wells, *Poetic Imagery* (New York, 1924); C. Day Lewis, *The Poetic Image* (London, 1947); Rosemund Tuve, *Elizabethan and Metaphysical Imagery* (Chicago, 1947).

[10]Winifred M.T. Nowottny, "Formal Elements in Shakespeare's Sonnets I-VI" *Essays in Criticism,* II (1952, 76-84).

[11]G. K. Hunter "The Dramatic Technique of Shakespeare's Sonnets," *Essays in Criticism,* III (1953), 152-164.

[12]Hunter, p. 157.

[13]As Rosemund Tuve demonstrated twenty years ago, this commonplace is in one large respect a misleading one.

[14]This essay follows the text of *Shakespeare's Sonnets,* ed. William G. Ingram and Theodore Redpath, 2d impr. (London, 1967). Our reading of l. 4 is defended in a note.

[15]*Antony and Cleopatra,* Phoenix ed. (1961), p. 100.

[16]Shakespeare is scarcely represented in these popular collections by a sonnet until well into the nineteenth century. Malone[1], the first important critical edition, appeared in 1780; Malone[2] in 1790. Vicesimus Knox's *Elegant Extracts* (the verse volumes, first issued in 1789, were the enormously popular "Golden Treasury" of the turn of that century) has three sonnets by Milton, a few each by Charlotte Smith, Helen Maria Williams, Bowles and Warton, and no others. Shakespeare is represented by extracts from the plays (108 pp. double column in the large 8vo. edition). I know of no later edition that included any of his sonnets. *Ellis's Specimens of the Early English Poets* (1790), designed to illustrate "the irregular compositions" of "these antiquated writers," has five sonnets by Daniel, three by Drummond, the familiar Drayton sonnet, and only one each by Sidney and Shakespeare (57); the other Shakespeare inclusions are songs, one of them a spurious attribution.

[17]My italics. Auden's talk was printed in *The Listener,* July 2, 1964, and published as the Introduction to the Signet Classic

Shakespeare edition of *The Sonnets,* ed. William Burto (New York, 1964). The statement quoted appears on pp. xxiv-xxv.

[18]My italics. In W.P. Ker, *Form and Style in Poetry,* ed. R.W. Chambers (London, 1928), pp. 139-140.

[19]Ker, pp. 173 ff.

[20]See above, n. 10.

[21]J.W. Lever has shown a developing interrelation of the images of the first group of sonnets and how this binds them into a "structural sequence of images" (op. cit., pp. 189 ff.).

[22]W.H. Hadow's Henry Sidgwick Lecture for 1925, *A Comparison of Poetry and Music* (Cambridge, 1926), p. 15.

NOTES TO NOWOTTNY

[1]Henry Morley and W. Hall Griffin, *English Writers,* XI, 333. In a note, p. 328, Griffin writes, "That the poems fall naturally into the three main divisions given above may be indicated by the fact that my own division had been adopted before I was familiar with that of Mr. Spalding." Spalding's essay, "Shakespeare's Sonnets," appeared in *The Gentleman's Magazine,* CCXLII (1878), 300-318. Both writers are cited in Hyder E. Rollins's *A New Variorum Edition of Shakespeare: The Sonnets,* 2 vols. (Philadelphia, 1944), II, 80, to which I am much indebted, as also to Alden's edition (see below), and to the corpus of scholarship generally. In a field so well-worked, to note specifically every point already made by a predecessor would make the footnotes about as long as the essay. When on any particularly notable issue I am indebted to or aware of prior work I try to make this clear.

[2]According to R.M. Alden, ed. *The Sonnets of Shakespeare* (Boston, 1916), p. 427.

[3]John Dover Wilson, ed. *The Sonnets,* The New Shakespeare (Cambridge, 1966), p. 207, and pp. lxxxiii ff. and 202 ff.

[4]Described and categorized by Claes Schaar, *Elizabethan Son-*

net Themes and the Dating of Shakespeare's "Sonnets" (Lund, 1962), pp. 84 ff.

[5]Tucker Brooke, ed. *Shakespeare's Sonnets* (New York, 1936), pp. 302-304 and p. 47.

[6]This quotation, from Dr. Orville Ward Owen's *Sir Francis Bacon's Cipher Story,* is taken from William F. Friedman and Elizabeth S. Friedman, *The Shakespearean Ciphers Examined* (New York, 1957), p. 64.

[7]Op. cit., p. 47.

[8]Edmund Dowden, ed. *The Sonnets of William Shakespeare* (London, 1881), p. 220. Alden and Rollins in their notes on Sonnet 108 cite Dowden's gloss, with "excited" (rev. ed., p. 270); C. K. Pooler cites it with "felt." The fact that there were two editions of 1881 is noted by Alden, p. 488.

[9]George Wyndham, ed. *The Poems of Shakespeare* (London, 1898), p. 313.

[10]Stephen Hawes, *The Pastime of Pleasure,* cited in the *New English Dictionary,* 1d.

[11]In William G. Ingram and Theodore Redpath's *Shakespeare's Sonnets* (London, 1964), p. 250 (notes to Sonnet 108), a sustained rendering of the sestet, making this application, is given (as one of "two concurrent meanings").

[12]Wyndham in a rather involved note (*op. cit.,* pp. 313-314) associates "page" (1.12) with "antique pen" in Sonnet 106. Alden in a long note (p. 254) in which he weighs the meaning "page of a book" against the meaning "page-boy" (each supported by several editors), points out that "Shakespeare never (unless here) uses the word "page" in that [i.e. the former] connection, but always 'leaf,'" and he sums up "I believe, therefore, that the line means simply 'makes old age his servant', instead of yielding it the mastery."

[13]Schaar (op. cit. [above, n. 4] p. 30), calling this a common theme, refers the reader to his earlier study, *An Elizabethan Sonnet Problem* (Lund, 1960), p. 21, n. 1.

[14]Martin Seymour-Smith, ed. *Shakespeare's Sonnets* (London, 1963), p. 161.

[15]Sonnets 63-68, with 19, 21, 100, 101 and 105 are deemed (after complex argument) a group in Brents Stirling's article "A Shakespeare Sonnet Group." *PMLA,* LXXV (1960), 340-349; in his reconstruction, he puts 100 and 101 at the beginning of his group,

and gives it as his view (p. 347) that when 100 and 101 have been removed (from their position in the 1609 text) "unity unexpectedly appears in 97-104." In a related essay, "More Shakespeare Sonnet Groups." published in *Essays on Shakespeare and Elizabethan Drama in Honor of Hardin Craig* (1963), pp. 115-135, he remarks (p. 126): "an attentive reader can determine for himself whether the two pairs. 113-14 and 115-16, nullify an ordered development" (i.e., in 109-12, 117-21). The limits of the scope of my essay preclude comment on Professor Stirling's analysis of "examples of close linkage" in his article "Sonnets 127-154" in *Shakespeare 1564-1964: A Collection of Modern Essays by Various Hands*, ed. Edward A. Bloom (Providence, R.I., 1964), pp. 134-153. When I wrote my essay I had not read Professor Stirling's article "Sonnets 109-126" in *Centennial Review*, VIII (1964) 109-120, nor his important book *The Shakespeare Sonnet Order: Poems and Groups* (Berkeley and Los Angeles, 1968), Chapter II of which includes rehandling of the substance of the above-listed articles.

[16]The idea is not, in principle, novel. In 1780 Edmund Malone (cited in Alden, Rollins, and others) made the following observations on Sonnets 153/154 (not quite on a par with other "pairs," because their case is complicated by the question of their relation to an ancient epigram—see Rollins [above, n. 1], I, 391-394): "[They] are composed of the very same thoughts differently versified. ... [The poet] ... perhaps had not determined which he should prefer. He hardly could have intended to send them both into the world." J.D. Wilson (op. cit., p. 203) makes it clear (in arguing for his grouping of 104 with 97-99) that he regards 104 as superseding other sonnets: "he turned to and composed a sonnet which left him with no desire to spoil it by sending the first three of the quartet along with it."

[17]G.K. Hunter's article "The Dramatic Technique of Shakespeare's Sonnets," *Essays in Criticism*, III (1953), includes discussion of it, pp. 163-164. Ingram and Redpath (op. cit., p. 222) call it "this splendid sonnet." Readers who dissent from my criticisms may welcome Edmund Hubler's remarks, in a note in his edition of *Shakespeare's Songs and Poems* (New York, 1959), p. 104: "Various editors find that this sonnet ... is hastily written. ... Yet it makes its impact and is, in part at least, unforgettable. It represents the triumph of poetic genius over the craft of analysis." Giorgio Melchiori in his edition of *Shakespeare's Sonnets* (1964), prais-

ing its pictorial quality, makes a comment on the stylistic resemblance between this and the "begetting" sonnets, which might be borne in mind if one were to go on from the idea of alternative versions, to speculate on their dates of composition: *"Questo sonetto . . . e piacevole sopr̲attutto per il numero è la vivacità delle immagini, ma stilisticamente si direbbe un'imitazione abile ed elegante della dizione e della* imagery *dei sonetti matrimoniali"* (p. 186).

NOTES TO PIRKHOFER

[1]This essay is a severely condensed abridgment of a book on the dramatic character of the Sonnets.

[2]See Anton M. Pirkhofer, "'A Pretty Pleasing Pricket'–On the Use of Alliteration in Shakespeare's Sonnets," *Shakespeare Quarterly,* XIV (1963), 3-14.

[3]For discussions of the role of the "substance-shadow" motif in Shakespeare's work, see Maria Rickert, "Das Schattenmotiv bei Shakespeare," *Anglia,* LXXI (1953). 274 ff.; Hilton Landry, *Interpretations in Shakespeare's Sonnets* (Berkeley, 1963), pp. 45-48.

[4]See my article on Shakespeare as a creative force in American literature, published as part of a *Festschrift* (with a summary in English), listed in the *Shakespeare Quarterly* Annotated World Bibliography for 1965 as no. 1030.

[5]Anton Pirkhofer, "Zur Einheit des dichterischen Impulses in Thomas Hardy's Kunsttheorie und Dichtung," *German.-Roman. Monatsschrift,* XXVI (1938), 232-246.

[6]See my contribution to "The Critical Forum," *Essays in Criticism,* XII (1962), 104-106, and Wolfgang H. Clemen, *Wandlungen des Botenberichts bei Shakespeare* (Munich, 1952).

[7]See Wolfgang Schmidt's "Sinnesaenderung und Bildvertiefung in Shakespeares Sonetten," *Anglia,* LXII (1938), 286-305.

[8]Cf. A. Nejgebauer's complaint in *Shakespeare Survey,* 15 (1962), 17, that "the study of the use of figurative speech in the sonnets is almost a blank in criticism" and that "nobody has as yet discussed their imagery as a whole." A laudable first attempt at filling the gap has been made by William G. Ingram and Theodore

Redpath in their essay on "Shakespeare's Use of Imagery in the Sonnets, and its Relation to the Structure and Texture" in their *Fifty-Five Sonnets of Shakespeare* (London, 1967), pp. 165-179.

⁹For these, see *A New Variorum Edition of Shakespeare: The Sonnets*, ed. Hyder E. Rollins, 2 vols. (Philadelphia, 1944), II, 74-116, 400-437.

¹⁰F. T. Prince, *Shakespeare, the Writer and His Work* (London, 1964), pp. 39-64.

¹¹Prince, p. 59. A more moderate view is taken by Francis Berry in Ch. VII ("Shakespeare's Voice and the Voices of His Instruments") of his *Poetry and the Physical Voice* (London, 1962). Berry maintains (p. 127) that "there is nothing we can call dramatic about the early sonnets" where the poet's voice "avoids dramatic expedients" (whatever these may be). By contrast, "the later sonnets show the most abrupt, or dramatic, peaks and troughs in the line of pitch . . . the sudden, and so dramatic, fluctuations of pitch and tone" (p. 129). Much as one may be in sympathy with Berry's fundamental tenet that "the sonnet was conceived as being heard from the voice of its creator . . . by an invited company in a small chamber" (but this hardly applies to the epistolary sonnets), one is cautioned against accepting Berry's findings by (a) contradictions in his statements in allowing for a certain dramatic quality even in the early sonnets (of which he discusses Sonnet 5 as a typical representative), as is indirectly admitted by his use of such terms as "dialectic" and "counter-statement" for those very sonnets; (b) the fact that what he says on the punctuation in the Quarto text of Sonnets 15 and 115 is not corroborated by a scrutiny of the text (the punctuation of both sonnets being, in point of fact, rather similar except for there being no semicolon in 15 as against one in 115); (c) the impossibility of isolating one formal aspect (namely, the "voice" as musical pitch, etc.) from others such as mood, attitude, imagery, and so on.

¹²Arthur Mizener, "The Structure of Figurative Language in Shakespeare's Sonnets,"*Southern Review,* V (1940), 730 ff.

¹³J. W. Lever, *The Elizabethan Love Sonnet* (London, 1956); G. K. Hunter, "The Dramatic Technique of Shakespeare's Sonnets," *Essays in Criticism,* III (1953), 152-164.

¹⁴Walter Mönch in his *Das Sonett, Gestalt und Geschichte*

(Heidelberg, 1955), pp. 37 ff. and elsewhere, also stresses the relationship between the sonnet and the drama in speaking of an "Exposition," a "Krisenpunkt" (climactic point), and a "Katastrophe." Like Th. de Banville, he characterizes the inner rhythm of the Shakespearean sonnet as a dramatic movement punctuated by "revirements," rising to a climax and falling away to a catastrophe —a bipartite movement, in short, of "tension" and "détente" which causes the sonnet to contain "within the smallest volume, the greatest mass of poetic energy" (p. 139). Mönch's further remarks, however, about the epigrammatic and didactic character of Shakespeare's sonnets, as well as his tendency to neglect the comic strain in them while overstressing their "daemonic" and "a-" or even "anti-Platonic" content, can hardly be accepted without reservation.

[15]Hallett Smith, *Elizabethan Poetry* (Cambridge, 1952), pp. 163-171.

[16]Waldo F. McNeir, "An Apology for Spenser's *Amoretti,*" *Die Neuren Sprachen,* XIV (1965), 1-9.

[17]See Pirkhofer, *Figurengestaltung im Beowulf-Epos* (Heidelberg, 1940), pp. 22-26.

[18]Cf. W.G. Ingram's pertinent comment on the differences between Shakespeare's and Sidney's use of imagery and mode of thought-progression in his contribution to this book.

[19]In a written communication Dr. Redpath agrees that this term is of interest and should have been annotated. Cf. the passage on the "world" in "Shakespeare in His Own Age," *Shakespeare Survey,* 14 (1961).

[20]In her article "Formal Elements in Shakespeare's Sonnets I-VI," *Essays in Criticism,* II (1952), 76-84, Mrs. Winifred Nowottny sees in Sonnet 1 a "litany of images" (which, she admits, is at the same time "a litany of considerations and arguments"). While objecting to her use of a liturgical term to describe the intense tone of worldly persuasion in Sonnet 1, I agree with her about the "modulation" of images in Sonnet 2, although even here she appears to overlook the forward thrust of the argument which culminates not in the second but in the third quatrain.

[21]See his *Kontrast und Polaritaet in den Charakterbildern Shakespeares* (Berne, 1951).

[22]On paired sonnets and sonnet clusters, see Landry's analyses, notably in Chs. 2, 3, and 5 of his *Interpretations* (above, n. 3).

[23]As to the use of pronouns in 12 and 13, there seems to be a palpable reason for employing "thou" in 12 and "you" in 13. This may be seen if the "thou" forms of 12 are tentatively replaced by "you" forms, which is possible without changing the rhyme words. The "thou" forms no doubt widen the gap between the generalizing and the personal strains in 12 so that the first "thy" of line 9 produces a shock of personal application which would be lost by the substitution of a more distant "your." Although in Sonnet 13 the "you" forms may be explained as conditioned by the necessity of rhyme-finding, the application of the substitution method here shows that the monotonous yet cumulative repetition of "you" forms (fourteen in the first two quatrains) achieves both a concentration of the second person (of the Friend) and the dramatic effect of an insistent urgency which would be dissipated by substituting a variety of "thou-thyself-thou-thine-thou-thyself" forms.

[24]See Professor Peter Ure's thoughtful inaugural lecture, *Shakespeare and the Inward Self of the Tragic Hero* (University of Durham, 1961), and R. B. Heilman, "'Twere Best not Know Myself," *Shakespeare Quarterly*, XV (1964), 89-98.

[25]Cf. Sir Edmund K. Chambers' dictum that "each sonnet is generally self-contained," *William Shakespeare* (London, 1930), I, 560.

[26]For details on this amusing if fanciful habit, see Appendix V of Rollins's *Variorum*.

[27]*Variorum*, I, 75 f.

[28]See the parallels cited in *Variorum*, I, 76.

[29]As for the epithet "swart Complexioned" in line 11, it appears to be an original variation of the phrase "blacke night" found in the preceding sonnet. Although torturers in the plays frequently appear in pairs, as they do in Sonnet 28, they are generally of the same sex (male). But the use of "swart," often applied to the complexion of a female (on the evidence of C. T. Onions' *Shakespeare Glossary*), together with the phrase "her old face" in 27 would rather point to the night of 28 being conceived as a female, too. It is in keeping with this interpretation that the poet uses "flatter" for his remonstrances with the female "torturing partner."

[30]Landry compares him to a court fool, op. cit. (above, n. 3), p. 77.

[31]See Landry's lucid account of the equivocal character of 58 (op. cit., pp. 72-76), and compare the edition of William G. Ingram and Theodore Redpath on line 7 (*Shakespeare's Sonnets* [London, 1964], p. 136).

[32]On the Elizabethan notion of time, see Professor Erwin Stuerzl, *Der Zeitbegriff in der Elisabethanischen Literatur* (Stuttgart, 1065), pp. 69-82, where he distinguished three roots of the Renaissance idea of time: the medieval idea of the transitoriness of life, the revival of a classical *topos,* and the cult of beauty. As regards Shakespeare, a distinctly personal element should be added to this triad, namely an intense realization of the destructive effect of time on the fundamental human values, among them "truth" and "beauty."

NOTES TO LANDRY

[1]Ransom's essay appeared in the *Southern Review,* III (1938), 531-553, and *The World's Body* (New York, 1938). For convenience, I follow the text reprinted in *A Casebook on Shakespeare's Sonnets,* ed. Gerald Willen and Victor Reed (New York, 1964) and cite their pagination. The sonnets are also quoted from their edition.

[2]*De Anima* and *Parva Naturalia,* among other treatises, in various editions and translations provide most of the basic ideas that Galen, Nemesius, Aquinas, and others modify and expand. A handy but scattered summary of the tradition appears in Burton's *Anatomy of Melancholy.*

[3]The reference to a deliberative aspect of imagination generally has been ignored.

[4]William Bates, *The Harmony of the Divine Attributes,* 3d ed. (London, 1688), p. 331. This neutral Puritan statement has thousands of parallels in Catholic and Protestant writing of the period.

See Pascal's *Pensées,* 82, for a severe attack on imagination and the sort of view Ransom has in mind in his fifth section.

[5]"Imagination," "fantasy" or "phantasy," and "fancy" are generally used as equivalent terms.

[6]See Richard Sibbes, *The Soul's Conflict with Itself,* 4th ed. (London, 1651), p. 170, on the imagination as first wheel of the soul as a mill; also Edward Reynolds' *Treatise of the Passions and Faculties of the Soul of Man* (London, 1640), ch. 4.

[7]Ed. cit., p. 179.

[8]Taylor's *Works,* ed. Heber, IV, 197-198. Taylor, the "metaphysical" prose writer, is at heart a medieval ascetic, as the bulk of his works reveal. Note that music, ornaments, perfumes, and so on are brought into the church to bribe the dangerous and shallow fancy with inferior things.

[9]"Shakespeare at Sonnets" in *A Casebook* (above, n. 1), pp. 211-212. Hereafter, page references will be given in parentheses after citation.

[10]C. D. Bowen's *Francis Bacon* (Boston, 1963). pp. 102-104, is among the recent works which go over this familiar ground.

[11]*The Poetical Works of Edmund Spenser,* ed. Smith and De Selincourt (London, 1912), p. 571.

[12]The poem is organized according to the rhetorical figure *carmen correlativum* or "the gatherer."

[13]Discussions of 66 and 129 appear in my *Interpretations in Shakespeare's Sonnets* (Berkeley, 1963), pp. 82-87, 96-104; hereafter cited as *Interpretations.*

[14]Santayana's comments (from *Reason in Society*) are made with an eye on Aristotle's discussion of friendship in the *Ethics.*

[15]See my "The Marriage of True Minds: Truth and Error in Sonnet 116," *Shakespeare Studies,* III (1967), 101-102, on the difference between these views.

[16]Winifred Nowottny's "Formal Elements in Shakespeare's Sonnets I-VI," *Essays in Criticism,* II (1952), 76-84, and her contribution, as well as those of several others, to this collection are much more satisfactory attempts to deal with problems of form.

[17]In the last line of 33 I have expanded "whē" to "when" and emended "stainteh" to "staineth."

[18] See I. A. Richards, *Speculative Instruments* (London, 1955), pp. 26 ff. and 32-33.

[19] See *Interpretations,* pp. 42-55, for a full discussion of 53 and 54.

[20] Such doubts are already present in Sonnet 48 under the guise of a fear that his friend might be stolen.

[21] Krieger's misreading of 53 and ignoring of 54 is discussed in my review of his *Window to Criticism* in *Shakespeare Studies,* I (1965), 330-331. Dover Wilson also takes 53 with 106, rather than 54, in his recent edition of the Sonnets (Cambridge, 1966).

[22] Ransom finds the compass figure unsatisfactory, perhaps because the focus shifts between tenor and vehicle.

[23] Does "line of action" refer to a poem's quasi-logical figurative argument?

[24] On Shakespeare's handling of figures, see Ransom's general remarks on p. 208.

[25] This sentence suggests that "action" is equivalent to Ransom's "object," with all that this term implies, or what would ordinarily be called the subject of the poem.

[26] On 125, see *Interpretations,* pp. 120-128, 134-137.

[27] See *Interpretations,* pp. 12-13, for remarks on Ransom's limited view of 94.

[28] Winters' "Poetic Styles, Old and New" was first published in *Four Poets on Poetry,* ed. D. C. Allen (Baltimore, 1959), pp. 44-75.

[29] These views, like much else in his lecture, go back to Winters' three-part essay in *Poetry* (1939), "The 16th Century Lyric in England."

[30] See my discussion of 57 and 58 in *Interpretations,* pp. 72-80.

[31] For discussion of 69 and 70, see *Interpretations,* pp. 28-41, 150-151.

[32] Some of Winters' clearest statements on these matters appear in "Preliminary Problems" from *The Anatomy of Nonsense* (1943), printed in *Critiques and Essays in Criticism, 1920-1948,* ed. R. W. Stallman (New York, 1949).

[33] See above, n. 15.

[34] Compare Plato, *Symposium,* 209, and Milton's *Areopagitica:*

"Books are not absolutely dead things, but do contain a potency of life in them to be as active as that soul was whose progeny they are; nay, they do preserve as in a vial the purest efficacy and extraction of that living intellect that bred them."

³⁵Since line 9 in Winters' text begins "Look! what . . .," he evidently fails to realize that "Look what" signifies "whatever."

³⁶As William G. Ingram and Theodore Redpath point out in their edition, "wastes of time" in Sonnet 12 does not mean "deserts." *Shakespeare's Sonnets* (London, 1964), p. 28.

³⁷See I. A. Richard, op. cit. (above, n. 18), pp. 26-38; and my discussion in *The Twenties,* ed. Langford and Taylor (Deland, Fla., 1966), p. 20.

NOTES TO LINDSAY

¹Paul Valéry, *Œuvres* (Paris, 1957), I, 456.

²Valéry, I, 451.

³Since this study is only indirectly concerned with textual problems in the original, citations from Shakespeare's Sonnets are to the edition in modern spelling by Hyder E. Rollins in the Crofts Classics series (New York, 1951).

⁴"The French sonnet form" is used here in the broadest sense and refers to the division into two quatrains and two tercets; Lafond's rhyme scheme is irregular.

⁵Omitted from this list of translations of Sonnet 73, but not from the general discussion, are the translations by Guizot (1862; "Death's second self" = *seconde édition de la mort*), Simone Arnaud (1891), Emile Legouis (1899), and Mélot du Dy (1943). The translations by Alfred Copin (1888) and Georges Roth (1926) were not available for this study. See the Bibliography for details concerning these translations.

⁶With preface by Gilbert Lely, biographer and editor of the Marquis de Sade. Lely includes his own translation of Sonnet 40, which is not without merit. One may note in passing that for Lely,

Shakespeare's "prise de possession virile de la réalité" is sufficient proof of heterosexuality (Coll. **"Les Phares"** [Paris], 1945, p. 16).

[7]This is common practice in the translations of this sonnet; only H. Thomas (1961) translates this word literally; see p. 206.

[8]Cf. *dans le repos* (Hugo, Legouis), *en son repos* (d'Uccle), *au grand repos* (Garnier). All of these translators use the same verb, *sceller.*

[9]Cited in the Introduction to the 1922 edition of Garnier's translation (Paris: J.M. Dent), pp. xxi-xxii.

[10]It is the d'Uccle translation of the Sonnets that Camus quotes, without reference to translator or sonnet number, in *Carnets, II* (Paris, 1964); he gives Sonnets 27.8 and 124.13-14. The entry falls between March and August of 1942, presumably shortly after d'Uccle's translation was published in Algiers by Edmond Charlot, who had published all of Camus' books through 1941.

[11]Of all the translators, Jouve is the best-known poet in his own right, and the introduction to his translation shows a keen appreciation of the poetry of the Sonnets and of the problems he faced as translator, *Il faut souligner,* he writes, *la présence d'une dialectique, qui le plus souvent supplante l'image.* His objectives in translating are in accord with such recent French theorists of translation as Georges Mounin (see his *Les Belles Infidèles* [Paris, 1955] and *Les Problèmes théoriques de la traduction,* préf. de Dominique Aury [Paris, 1963]). With regard to the modalities of literal and free translation, he states that "en s'éloignant comme il le faut de la lettre, [une traduction] approche l'esprit: elle doit établir d'abord un poème français, avec tout l'appareil de ses correspondances, et ce poème doit être en outre constamment nourri de la *substance* du poème étranger. Il faut faire le contraire de 'franciser'; il faut porter la poésie française jusqu'aux moyens poétiques d'une autre langue, et qu'elle rivalise avec l'étrangère. C'est un tournoi."

[12]There is a formal innovation here in the mixing of Alexandrines and lines of 14 syllables.

[13]See Gide's remarks on verbal ambiguity and translation in his *avant-propos* to the first volume of Shakespeare, *Œuvres complètes,* Bibliothèque de la Pléiade (Paris, 1959).

[14]There are, of course, bad translations of the line such as the

following by Baldensperger: *Puis passe, allégrement, hors de la souvenance.*

[15]But not *hymen* (Lafond, Arnaud) or *épousailles* (Guerne), which are something like "wedlock" or "matrimony."

[16]Strictly speaking, Garabedian's version belongs here: *Qu'entrave au marier d'esprits vrais point admise / Ne soit par moi;* but aside from the *que* and present subjunctive, the syntax is not French.

[17]I should like to acknowledge my indebtedness in this discussion of Sonnet 94 to Hilton Landry, *Interpretations in Shakespeare's Sonnets* (Berkeley, 1963), pp. 7-27. Professor Landry's critical orientation to the Sonnets can, I believe, be felt at many points in this study.

NOTES TO RAMSEY

[1]I wish to thank the University of Chattanooga for a research grant that was used in part on the research for this paper, and Dr. Louis B. Wright (now retired) of the Folger Shakespeare Library and his staff for many courtesies, including permission to quote from photographic copy made for me at the Folger of one of their copies (with facsimile title page, Aspley imprint) of the 1609 edition of Shakespeare's Sonnets. All quotations from the Sonnets in this paper are from my photographic copy of that edition. I also owe a strong professional and warm personal debt of gratitude to Professor Edward R. Weismiller of George Washington University, who gave me some crucial hints and who also generously gave me access to his massive research files compiled while dealing with similar matters in his work on Milton's prosody for the forthcoming Variorum Milton Commentary.

[2]George Saintsbury, *History of English Prosody* (London, 1923), II, 61; Laura Riding and Robert Graves, *A Survey of Modernist Poetry* (London, 1927), p. 66.

[3]Jakob Schipper, *A History of English Versification* (Oxford,

1910), pp. 165-166; Norman Ault, ed. *Elizabethan Lyrics,* 3rd ed. (New York, 1949), pp. xiv-xv; A. W. Partridge, *Orthography in Shakespeare and Elizabethan Drama* (London, 1964), esp. pp. 95-96; C. H. Herford et al., ed. *The Works of Ben Jonson* (Oxford, 1932), IV, 338-342.

⁴William G. Ingram and Theodore Redpath, ed. *Shakespeare's Sonnets* (London, 1964), p. xxxiv.

⁵Baastian A. P. van Dam and Cornelis Stoffel, *Chapters on English Printing, Prosody* . . . (Heidelberg, 1902), pp. 49-113; Helge Kökeritz, *Shakespeare's Pronunciation* (New Haven, 1953), pp. 25-31.

⁶See Sister Miriam Joseph, *Rhetoric in Shakespeare's Time* (New York, 1948), esp. pp. 293-294.

⁷Thomas Campion, *Observations in the Art of English Poesie* (London, 1602), p. 5, from a microfilm of a British Museum copy.

⁸Kökeritz, p. 30.

⁹Kökeritz, p. 25.

¹⁰Partridge, p. 155. Partridge also places much reliance on Evelyn H. Scholl's essay, "New Light on Seventeenth Century Pronunciation . . .," *PMLA,* LIX (1944), 398-445, which shows some extra syllables were sung. This seems to me not very relevant since music, unlike the poetic foot, has of course no syllabic requirement. In a line from Campion quoted on p. 443 of Scholl's essay, "t'a-" of "t'adorn" is set to two notes of music, but so are each of the following single syllables in the same line: "coun-" of "counsel'st," "sel'st" of "counsel'st," and "-dorn" of "t'adorn."

¹¹Partridge, pp. 87, 96.

¹²E. A. Abbott, *A Shakespearian Grammar* (New York, 1966), p. 328, sec. 452. Reprint of 1870 ed.

¹³Seymour Chatman, *A Theory of Meter* (The Hague, 1965), p. 111.

¹⁴This feeling that poetry should be formal is probably more prevalent in somewhat earlier writers, e.g., Matthew A. Bayfield, *A Study of Shakespeare's Versification* (Cambridge, 1920), but it is an important cause of the later modern prejudice against disyllabism.

[15] Alexander Hume, *Of the Orthographie and Congruitie of the Briten Tongue* (c. 1617), ed. Henry B. Wheatley, Early English Text Society (London, 1865), p. 20.

[16] The following metrical sigla are used: / metrically stressed syllable; x metrically unstressed syllable; __ (under other sigla), foot; *i* iamb; *t* trochee; *a* anapest; *d* dactyl; *b* amphibrach.

[17] John Heminge and Henrie Condell, ed. *Mr. William Shakespeare's Comedies, Histories, and Tragedies* (New York, 1968) sig. A3ʳ. Facsimile of 1623 ed. prepared by Charlton Hinman.

[18] Partridge, pp. 86-87.

[19] Puttenham, *The Arte of English Poesie* (London, 1589), p. 105.

[20] Puttenham, p. 108.

[21] Van Dam, p. 63.

[22] James I, King of Great Britain, "The Revlis and Cavtelis . . . in Scottis Poesie," *The Essays of a Prentise* (Edinburgh, 1584), sig. L2ʳ.

[23] "Certayne Notes of Instruction . . .," *The Poesies of George Gascoigne* (London, 1575), sig. T3ʳ.

[24] Campion, p. 1.

[25] Samuel Daniel, *A Defence of Ryme* (London, 1603), sigs. H1ᵛ, F3ʳ.

[26] Abraham Fraunce, *The Arcadian Rhetorike* (London, 1588), ed. Ethel Seaton (Oxford, 1950), p. 26.

[27] William Webbe, *A Discourse of English Poetrie* (London, 1586), sig. D2ʳ. Photographic copy of Huntington Library copy. See Dorothy L. Sipe, *Shakespeare's Metrics* (New Haven, 1968). pp. 13-15, where evidence from contemporary prosodists is also summed up. Sipe's book, which appeared after this essay was completed, comes to conclusions similar to mine about Shakespeare's metrics, although, since she discusses only the plays, strictly speaking our work does not overlap.

[28] John Palsgrave, trans. *The Comedye of Acolastus* . . . (London, 1540), sig. E3ʳ.

[29] E. J. Dobson, *English Pronunciation 1500-1700,* 2 vols. (Oxford, 1957), esp. II, 887-891.

[30] Gascoigne, sig. U1ʳ.

[31]Henry Peacham, *The Garden of Eloquence* (London, 1577), sig. E3^r.

[32]Campion, p. 38.

[33]In n. 4 and relevant text.

[34]Ben Jonson, *The English Grammar,* p. 70, in *The Workes of Benjamin Jonson* (London, 1640), vol II. Pagination is not continuous throughout the volume.

[35]I count over fifty errors, not including metrical inconsistencies and errors in punctuation. Other scholars count otherwise, but there are a significant number by any count.

[36]Claes Schaar, *An Elizabethan Sonnet Problem* (Lund, 1960), p. 149 n.

[37]Peacham, sig. E2^v.

[38]Peacham, sig. E1^v.

[39]See Partridge, pp. 94-95; Abbott, pp. 361-363, secs. 475-476; John Thompson, *The Founding of English Metre* (London, 1961), p. 79, where he shows some puzzlement at an example, calling it a "cavalier inconsistency." Professor Edward Weismiller has collected a number of examples of such variant doublets.

[40]Kökeritz, pp. 248-249.

[41]Cf. Shakespeare's *ev'* used for *ever* in Shakespeare's presumed autograph section of *Sir Thomas More,* according to Partridge, p. 57. See also Partridge, p. 24. End curtailment is an outside possibility at best.

[42]Kökeritz, p. 322, and *OED* for *neither, ner.*

[43]There is, in my judgment, one likely anapest in fact though not in intent in Shakespeare's sonnets, but of a peculiar sort that does not affect the argument. The likelihood of rhetorical stress in context on the feminine ending of 42.7, "And for my sake euen so doth she abuse *me,*" yields the scansion *itiia.*

NOTES TO REDPATH

[1]Douglas Bush and Alfred Harbage, ed. *The Sonnets* (Baltimore: Penguin Books, 1961).

²Aldus Manutius the Elder, "Interpungendi Ratio," in *Orthographiae Ratio* (Venice, 1561), p. 52.

³Puttenham, *The Arte of English Poesie* (London, 1589), bk. II, ch. 5.

⁴Laura Riding and Robert Graves, *A Survey of Modernist Poetry* (London, 1927), pp. 63-82.

⁵Walter W. Greg, "An Elizabethan Printer and his Copy," *The Library*, 4th ser., IV (1924), 102-118; see also E.J. Howard, "The Printer and Elizabethan Punctuation," *Studies in Philology*, XXVII (1930), 220-229.

⁶This is certainly my personal impression from a spot check on samples of Eld's printing in about a dozen of the books printed by him that are in the Library of Trinity College, Cambridge. I was much helped in this small piece of research by the valuable manuscript list of early books in the Library (classified under their printers) compiled by Mr. H.M. Adams, formerly Librarian and now Honorary Fellow of the College.

⁷*A Transcript of the Registers of the Company of Stationers of London, 1554-1640*, ed. Edward Arber, 5 vols. (London, 1875-1877; Birmingham, 1894), III, 699. Hereafter volume and page numbers are cited in text.

⁸See A.W. Pollard, G.R. Redgrave et al., *A Short-title Catalogue of Books Printed in England, Scotland and Ireland, 1475-1640* (London, 1926); and Paul G. Morrison, *An Index of Printers, Publishers, and Booksellers Named in the Short-title Catalogue* (Charlottesville, Va., 1950), p. 27.

⁹Morrison, p. 27, and *Short-title Catalogue*, STC 17430.

¹⁰I have taken a figure of about 10,000 ens per day. For further information about typesetting speeds see Charlton Hinman, *The Printing and Proof-Reading of the First Folio of Shakespeare* (Oxford, 1963).

¹¹Rowland Vaughan's *Water workes*, entered on November 14, 1609 (Arbor, III, 424).

¹²John Selden's *The Duello*, entered by John Helme on December 22, 1609 (Arber, III, 426).

¹³It seems very unlikely that Eld could have dealt with the heavy load of work simply with two apprentices. He would almost certainly also have needed a journeyman. With regard to apprentices,

by a decree of the Court of Star Chamber of 23 June 1586, the number of apprentices to be kept by Freemen of the Company was limited. (See Marjorie Plant, *The English Book Trade* [London, 1939; 2nd ed., 1965], pp. 133-134. I am indebted to Dr. Philip Gaskell, Fellow and Librarian of Trinity, for this reference.) A member of the livery could only keep two apprentices, and a yeoman only one. It seems likely that Eld was by 1609 a liveryman. Indeed, he was already officially keeping two apprentices in 1604 (Luke Norton, shortly to be mentioned, and Robert Roworth, who had been bound to Eld for eight years from 24 June 1604 [Arber, II, 282]). Roworth evidently did not serve out his term (see D. F. McKenzie, "A List of Printers' Apprentices, 1605-1640," in *Studies in Bibliography* [Charlottesville, Va., 1960], p. 120).

[14] See McKenzie, art. cit., p. 120, and his *Stationers' Apprentices, 1605-1640* (Charlottesville, Va., 1961), p. 15.

[15] *Stationers' Apprentices,* p. 15.

[16] On this whole matter see John Dover Wilson, ed. *The Sonnets* (Cambridge, 1966), pp. xvii-xlii, and especially the support given on p. xlii to F. Mathew's hypothesis, in his *An Image of Shakespeare* (London, 1920), p. 114, that the publication was quickly suppressed.

[17] Aspley and Thorpe had, for instance, jointly entered their copy of Marston's *Malcontent* in 1604 (Arber, III, 268) and of *Eastward Ho* in 1605 (Arber, III, 300), and Eld had printed three editions of the latter play the same year. Eld had also printed Jonson's *Sejanus* for Thorpe in 1605, and Chapman's Byron plays for him in 1608. He had also printed *The Retourne from Pernassus* for Wright in 1605, and *Julius Caesars Revenge* for the same publisher in 1606. It is harder to establish a close connexion between Thorpe and Wright before 1609, and any such connexion was probably less direct, and, indeed, possibly through Eld. There is an interesting entry in *The Stationers' Register* for 6 August 1607 (Arber, III, 357-358). The entry on that day is for the copy of five books, of which three were plays. Three of the books were entered by Eld, one by Wright, and one by Thorpe. In the same year Eld printed two of his three, and also the books entered by Wright and Thorpe. Thorpe, Aspley, Eld, and Wright were all Freemen of the Stationers' Company at the time, having been admitted to the Freedom in that order. Eld evidently specialized in printing and publishing,

Thorpe in publishing, and Aspley and Wright in both publishing and bookselling. In the case of Shakespeare's Sonnets the part of Aspley and Wright in the venture was the sale. (The information in this note concerning Eld's printing activities was gleaned from the *Short-title Catalogue* with the help of Morrison's *Index* cited above [n. 8].)

[18]Tucker Brooke, ed. *Shakespeare's Sonnets* (London: Oxford Univ. Press, 1936), p. 58, n. 1.

[19]Brooke, pp. 57-64.

[20]Riding and Graves, op. cit. (above, n. 4), pp. 63-82. Hereafter, page references will be given in the text.

[21]It is necessary to add this qualification, since Riding and Graves omit a comma that *The Oxford Book* prints in line 9 after "pursuit." They also, incidentally, print the Quarto's "inioyd" (line 5) as "injoyd," a point that would, however, be hardly worth mention were they not such fanatical sticklers about spelling.

[22]Martin Seymour-Smith, ed. *Shakespeare's Sonnets* (London, 1963), p. 105; Wilson, ed. cit. (above, n. 16), pp. 67, 248.

[23]A. Schmidt, *Shakespeare-Lexicon,* 3rd ed., 2 vols. (Berlin, 1902), I, 99.

[24]*Metamorphoses,* VII, 20-21.

[25]Percy Simpson, *Shakespearian Punctuation* (Oxford, 1911).

[26]See especially the excellent article by R.M. Alden, "The Punctuation of Shakespeare's Printers," *PMLA,* XXXIX (1924), 557-580, and the important pages on Shakespearean punctuation in E.K. Chambers, *William Shakespeare,* 2 vols. (Oxford, 1930), I, 190-198. See also C.C. Fries, "Shakespearean Punctuation," in Michigan *Studies in Shakespeare* (1925), 67-86; and E.J. Howard, "The Printer and Elizabethan Punctuation," *Studies in Philology,* XXVII (1930), 220-232.

[27]Wilson, Ed. cit. (above, n. 16), p. cxxiv.

[28]H.C. Beeching, ed. *The Sonnets of Shakespeare* (Boston and London, 1904), pp. lix-lxiii; R.M. Alden, ed. *The Sonnets of Shakespeare* (Boston and New York, 1916), and his "The Punctuation of Shakespeare's Printers," *PMLA,* XXXIX (1924), 557-580; Chambers, op. cit. (above, n. 26), I, 190-198.

[29]Seymour-Smith, ed. cit. (above, n. 22), p. 109; and Wilson, ed. cit. (above, n. 16), p. 71.

[30]Simpson, op. cit. (above, n. 25), p. 31. Hereafter, page references will be given in the text.

[31]Simpson's failure to realize this was one of his primary mistakes. Cf. Alden, art. cit. (above, n. 26), and Chambers, op. cit. (above, n. 26), I, 193.

[32]Alden, p. 565.

[33]Simpson also quotes a fourth passage (7.11-14), but this does not seem to be of quite the same kind, and is not of equal interest.

[34]Constable, *Diana,* 3rd Decad, Sonnet V, 11-12.